A Complete Guide to

STREET SUPERCHARGING

Pat Ganahl

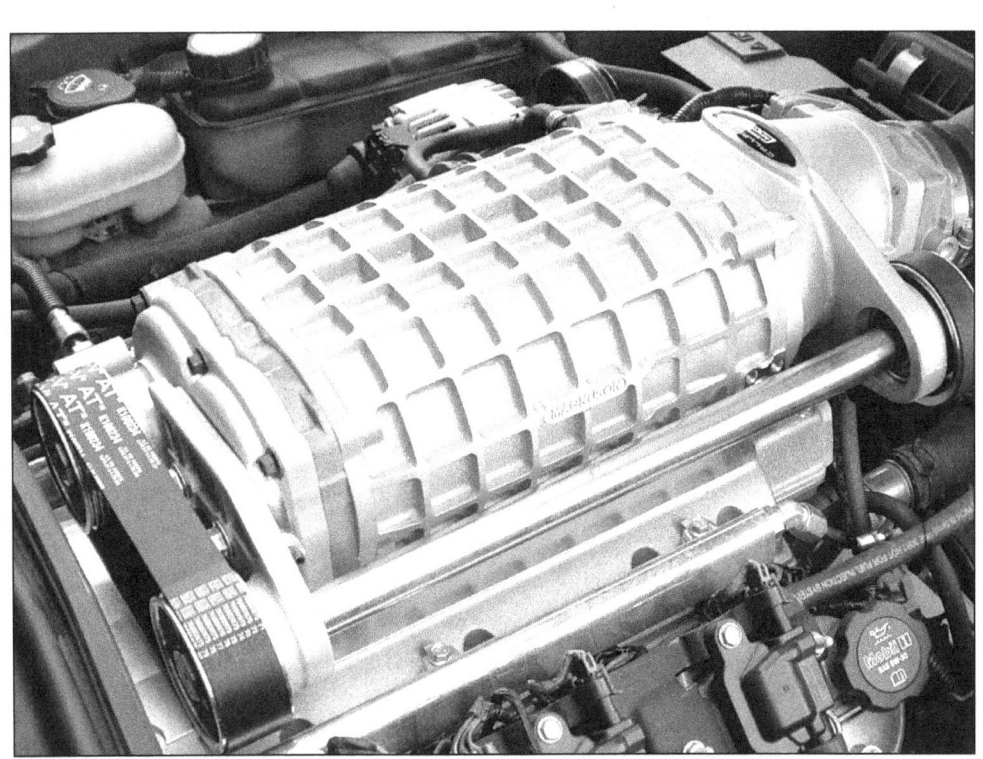

CarTech®

CarTech®

CarTech®, Inc.
39966 Grand Avenue
North Branch, MN 55056
Phone: 651-277-1200 or 800-551-4754
Fax: 651-277-1203
www.cartechbooks.com

© 2009 by Pat Ganahl

All rights reserved. No part of this publication may be reproduced or utilized in any form or by any means, electronic or mechanical, including photocopying, recording, or by any information storage and retrieval system, without prior permission from the Publisher. All text, photographs, and artwork are the property of the Author unless otherwise noted or credited.

The information in this work is true and complete to the best of our knowledge. However, all information is presented without any guarantee on the part of the Author or Publisher, who also disclaim any liability incurred in connection with the use of the information and any implied warranties of merchantability or fitness for a particular purpose. Readers are responsible for taking suitable and appropriate safety measures when performing any of the operations or activities described in this work.

All trademarks, trade names, model names and numbers, and other product designations referred to herein are the property of their respective owners and are used solely for identification purposes. This work is a publication of CarTech, Inc., and has not been licensed, approved, sponsored, or endorsed by any other person or entity. The Publisher is not associated with any product, service, or vendor mentioned in this book, and does not endorse the products or services of any vendor mentioned in this book.

Layout by Chris Fayers

ISBN 978-1-61325-131-7
Item No. SA17P

Library of Congress Cataloging-in-Publication Data

Ganahl, Pat.
  Street supercharging / by Pat Ganahl.
     p. cm.
  ISBN 978-1-932494-93-8
 1. Automobiles—Motors—Superchargers. I. Title.

TL214.S8G36 2009
629.25—dc22   2009001267

Title Page:
A new MP 2300 Magna Charger fitted to a Corvette.

Back Cover Photos

Top Left:
How many people make Jimmy blower kits for 500-inch Cadillacs? BDS does. Note the individual-runner, cast-aluminum intake manifold mounting the BDS 8-71 blower, with a pair of EFI throttle bodies on top of that. Although not installed here, BDS makes the complete Gilmer belt drive, too, of course.

Top Right:
This Vortech application on an LS7 Corvette is one of the few that uses a large, aluminum air-to-air intercooler mounted just ahead of the car's radiator. Also note the large, low-restriction air cleaner for the blower's intake, mounted in the fresh-air stream.

Middle Left:
A cutaway of a ProCharger D-1SC clearly shows the 4.1:1 step-up gears and bearing shafts, as well as the scroll housing and impeller (from the backside). Since this unit self-contains oil in the gear case, the thinner cogged wheel aerates and pumps oil onto the gears. From this angle, the drive pulley turns clockwise (same as the engine crankshaft), while the impeller turns the opposite direction due to the gear drive. The scroll outlet is beyond the larger section of the cutaway.

Middle Right:
While Magna Charger stresses the latest technology, and most systems are designed to directly interface with existing EFI and serpentine belts on late-model vehicles, Magnuson has a soft spot for traditional hot rods, as exemplified by the MP 112 carbureted kit seen on a display motor and completely assembled on Jerry's own 1929 roadster pickup.

Bottom Left:
Don't think that modern superchargers are just made for V-8 engines. Even though belt-driven blowers can be easily adjusted by changing pulley ratios, they should still be sized to the engine for optimum performance. This small, shaft-driven, intercooled Vortech makes big muscle from a tiny Honda 4-cylinder, and illustrates the versatile mounting possibilities of today's superchargers.

Bottom Right:
Earlier Whipples used Opcon and then Lysholm compressors from Sweden, but now Whipple makes its own rotors and rounded, finned cases in the United States. Current Whipples are made in 2.3L and 3.3L sizes.

TABLE OF CONTENTS

Chapter 1: Blower Basics 4
   The Air Engine 5
   Street Supercharging 9
   What is a Supercharger? 10
   What a Supercharger Does 12
   Types of Superchargers 15

Chapter 2: Blower Background 19
   A Short History of Supercharging 19
   Blowers in Europe 20
   Superchargers in the United States 22
   Hot Rod Supercharging 23
   Street Supercharging 25

Chapter 3: How Blowers Work 29
   Density, Volume and Pressure 30
   The Gas Law 31
   The Problem of Heat 31
   Blower Efficiency 33
   The Air Density Ratio 38
   The Limits of Supercharging 39
   Expansion Ratio and Thermal Efficiency 41
   Let's Get Practical 42

Chapter 4: Vintage Superchargers 44
   Early McCulloch Blowers 45
   The Frenzel 48
   The S.Co.T./Italmeccanica 48
   Early GMC Kits 49
   Other Roots Blowers 50
   The Judson and Other Vane Types 52
   Latham 54

   Magna Charger 56
   B&M Automotive 57

Chapter 5: The New Centrifugals 62
   Centrifugal Superchargers vs.
      Turbochargers 68
   Vortech and Paxton Superchargers 69
   ATI ProCharger 76

Chapter 6: Modern Roots Blowers 78
   GMC Blowers 78
   GMC Blower Builders 82
   New Old Roots 91
   The New Roots 92

Chapter 7: Screw-Type Superchargers 104
   Whipple 106
   Kenne Bell 109
   Vortech-Lysholm 111

**Chapter 8: Building the
Street-Supercharged Engine** 112
   Block, Crank, Rods 115
   Pistons and Rings 117
   Cylinder Heads 120
   Camshaft and Valvetrain 122
   Fuel System 124
   Air Cleaners and Intercoolers 125
   Ignition 125
   Exhaust 126

Source Guide 128

CHAPTER 1

BLOWER BASICS

"No single performance modification to an internal combustion engine is more practical or effective than the addition of a supercharger."

That was the opening statement of this book when it was first written in 1984, and again when it was revised in 1999. Now, as we are well into a new millennium and the automobile is celebrating its second century of production, that statement is as true as ever. It is even more relevant to performance vehicles of all types, whether they are built on an assembly line or modified in your local "speed shop" or home garage.

That might sound like technological bragging or advertising hype, but you'd get little objection from engineers, engine builders, or race car drivers. The supercharger's effectiveness has been known almost since the engine was invented.

So why haven't auto manufacturers put blowers on all cars? It has always been a matter of economics. Buyers of mass-produced transportation vehicles have always been more motivated by bottom-line cost than performance and, until recently, the cost of gasoline in America has been so low that little emphasis had ever been put on significantly increasing engine efficiency. If you want more power, make the engine bigger! Well, we're finally learning that adding a supercharger to a smaller engine can do the same thing. Manufacturers and typical buyers are also learning that smaller, more-nimble cars are

The audio-visual effects of a big, shiny, whining supercharger are sure to draw a crowd and admiring glances at the local cruise night, especially when it's out in the open, not under a hood. The 302 small-block in this early Mustang doesn't need a 6-71 with two 4-barrels, but note the large pulley on the blower to underdrive it. Belt-driven blowers are easily adjustable to make them very drivable, and the best part is that they work even better than they look.

not only more efficient, but they also perform much better than the big, lumbering vehicles of a couple decades ago—or more recent SUVs and crew-cab pickups. Yes, today more and more new-car manufacturers are supplying vehicles with superchargers of several types.

Better yet, those of us who are of the hot rod or do-it-yourself automotive-performance-enhancement persuasion can now choose from a widening variety of supercharger types and sizes. New superchargers have significantly improved power/efficiency accessories such as intercoolers and electronic fuel injection (EFI), to either immediately pump up the muscles of an undernourished small or medium-size motor, or put a big, already muscular motor on an amazing-to-ridiculous dose of steroids.

The Air Engine

Before we can even begin to discuss what a supercharger is, what it does, and why your street-driven engine should have one, we need to dispel a major myth about the internal combustion engine itself.

You probably think the engine in your car runs on gasoline. Most people do. But it doesn't. It runs on air—expanding air. That's what pushes the pistons and turns the crank. All the gasoline does is make a very hot fire to heat the air. Heating the air makes it expand.

You probably think of the fire in the cylinder, when the spark plug ignites the compressed air/gasoline mixture, as an explosion, and that this powerful explosion "blows" the piston down the cylinder on the power stroke. Well, this explosion is nothing more than very rapidly expanding air (which has been rapidly and extremely heated). That's what an explosion is, by definition: very

A 16-plug, dual distributor, 426-inch Chrysler Hemi is a plenty impressive piece of machinery, but a big, polished, 6-71 GMC supercharger adds a whole new dimension to such a motor, figuratively as well as literally in terms of its air-capacity volumetric size—and power.

While a supercharger can make a big engine bigger, the real beauty is that it can make a smaller engine act like a big one. Obviously, the blower size should be matched to engine capacity. This well-manicured example is a 110-ci early Magna Charger on a 231-ci Buick V-6.

CHAPTER 1

rapidly and forcefully expanding air, which "blows" things apart. The word is more appropriate than you might have thought.

There are two primary points to consider here (we'll get more technical later...which you can skip if it doesn't interest you). The first is that the size of an engine is measured in cubic inches (ci). Cubic inches of what? Air. Let's say you have a 300-ci engine and it has 8 cylinders. That means each cylinder has a volume of 37.5 ci when the piston is at the bottom of its travel. If this engine had 100-percent volumetric efficiency (VE), the cylinder would draw in a total of 37.5 ci of air on each intake stroke. Through one full cycle of the firing order, this engine would draw in, "breathe," or consume 300 ci of air in its eight cylinders.

We don't need to get more technical than that right now. What you know is that the "bigger" the engine—the more total cubic-inch volume (or displacement) of its cylinders, the more powerful it is. We all know that. In fact, we know that, in general, a 400-ci engine is about twice as powerful as a 200-ci one, other things being the same. So the power of an engine is based on the amount of *air* it holds, processes, or consumes, not the amount of fuel it uses. In fact, if you know anything about tuning gasoline engines, you know that if you try to add too much fuel to the mixture—that is, make it run rich—it will start losing power, significantly. So, adding more fuel to an engine doesn't make it more powerful; adding more *air* to it does. You can probably see where we're going with this.

The second point, which can get complicated, is that air, like any gas, is elastic. It expands and contracts, and it can be compressed. This is critical to supercharging. In fact, it's

This Nostalgia Top Fuel dragster demonstrates two things: first, drag racers have known since the 1950s that blowers work, big time. Second, you can readily see from the gaping injectors that the blower's job is to gulp a whole lot of fresh air and pump it into the motor to make more power. Even limited to "small" 6-71 GMC blowers, these cars run 250+ mph with obsolete Chrysler engines.

what the whole process of supercharging is based on.

To begin at the most basic, all the "stuff" in the world—technically known as matter—is made of atoms and molecules. And most of this matter can exist in one of three forms, depending on its temperature: solid, liquid, or gas. Solids can be melted into liquids, and liquids can be "boiled" (or evaporated) into gases, and vice versa. At normal atmospheric (or "room") temperatures, certain substances exist as solids, some as liquids, and some as gases. Even though we usually can't see it or feel it, air is a gas. It is matter made up of atoms and molecules. The air that we breathe, as you know, contains about 21 percent oxygen. Another 78 percent or so is nitrogen. The remaining 1 percent contains obviously small amounts of argon, carbon dioxide, methane, etc. And that's if the air is clean and dry.

But the point is that air is matter; it's made of stuff (atoms and molecules) and it has weight (or "mass" as the physicists call it). If you don't believe it, consider that air can mess up your hair, it can knock you down, or it can even rip the roof off your house if it's blowing hard enough. Air can be quite forceful. It has mass, even though you can't see it. The dynamics of air moving inside your engine are a bit different than those of wind in a hurricane, but it's the same stuff doing the work. Air packs a punch. It's what makes the horsepower in your engine and moves your car. That's what we're talking about.

We said that air has weight. Since this weight presses on everything at the earth's surface equally, from all sides (like the weight of water at the bottom of a pool or the ocean), we measure it as pressure—so much weight per square inch. You probably know that the weight of air varies with its temperature. Warmer air is lighter (less dense) than cold air. This has a lot to do with supercharging, and we'll discuss it much more in Chapter 3. But for now, understand that this is what we call barometric pressure and differences in air pressure (due to temperature) between one place and another is what causes wind—sometimes very strong wind. You probably also know that the higher up you go in altitude, the "thinner" (that is, lighter) the air gets. That makes sense, since the higher you go from the earth's surface, the less air there is above you pressing down.

OK, the point of this little lesson is that the normal, or average, pressure of air at the earth's surface is about 14.7 pounds per square inch (psi). Since this amount is considered normal, most air pressure gauges start at this amount as zero, and read increases in air pressure above that. Therefore, a reading of 14 to 15 psi on a typical air pressure gauge is really about 28 to 29 pounds of actual air pressure (which scientists call "absolute" pressure; the reading on the gauge is called "gauge" pressure). That means if an air pressure gauge reads about 15 psi, whatever it's hooked up to—say the tank on your air compressor—contains about twice as much air as it did when the gauge read 0 psi. In other words, if your air compressor has a 5-gallon tank, and you run it until the tank gauge reads about 15 psi, then that tank has the equivalent of 10 gallons of air in it. You can't put 10 gallons of water in a 5-gallon tank, just like you can't put 50 pounds of solid, um, stuff in a 5-pound bag, because liquids and solids won't compress. But air, like any gas, will.

The point we're making about engines and superchargers should be obvious by now. The internal combustion engine runs on air. The more air it holds (the bigger the displacement), the more power it makes. And a supercharger can pump more air

And if anything worked better than Roots-style blowers, today's Top-class dragsters and Funny Cars would use it. But nothing does. They've tried. Even limited to 14-71 length and 60-degree helix, GMC-type blowers now push these still-obsolete Chrysler-based engines to well over 300 mph with something like 3,000 hp.

There's no question GMC-style blowers work, but there are lots of types of superchargers, and several of today's are more refined and more efficient—and don't have to stick out of the hood. Some say the downfall of centrifugal blowers is that they don't make low-end power. But looked at it another way, their power output increases geometrically with blower speed. A setup like this Vortech blowing into an aftermarket EFI throttle body through an intercooler can produce upwards of 1,200 hp from this Duttweiler small-block, in a hurry.

CHAPTER 1

Engines like these look impressive and can run strong in a high-RPM power range. But they run very poorly at street-driving speeds, are difficult to tune and maintain, and can actually cost considerably more to build—especially if trick heads are included—than simply bolting on a supercharger. Blowers are more practical and efficient, especially for the total price.

more fuel in? No, to get more *air* into the cylinders. Once we get more air in, *then* we have to add more fuel to keep the air/fuel ratio (fuel mixture) correct. We also know that we can bore and stroke the engine to make it hold more air, and thus make more power.

Before going any further, let's dispel another engine myth. You've undoubtedly heard the old saw that an internal combustion engine is basically an air pump. I'm not sure where that analogy came from or what it's really supposed to mean, but it's 180-degrees wrong. An internal combustion engine doesn't *pump* air, it *sucks* air. That's its basic problem, which a supercharger—which *is* an air pump—can quickly and easily solve.

The problem is that a "naturally aspirated" engine has only the outside air pressure to push air into the cylinder when the piston moves down on the intake stroke. Looking at it the other way around, the piston moving down in the bore creates a vacuum, which sucks the outside air into the cylinder. (That's just two different ways of saying the same thing.) But it has to suck that air past an opening valve, through a long port, through a usually convoluted intake manifold, past the venturis of a carburetor (or through a throttle body), and through a restrictive air cleaner of some sort. And the faster the engine turns, the less time it has to do all this.

If a 300-ci engine could fill its cylinders with 300 ci of air on each full intake cycle, that would be called 100-percent volumetric efficiency (VE). But you can see why most naturally aspirated engines don't come close to 100-percent VE.

But we traditional (dare I say, stubborn?) hot rodders have been porting and relieving, adding more or bigger carbs and manifolds, grinding bigger cams, even boring and stroking for bigger displacement—

into the engine than the natural atmosphere can—lots more.

Yes, but we hot rodders, like Detroit engineers, sometimes think too traditionally. We know that we can add more or bigger carburetors, increase the size of the ports, or hold the valves open higher and longer with a bigger camshaft to make more power in a given engine. Why? To get just to try to fill the engine with as much air as it will hold. That is, to try to get closer to 100-percent volumetric efficiency. Given natural air pressure, that's the best you can do. That's the limit.

So why not just bolt some sort of air pump on the engine and *force* more air into it? Bingo! It doesn't really take a genius to figure this out. That pump is called a supercharger, and it's the simplest, most-effective single piece of equipment you can add to your engine to dramatically increase its efficiency and power.

Yes, a supercharger might be the single most expensive piece of equipment you can add to your engine, but compare it to all the work and expense of traditional modifications it can not only replace, but actually supersede. Adding a mild-boost (5 to 7 psi) blower to any stock engine can easily achieve or exceed 100-percent VE without any other modifications. Such boost levels won't tax the engine mechanically, and will keep it tame and very tractable on city streets or the highway. As already mentioned, increasing blower boost (by a simple pulley swap, in most cases) to 14 to 15 psi is effectively the same as doubling the size—and power—of your engine. In the case of most modern powerplants the only limiting mechanical factor to doing so is the available-gasoline's octane rating.

Or, if you're a typical hot rodder who always wants more power, supercharging is really the only way to do it in a given engine. Yes, you'll have to make traditional modifications to help the engine breathe the extra air you're forcing into it, and to make parts like pistons and rods withstand the extra force it will create. But boost levels up to 30 psi aren't out of the question, especially for short bursts of speed, which is how most blowers are used.

Although it took hot rodders a while to appreciate what blowers could do, they started to experiment with them shortly after World War II, as this GMC 2-71, cleverly and cleanly adapted to a Willys Jeep, attests.

Look at it this way. The ultimate, most unrestricted form of automotive competition—and by far the most powerful—is the Top Fuel class in drag racing. And every one of those cars uses a big, belt-driven supercharger. Need we say more?

Street Supercharging

The main reason superchargers of some sort aren't used in all forms of racing is that rules regulate against it. But there are no such rules for street-driven vehicles.

In the following pages we will discuss some of the history and theory of supercharger development, but we will be primarily interested in showing you the several varieties of superchargers and complete kits currently available for street performance engines, how they should be installed and maintained, and how the package can be tuned for maximum performance and efficiency. We will also study the types of changes that should be made to a typical street motor (and those that shouldn't) before a supercharger is installed, as well as a rundown on the best ancillary components for both the engine and the blower (drive systems, linkage, ignition systems, camshafts, exhaust systems, intercoolers, and so on).

While we don't really recommend buying a used blower at a swap meet (or unseen over the Internet), given the strong interest in vintage engines and equipment these days, we will give an overview of the wide variety of superchargers that have been available on production automobiles as well as through the aftermarket over the past several decades. Plus, surprisingly, we will even look at some brand-new and improved reproductions of these early blowers that are now available.

And while the current trend, given today's proven and efficient electronically fuel-injected engines, is toward

CHAPTER 1

But even hot rodders were a bit incredulous when Tom McMullen's blown, flamed, street-driven 1932 roadster hit the cover of Hot Rod *magazine in 1963. It won class at the NHRA Winternationals, set lakes records at El Mirage, raced on the street and strips every weekend, yet still drove to work. Superchargers could do that then, and they can do it now.*

centrifugal, screw-type, or smaller and more-efficient Roots blowers integrated into an EFI system—especially with a highly effective intercooler—we will see that there are still plenty of ways to supercharge your engine. These include a big, polished, 6-71 or 8-71 "Jimmy" sticking through the hood, Gasser-style, with either a pair of 4-barrels on top or a Hilborn- or Enderle-style injector converted to programmable electronic operation. But no matter which approach you take, as long as you follow the several hints and guidelines offered here to get the system matched and tuned properly, you will certainly agree that no other single performance upgrade can compare with supercharging.

What is a Supercharger?

If we are going to spend the rest of this book talking about superchargers, we had better start by determining exactly what a supercharger, or "blower," is. In the broadest sense, a supercharger is anything that will force more air into the cylinders of an engine than would be drawn into the cylinders naturally by the suction of the pistons during the intake stroke. At sea level, atmospheric pressure is approximately 14.7 psi. Air exerts this much naturally on everything near the surface of the earth (because of the air's weight). When an engine is "naturally aspirated" (not supercharged), it must rely on this pressure to push the air into the carburetor or throttle body, through the manifold, into the intake port, past the opening valve, and then into the cylinder as the piston "opens" the cylinder to maximum volume when it moves downward on the intake stroke.

We've touched on volumetric efficiency, but let's study it further, because it's the natural law of physics the supercharger can break, and thus do more good for your engine than any other mechanical modification. Because of the restrictions and bends along the path, friction, turbulence, incomplete evacuation of the exhaust from the cylinder, and several other factors, the naturally aspirated cylinder is never able to completely draw in a full "charge" of air/fuel mix.

Let's say the total volume of the cylinder is 40 ci. If you turned the engine by hand to bottom dead center (BDC) on the intake stroke, and left it there, the cylinder would fill with 40 ci of air through the open intake valve. Atmospheric pressure pushes the air in (which is exactly the same as saying the downward-moving piston sucks the air in). Whenever you create a space that has nothing in it—that is, a vacuum—atmospheric pressure will immediately push air into that space through any available opening. The force pushing the air in will be approximately 14.7 psi at sea level; less at higher altitudes. But when the engine is running at speed, atmospheric pressure is not great enough to push 40 ci of fresh air/fuel mixture into the cylinder before the intake valve closes and the compression stroke begins.

What we are describing is the volumetric efficiency of the engine, which is a comparison of the total amount of air a naturally aspirated engine could draw in (total cylinder volume), to the amount (volume) that it actually does draw in under given operating conditions. Other factors being equal, an engine's power output is directly proportional to its volumetric efficiency, and the vast majority of our traditional hop-up tricks are directed at increasing this figure: carburetion (or injection), intake manifolding, porting, polishing, valve size, camshaft design, exhaust scavenging, and so on.

But no naturally aspirated engine can attain 100-percent volumetric efficiency (except in rare cases when a perfectly tuned ram-induction intake manifold can accelerate the intake charge sufficiently to "ram" it into the cylinder at a certain, narrow span in the RPM range). By increasing intake tract and port sizes, streamlining passages, and evacuating exhaust, we can reduce losses and increase the efficiency to a certain point. But as long as we are relying on atmospheric pressure to push the air/fuel charge into the cylinder—if that remains constant—we can very rarely (if ever) reach 100-percent efficiency.

After you have done everything you can to help the engine draw as much air into the cylinders as possible by normal suction, there remains only one way to get more air/fuel charge in—and it's a simple deduction: increase the pressure pushing the air into the motor; force the air in; and pump the air in. That is what a supercharger is—an engine air pump.

So in the broadest sense a super-charger is any device or means for increasing the cylinder-filling (volumetric efficiency) in the engine beyond that possible by the normal suction of the pistons; that is, beyond that possible under the force of atmospheric pressure.

Given this broad definition, we could say that any sort of pump, fan, or wind-blowing device that can force a greater volume of air through the intake system, and/or get a greater volume of air/fuel charge into the cylinder, than is possible under atmospheric pressure, is a super-charger. Under this definition we might say that a tuned ram-induction intake manifold, or even a good air

What in the world is this? Yes, it's Big Daddy Roth's wild, bubble-topped, fiberglass Beatnik Bandit *from 1961, and it has a fully chromed and polished Cragar 4-71 blower kit (from Bell Auto Parts) with two 97 carbs on top of an Olds V-8. You might think this is a typical "show only" setup, but Roth actually fired this thing up at shows (with a remote-control button, no less) about every half hour, and revved it up, to draw a crowd to his booth. It sounded—and ran—great.*

It took a very long time for new-car manufacturers to learn how simply and flawlessly super-chargers can work. Literally millions of new cars, worldwide, now come with belt-driven blowers. But, after a few high-dollar cars in the 1930s, one of the few timid pioneers in factory super-charging was the 1963 R-3 Avanti, which used a Paxton centrifugal blowing into an AFB 4-barrel through a bonnet. In 1957, Fords used a similar arrangement on very limited models.

CHAPTER 1

Paxton continued making its historic ball-drive centrifugal superchargers through the 1990s. The difference, as seen on this 5.0L small-block in an early Mustang, is that it could be hooked up to blow directly into an EFI throttle body, instead of a carburetor.

scoop on a fast-moving race car, is a sort of supercharging device. Likewise, it might be argued that nitrous oxide injection is a form of supercharging because the super-cooling of the evaporating nitrous greatly increases the density of the air charge entering the cylinder, which is slightly different than increasing the volume. (Running your car on a cold night, or at low altitude, produces the same effect in smaller proportion.) Mickey Thompson once even tried feeding his Funny Car engine with very highly compressed air carried in on-board tanks with some success!

But none of these methods is strictly considered supercharging. For the purposes of this book, we will define a supercharger as a mechanical air pump capable of producing a positive boost pressure in the manifold of the engine at some point in its operating range.

What a Supercharger Does

Obviously, we have already discussed to some extent what a supercharger does. It pumps air, or air/fuel mixture, into the engine at a rate faster than the engine can draw it in under atmospheric pressure. Therefore, instead of loading the cylinder with a partial air/fuel "charge" before compression and combustion, a blown engine can fill its cylinders with a *supercharge*, which can attain or usually exceed 100-percent volumetric efficiency.

As we stated, the supercharger can, therefore, do the job of several other traditional performance modifications aimed at increasing the engine's volumetric efficiency. If you are going to add a supercharger to an engine for street use, be it a 500-ci big-block, a medium-size small-block, or a pint-size 4-cylinder, you will very likely be able to pump in all the extra performance you need without doing any other significant (and expensive) modifications to the engine. If you are building an all-out race motor, or if the intake passages or cam profile of your engine are particularly restrictive, you will want to make sure that no single component in the intake or exhaust system "fights" the supercharger by overly constricting airflow into or out of the cylinders. Since the days of high-compression engines and high-octane pump gas disappeared in the 1970s, nearly all of our recent and current factory powerplants are ripe for supercharging just the way they are.

Not surprisingly, carburetors began disappearing from factory engines about the same time. Our current EFI systems, using an electronic mass-airflow sensor (MAF), are perfect for supercharging. Whether the supercharger is installed to blow air into the MAF, or draw air through it, it senses the actual amount of air passing through it into the engine, and increases fuel flow through the injectors proportionally—automatically. Likewise, even old mechanical carburetors, using the venturi system, draw fuel into the intake stream in proportion to the amount of air passing through them.

Carburetors may take a bit more fine-tuning of various circuits when used with a supercharger, but in either case the existing fuel system is designed to meter gasoline into the airstream in proportion to the volume of air it "reads" passing through it, and it will automatically increase fuel supply when the airflow is increased by a supercharger. The only limitation in this regard is if the blower increases airflow to the point that it exceeds the fuel flow capacity of the injectors or carburetor, in which case higher-flow injectors or larger carburetor(s) will be needed.

Since the blower pressurizes the entire intake manifold and port runners, there is usually no need to streamline, tune, or otherwise enhance intake flow. In fact, the air/fuel mixture no longer really flows through the manifold in a blown engine. Instead, you might think of the manifold as a pressurized reservoir of air or fuel/air mix ready to burst through the valve as soon as it opens. As a matter of fact, some supercharged engines have problems keeping the intake valves shut and require stronger valvesprings to do so.

Because the intake charge is so eager to get into the cylinder of a supercharged engine, there is little need to increase the valve timing or lift with a special camshaft. Naturally, certain camshaft profiles will work better than others in blown engines, and we will discuss some of these fine points later. But in general, a supercharged engine is far less touchy about camshaft profile than a naturally aspirated engine (the worst thing for a blown motor is a super-long-duration, big-overlap cam, since it will allow much of the blower's forced induction to go right out the exhaust port). With milder cam timing, however, the supercharger will still help blow residual gases out of the cylinder as it forces fresh fuel/air mix in to take its place. Therefore exhaust valve size, port shape, and tuned headers are much less important on a blown motor. The supercharger will actually help pump the exhaust out of the engine.

By pumping a greater amount of air/fuel charge into the cylinder, the supercharger effectively raises the compression ratio of the engine (since a larger volume of air will be compressed into the same combustion chamber volume at top dead center/TDC). Consequently, the static compression ratio (the physical ratio of the open cylinder volume at BDC to the closed cylinder volume at TDC) in a supercharged engine must be considerably lower than that in a naturally aspirated high-performance engine. Adding a blower to a 10:1 or 12:1 motor will literally blow it because of excessively high cylinder pressures. However, current production engines with compression ratios in the 9:1 range are just right for the addition of a typical street blower making 6- to 8-psi boost. (The foremost consideration is whether the factory pistons and rings are strong enough to withstand the higher pressure and heat levels produced in the cylinder by the blower, or, perhaps more accurately, by the actuation of the driver's right foot once the blower is installed.)

Here's a very similar, yet more contemporary, installation of a Vortech centrifugal blowing directly into a similar EFI intake on a small-block Ford in this Saleen version of a late-model Mustang.

While integrating a supercharger with EFI is more common these days, don't think that carburetors are dead, especially for high-flow, big-horsepower racing setups. Vortech/Paxton still prefers to put the carb inside a pressurized box, as seen on this recent, sanitary installation. ProCharger likes to blow directly into the top of the carb with a bonnet attachment.

You may wonder at the logic of reducing the static compression of an unblown high-performance engine so that you can raise the compression back up to a comparable level with a supercharger. If that's all a blower did (raise the compression), it would be a waste of time and money (and engine horsepower to turn it), since a set of high-compression pistons costs considerably less than a supercharger. But don't forget that the naturally aspirated engine, no matter what its compression ratio, can only draw so much air into the cylinders under atmospheric pressure. It cannot achieve 100-percent volumetric efficiency. It just squeezes the same

CHAPTER 1

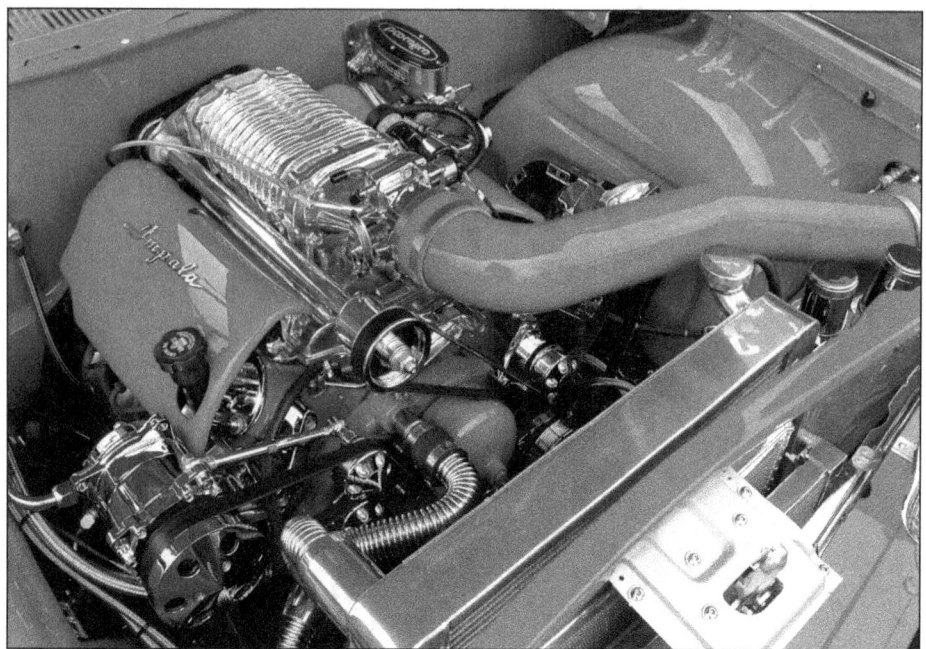

Speaking of sanitary installations, this polished 112 Magna Charger mounted on an LS-style small-block in a 1959 Chevy looks as good as it performs. Based on the new-generation Eaton Roots blower, this healthy yet compact unit draws fresh air through the factory MAF/throttle body at the blower's inlet, and injects fuel into the manifold below it using factory, or higher-flow, electronic injectors. Being the first redesign of a Roots for automotive performance, ever, it can deliver the same boost as a big Jimmy, but at a lower air temperature, with less horsepower drain.

volume of air into a smaller space with a tall piston dome. Consequently the higher-compressed charge will fire with a bigger "bang," producing more power than the same charge in a lower-compression motor. In a blown motor of the same displacement, however, you start with a larger volume of air in the cylinder, and then compress it into a larger combustion chamber, arriving at the same proportional compression ratio. So you get the same "bang" as in the high-compression engine, but you have a larger charge of air to expand and push the piston down. And, as we have seen, the more air you put into each cylinder, and make expand with the proportional fuel charge, the more power that engine will make. This is what a supercharger does.

Although we've already stated this, it bears repetition: you can think of a supercharger as a device that effectively increases the displacement of a given engine. That is, if you compare an unblown 450-ci engine with a supercharged 350-ci engine, you would very likely find that the smaller blown engine is pumping the same air/fuel charge into its cylinders as the larger one can draw in naturally. The power produced by an engine is directly proportional to the mass (or weight) of air it can ingest, compress, and expand (through ignition) per cycle, other things being equal. That is why larger-displacement engines make more power than smaller ones. But rather than making the cylinders bigger, we can use a supercharger to pump more air into the smaller motor, thereby making it perform just like an engine of much larger displacement.

Better yet—and this is increasingly important today—the smaller-displacement supercharged engine can be smaller externally and lighter, thereby allowing for a smaller and lighter vehicle package, which will increase performance, economy, and overall vehicle efficiency tremendously. This is exactly the kind of performance we are looking for today, and superchargers will certainly play a growing role in the small-car era. Further, superchargers help atomize the fuel charge in the airstream, which promotes even and complete combustion, and cleaner burning for lower emissions.

However, we must be fair and point out that not all contributions made by a supercharger are positive. To begin with, all belt-driven superchargers necessarily consume a certain portion of the engine's power, since they are driven by the crankshaft. At high boost levels, this power drain can be considerable, but the extra power produced by the blower more than offsets this drain. A good supercharger gives much more than it takes. Turbocharger devotees point out that turbos deliver "free" horsepower, unlike belt-driven blowers, but the truth is that turbos do cost something in backpressure.

A Roots-type blower, on the other hand, will "windmill" under high-vacuum driving conditions, such as constant-speed cruising. In other words, when the engine is running with the throttle closed, or only slightly open, vacuum rather than boost will be produced in the intake manifold (which can readily be seen on the boost gauge), and this vacuum will turn the supercharger rotors like a windmill. Under such circumstances, the blower will not be using up crankshaft horsepower. To prove this point,

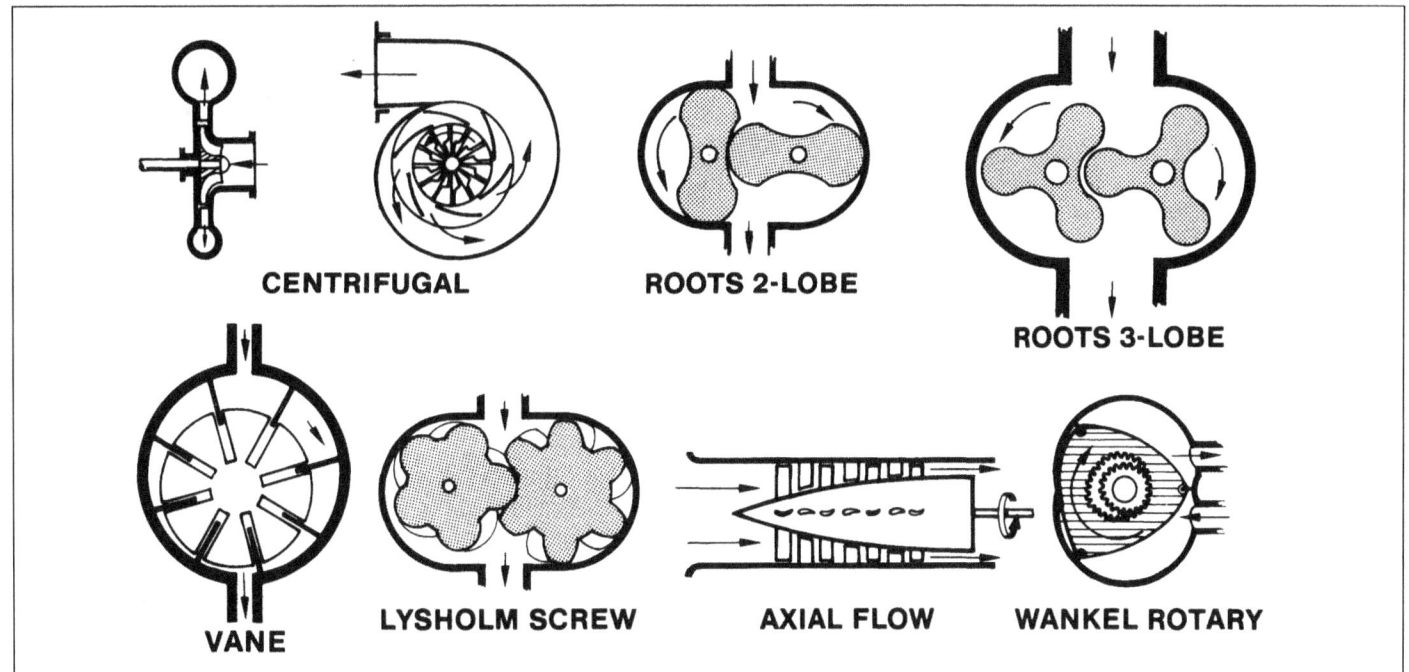

you can disconnect the belt from a Roots blower (or other types), and watch the drive pulley spin by itself while the engine is running.

Finally, all superchargers raise the temperature of the intake charge as they pressurize it, because the temperature of any gas rises when it is compressed. The amount of intake-charge temperature increase will vary with the amount of boost being produced and the efficiency of the supercharger (which we will discuss more fully later). This increase in intake temperature can lead to detonation in the combustion chamber, and possible parts damage, if not controlled. Fortunately, however, this is not a concern at typical street-boost levels, plus the efficiency of today's superchargers has increased significantly, and their design makes the use of intercoolers much simpler and more effective.

Types of Superchargers

There are any number of ways to pump things. Just think of the numerous types of water pumps or air fans you have seen. Most of the designs that have been used for engine superchargers over the years, including current styles, were actually intended for some other purpose originally. You have probably heard the story that the Roots blower was originally used to pump fresh air into mine shafts. Actually, it was first used to blow air into forges, as were several varieties of centrifugal types, well before the internal combustion engine was even invented. Roots blowers have also been used for such varied purposes as pressurizing airplane cabins and pumping flour or molasses, just to name a couple.

We mentioned that internal combustion (piston) engines have been likened to an air pump, because

A majority of today's new supercharger systems are designed to integrate as seamlessly as possible with modern EFI engines in crowded compartments. This ProCharger centrifugal package adds more than V-8 punch to a V-6-powered 2005 Mustang without altering much else. You can see the fresh-air inlet to the blower at lower right. What you can't see is the air-to-air intercooler (mounted behind the grille) the blower pumps pressurized air into, before it is routed back to the stock EFI inlet.

a piston-and-valve arrangement—like most air compressors—is a common air-pumping device. Consequently, some early designers tried to use a couple of cylinders in an engine to supercharge the other cylinders, but both the mechanical efficiency and the pumping rate of such a design were too low to be practical. A piston-and-valve air pump is good for high-pressure/low-volume work (such as an air compressor, which uses a large storage tank), while an engine supercharger needs to pump a large volume of air at a relatively low pressure.

Of course there are other types of internal combustion engines besides the piston variety, and some of them can be used as superchargers. The Wankel rotary engine, for instance, was first designed as a supercharger and used very effectively on some record-setting NSU motorcycles years ago. The jet engine, or "radial fan," is also a type of blower, and this same principle was used in the Latham "axial flow" supercharger made in the 1950s and 1960s.

Countless other varieties of pumps, compressors, blowers, and variations on each have existed in the past and may well appear in the future. But at present three types of blowers are the most commonly used: the Roots, the centrifugal, and more recently the Lysholm screw.

Roots

The type of supercharger most readily associated with hot rod engines is the Roots type. GMC blowers are of this design, which may be described as a bi-rotor, inter-meshing gear pump. A pair of rotors turns inside a closed housing (with an intake opening on one side and an outlet on the other) in opposite directions, meshing like a pair of gears. Most Roots blowers have two or three lobes per rotor (though they could have more). The open space between the lobes "catches" the air at the intake opening, carries it around as it rotates, sealed in by the wall of the case, and then "pushes" it out the exit opening on the other side. The meshing of the rotors in the center of the blower seals that area so the air cannot escape back up the middle. A Roots blower is called a positive-displacement pump since it theoretically moves the same volume of air through it on each revolution. The oil pump in most automotive engines works on exactly the same principle as the Roots blower.

Another positive-displacement air pump that has been used in the past for automotive supercharging is the vane type. There have been several variations on this design, but basically it consists of a cylindrical housing with a single, slightly smaller cylindrical "rotor" that turns on an offset axis. The rotor is slotted for a number of protruding vanes (usually three or four) that maintain light or near contact with the case wall at all times. Thus, as the rotor spins, the vanes sweep air into the case through an inlet port, pushing it around between the rotor and the case. At the same time, the offset rotor moves closer to the case wall as it turns, compressing the air trapped between the vanes, before pumping it out the outlet port. Several types of vane superchargers were made during the 1930s and 1940s. Two types, the Shorrock in England and the Judson in the United States, were aftermarket types made in the 1950s and early 1960s, but none have been produced since then. Both the Roots and the vane blowers are utterly simple types of pumps in terms of design and construction, though both are highly effective. The big advantage of the Roots blower is that it will pump a large quantity of air per revolution.

To make a clean application in the tight quarters of a C5 ZO6 Corvette, this polished, reverse-rotation ProCharger is mounted backward (belt at the back, inlet at the front). It still routes through an intercooler ahead of the radiator, before being ducted into the factory MAF/throttle body, as you can clearly see.

Vortech prefers water-to-air intercoolers, which place one heat exchanger up front, flowing cooled water into another placed between the blower and the engine's intake, as seen in this example installed on a late-model 6.1L Dodge Hemi. This all still fits neatly under the stock hood.

The vane type doesn't move as much air, but its advantage is that it compresses the air internally while pumping it.

Centrifugal

The second common type of supercharger used today—and throughout the history of this subject—is known as the centrifugal blower. It moves air by means of a bladed fan that spins at high speed inside a spiral housing shaped sort of like a snail's shell. Air enters at the center of the fan (called the impeller), is picked up by the spinning blades, and is then rapidly accelerated by centrifugal force before being flung out the outlet port. Although it only has, essentially, one moving part (the impeller), the centrifugal supercharger is not a positive-displacement type, and is much more complex in design and function than the Roots "pump."

The volume of air delivered at the outlet of the centrifugal blower increases as the square of the rotational speed of the impeller. Unlike the Roots, they do not pump much air at slow speeds, and therefore must be turned at very high speed, relative to engine RPM, to produce usable boost. And, because of the exponential increase in boost with impeller speed, it consequently produces little boost at lower engine RPM. The primary advantages of the centrifugal supercharger are that it takes much less engine horsepower to drive it, even at high boost, and that it can make large amounts of boost at higher RPM (this could be a problem, but it can be controlled by a waste-gate system).

Centrifugal superchargers were used on many race cars of the 1920s–1930s, such as Miller Indy cars and Mercedes/Auto Union Grand Prix machines, and World War II aircraft. The first aftermarket centrifugal blower common in the United States was the McCulloch/Paxton, which even found its way onto certain Ford and Studebaker models during the 1950s.

Of course all of the common types of exhaust-driven turbochargers, which have received so much attention from race car builders, not to mention production automobiles from the 1960s to the present (and now especially diesel-powered

Don't think that modern superchargers are just made for V-8 engines. Even though belt-driven blowers can be easily adjusted by changing pulley ratios, they should still be sized to the engine for optimum performance, as these two examples from Vortech/Paxton illustrate. The big reverse-rotation Paxton Novi pumps huge power into a Viper V10, while a smaller, shaft-driven, intercooled Vortech makes big muscle from a tiny Honda 4-cylinder. These examples also show the versatile mounting possibilities of today's superchargers.

trucks), are centrifugal superchargers. The only difference is that they are operated by a common-shaft turbine, driven by the engine's exhaust rather than by a belt (and step-up gearing) connected to the engine's crankshaft. Although we may make several comparisons between belt-driven superchargers and turbochargers later on, we will not discuss turbos in this book. The subject has been covered in great detail elsewhere, and certainly deserves separate study. However, the strong focus on turbocharging, for racing and production vehicles, has produced significant technical gains in that field, which have finally carried over to belt-driven centrifugal supercharging today.

Consequently, for these and other reasons (such as mounting location options, intercooling, and adaptability to factory EFI), highly improved centrifugal superchargers from Paxton, as well as from relatively new manufacturers such as Vortech, Powerdyne, and others, have become increasingly popular in today's street supercharging world, especially on smaller cars.

CHAPTER 1

The only real problem with street super-charging is that it's easy to get carried away. The shotgun-injected, 10-71 blown, alky-fed big-block Corvette even has nitrous added, if that weren't enough to make noise at fairgrounds events. The 14-71-blown K-B Hemi in the '32 roadster with no less than two mags and three 4-barrel carbs could probably be tuned to drive around OK, but this is an obvious exercise in excess spending.

The Lysholm-design twin-screw compressor, finally becoming more common for aftermarket (and factory) supercharging today, looks much like a modern Roots blower on the outside, but works quite differently. This Kenne Bell version mounts on a recent SOHC Ford engine in an early Mustang, drawing air through an enlarged throttle body (with the MAF sensor located upstream), and blowing into a manifold fed by stock EFI injectors and fuel rails.

The best thing about hot rodding is that it accepts everyone. At the opposite end of the spectrum, this 1940 Ford owner grabbed a small Eaton blower off of some new car, machined his own manifold, drive, and carb adapter, and makes all the power he can use from his simple 350 small-block Chevy. That's the beauty of supercharging.

Screw

Finally, a third type of relatively sophisticated supercharger that has become more or less common today is the Lysholm screw. If it weren't for significant advances in computer-aided design and machining (CAD-CAM), this complicated supercharger would not be practical to produce at all, let alone in a size (and price range) that would work on today's street performance vehicles. Actually, the supercharger itself is not complicated, since it has only two primary moving parts: a pair of multi-lobed, meshing rotors inside a case similar in size and shape to a Roots blower. However, these rotors are quite different from those in a Roots, as well as from each other. It's hard to describe, but one rotor has concave lobes, while the other's lobes are convex. Both are "twisted," and mesh in such a way that they not only draw in and pump air with each revolution, but also compress it between the rotors at the same time. This internal compression raises the efficiency of this type of supercharger, which we will discuss more fully in chapters 3 and 7.

When this book was last revised in 1999, we were still lamenting that supercharger design was sorely lagging, not only in technical advances in the blowers themselves, but also in the realm of peripheral equipment such as intercoolers and interfacing with modern electronic fuel injection. Finally, we can say that the state of street supercharging today is at the front of the curve of automotive technology in general. In fact, it could well be that supercharging is the future of modern, more efficient, hopefully more-responsive and fun automotive technology, which could use a good boost.

CHAPTER 2

BLOWER BACKGROUND

A Short History of Supercharging

Most types of superchargers, in elementary forms, were used for some other purpose well before cars were invented. They were used to pump water, to be pumped by water (as a water wheel or mill), or to blow air for ventilation, for furnaces, or for other purposes. The Roots blower design, the type used by GMC and several other automotive supercharger manufacturers, traces its origin to two American brothers, Francis and Philander Roots, who were trying to design a better waterwheel to power their woolen mill in 1854. Their bi-rotor gear pump was not successful as a water mill, but they later found it to be very good for pumping large volumes of air at relatively slow rotor speeds as a blast blower for a foundry furnace. The Roots brothers patented their blower in 1860, updating the design with 16 more patents by 1884. The Roots blower has been used in a wide variety of industrial applications, including blowing fresh air into mine shafts, ever since. The company is still operating as the Roots Division of Dresser, Inc., of Addison, Texas.

The first noted example of a blower being fitted to an internal combustion engine was in 1901 when Sir Dugald Clerk, the pioneer of two-stroke engine design, used a pumping device to force more air into the engine to supposedly lower the maximum combustion temperature. As we shall see, blowers actually raise the temperature of inlet air and of combustion in the cylinder, but Clerk found that the blower ultimately increased the power of his two-stroke engine by six percent. Thus the power-producing capabilities of supercharging were discovered. In 1902,

Supercharger development in the U.S. centered around centrifugal blowers. Blown Duesenberg and Miller straight eights totally dominated the Indy 500 throughout the 1920s. This is a Goosen-designed, Offenhauser-built Miller 91 circa 1927 showing the flywheel-driven blower at the back with a single updraft Miller barrel-valve carburetor. Note the increasing diameter of the blower scroll housing.

One of the more radical Indy designs was the Duesenberg "Sidewinder" introduced in 1927, using a side-mounted, shaft-driven centrifugal blower. The fins on the blower case and the tall intake manifold weren't just for looks. Their purpose was to dissipate heat generated by the blower—one of the first intercoolers.

A COMPLETE GUIDE TO STREET SUPERCHARGING   19

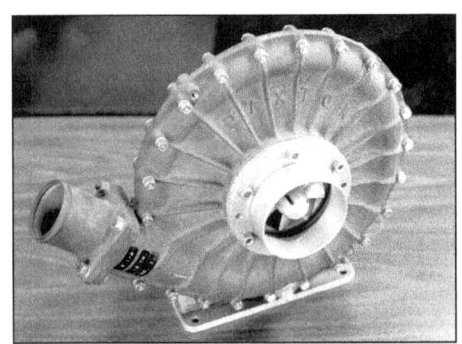

This is a very early Paxton-McCulloch centrifugal blower made specifically for extremely high boost on the Novi Indy cars. Note the similarity to the Miller Indy blower.

Louis Renault patented a supercharging system in France that used a centrifugal compressor to blow air into the carburetor.

The first example of supercharging in the United States, the first supercharged car to win a competitive event, and the first application of a supercharger for production vehicles all fall to Lee Chadwick of Pottstown, Pennsylvania. He had been manufacturing Chadwick automobiles since about 1900. In 1907, he and engineer John Nichols mounted a centrifugal blower to the 1140-ci Great Chadwick Six, producing a certified top speed in excess of 100 mph. The initial Chadwick design drove the supercharger with a leather belt from the flywheel at nine times crankshaft speed, blowing dry air into the carburetor. A second version used a three-stage centrifugal compressor with three 10-inch-diameter impellers of 12 blades each (but of increasing widths for 3-stage compression). This car won the Wilkes-Barre Hill Climb in 1908, the first event in which a supercharged car was ever entered, and it went on to score many other victories before Chadwick ceased production in 1911 after making some 260 cars. Also, the Chadwick was obviously our first street supercharged vehicle.

Blowers in Europe

Supposedly Chadwick had considered an exhaust-driven centrifugal supercharger (that is, a turbocharger) before deciding on the belt-driven type. However, a Swiss engineer named Buchi is generally credited with the invention of the turbocharger. He adapted an exhaust-driven blower to a diesel engine in 1909.

In 1911, a Frenchman named Sizaire carried out experiments with centrifugal blowers, and the following year Marc Birkigt designed a Hispano-Suiza for the Coupe de l'Auto race that used two of its six cylinders to supercharge the other four. This experiment was not very successful.

Further automotive applications for superchargers were eclipsed by the outbreak of World War I. This was the first air war, and air superiority relied heavily on supercharging, because the higher an airplane flies, the less dense the air becomes to feed the engine. Supercharging was immediately seen by the Germans as a practical means for maintaining engine power at higher altitudes by mechanically forcing a denser charge into the cylinders. Similar supercharger developments followed in other European countries and in the United States.

Naturally, most leading auto designers and manufacturers were involved in the war effort in Germany and elsewhere. Not long after the war's end, superchargers of various types began showing up on race cars.

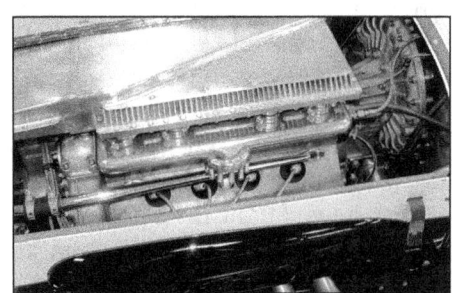

The Novi cars came a little later in Indy history. This one was built on one of the 1935 Miller-Ford V-8 front-drive chassis by Lewis Welch and Bud Winfield. They hired Fred Offenhauser to build a new, supercharged V-8 for it in 1941, designed by Leo Goosen. With its 10-inch Paxton centrifugal blower overdriven 5.35 percent, this ground-breaking Novi produced 450 hp from 181 ci at 8,000 rpm. With front-wheel drive and the tires available, the power was basically unmanageable, and veteran driver Ralph Hepburn used a wood block as a throttle stop in order to wrangle the car to a very respectable 4th place finish in the '41 500.

BLOWER BACKGROUND

One of the first companies to use superchargers for automobiles in Germany was Daimler (which made the Mercedes cars, later to merge with Benz in 1926). With the assistance of Dr. Porsche, who worked for Daimler at the time, they developed the 28/95 Mercedes 6-cylinder, which won the 1921 Coppa Florio—the first victory for a supercharged car since the Chadwick. The 28/95 Mercedes, like several later models including the famous SS and SSKs, used a Roots-type blower mounted vertically at the front of the engine, driven by a bevel gear and cone clutch from the crankshaft. The blower was engaged only at full throttle, and blew into the carburetor. When the blower was engaged, power was reportedly increased 50 percent with a pressure boost of approximately 6 to 7 psi. A considerable amount of Roots blower technology was compiled by Mercedes-Benz between World War I and World War II.

In 1923, Fiat added a Wittig vane-type supercharger to its 8-cylinder Grand Prix car. The blower was front-driven by the crankshaft and, like the Mercedes, blew into the carburetor only at full throttle. This early vane-type blower did not work well (possibly because oil had to be injected into the blower to lubricate the vanes, causing detonation in the engine). Later the same year Fiat switched to a Roots-type blower with an intercooler and did much better, finishing one-two in the Italian Grand Prix and setting a new lap record just shy of 100 mph at Monza.

In 1924, Sunbeam and Alfa Romeo both introduced Roots-blown Grand Prix cars, with the Sunbeam being the first to place the Roots supercharger between the carburetor and the intake manifold (that is, in a draw-through rather than a blow-through arrangement), discovering through testing that this design netted a 20-percent

European manufacturers preferred positive-displacement Roots-type blowers. One of the more famous early blown cars was the Mercedes SSK (this is a '29 Model), which used an upright supercharger driven by a bevel gear from the crank, with a clutch to engage the blower only at full throttle. Although the car won many races, it was outfitted and sold as a street vehicle, as were most of the early supercharged "sports cars."

In an arrangement similar to the famous Blower Bentley, also from England, this 1934 MG K-3 "Brooklands" used a front-drive Roots blower (A Marshall), with a single SU carburetor, mounted in front of the radiator, between the frame rails. Something like this could be striking—and effective—on a hot rod today, wouldn't it?

increase in horsepower over the blow-through configuration. The cooling effect of the vaporizing fuel in the blower, plus, the better atomization of the fuel particles as they passed through the rotors, were the main factors in the power increase.

After this, until a rules change in 1952 virtually banned the too-dominant blowers, supercharged cars

This '37 Mercedes 540 K mounts a Roots blower horizontally beside the straight eight engine, at the front. Note the fins on the blower and carburetor ducting for cooling.

totally dominated Grand Prix racing in Europe, and the majority of these used Roots-type blowers.

Superchargers in the United States

In the United States, by a series of coincidences, supercharger development centered around the city of Indianapolis. Prior to World War I, Dr. Sanford Moss, working for the General Electric Company, had been experimenting with Roots-type blowers and centrifugal turbochargers. He was also a pioneer in the two-stage blower concept. Dr. Moss, as well as Kerr and LeBlanc, who were designing a gear-driven centrifugal blower for the Liberty aircraft engine, were working for the U.S. government at McCook Field, near Indianapolis. Allison Engineering, manufacturer of the Liberty engine and other subsequent supercharged aircraft engines, was also located near Indianapolis, and the company's owner, James A. Allison, was one of the owners of the Indianapolis Motor Speedway. Thus much of the pioneering supercharger development in the United States was occurring in the same city as most of the pioneering race-car development, even if for different reasons.

Meanwhile, brothers Fred and August Duesenberg had opened their new automobile manufacturing company in Indianapolis in 1912 and were involved in building one-off race cars. In 1924, the Duesenbergs fitted a centrifugal supercharger to their already highly successful straight-8 racing engine. The blower was gear and shaft driven and was the first recorded example in the United States to place the carburetor ahead of the supercharger in a draw-through layout. This supercharged Duesy was a winner, and all subsequent Duesenberg racing engines were similarly supercharged. After Errett Lobban Cord bought into the Duesenberg company in 1928, as he had with Auburn previously, they introduced the famous J and SJ production models, which came equipped with shaft-driven centrifugal superchargers mounted horizontally above the engine. Models of the Auburn, the V-8 Cord, and the Hollywood Graham also came factory-equipped with similar centrifugal blowers.

The Italians were also big on Roots blowers, and most of the manufacturers made their own. They knew how to make power, and they also knew how to make engines beautiful. They still do. This DOHC '34 Bugatti Type 55 uses a blower mounted at the side of the engine, under the intake, driven by a shaft from the front of the crank.

Shortly after the Duesenbergs unveiled their blown engine at the 500, a Los Angeles-based engine builder and a fierce competitor of the Duesenbergs, Harry Miller, came up with a centrifugal supercharger for his straight-8 racing engines. Designed by Leo Goosen and built by Miller machinist Fred Offenhauser, this flywheel-driven blower was relatively advanced for the time in terms of impeller, diffuser, and scroll-housing design.

The most interesting point about this period of supercharger activity in motor sports (roughly between World War I and World War II) is the fact that Roots-type blowers were used almost exclusively in Europe while centrifugal blowers were predominant in the United States. The Europeans used other types of blowers to begin with, as did the Americans, but each group soon discovered which type of supercharger worked best for the particular style of racing predominant in that part of the world.

In Europe, the Grand Prix, or road racing, was the ultimate in auto competition. The twisting and turning road course required a broad horsepower range in the engine, as well as instant throttle response and good low-end torque for accelerating from slow corners. In the United States, however, the ultimate was the Indy 500, a long, fast oval with sweeping curves that kept a racing engine operating in a narrow RPM range. From the turn of the century on, auto racing in the United States was done primarily on circle, oval, or board tracks, and therefore mostly at wide-open throttle. The Roots blower gave the Europeans the kind of power they needed, while the centrifugal blower, which was more efficient in a narrower RPM range, gave the American cars the top-end boost they required.

The period between the two World Wars was the heyday of supercharging. Not only did the major race cars of the time run blowers but, as you might expect, so did several of the more racy production models, both in the United States and in Europe. However, the 1930's economic Depression and then World War II finally put an end to supercharged luxury sports cars and, shortly after war's end, rules changes stifled the supercharger's advantage in racing. Consequently, after the early 1940s, superchargers virtually disappeared from the automotive scene.

Hot Rod Supercharging

Just before and after World War II was when hot rodding really began to develop. The young kids who raced stripped-down Model Ts and As on dirt ovals and dry lake beds were a far cry from the sophisticated European Grand Prix and the U.S. Indy race car builders, but they had paid close attention to the way the experts built racing engines and they knew the effectiveness of superchargers. In hot rodding there was no ban on blowers. The major determinant then, even more than now, was cost (not to mention scarcity of equipment).

There were a few examples of blowers being run on roadsters at the dry lakes, even in the Depression days before the war. A few rodders acquired centrifugal blowers from production American cars such as the Graham, and adapted them to the Ford flathead V-8. However, Graham production blowers produced very little boost, and when hot rodders tried to spin them faster to get more pressure out of them, they usually ended up stripping the blower's step-up drive gears. McCulloch also introduced a centrifugal supercharger as an aftermarket bolt-on kit for the Ford V-8 about this time (probably the first aftermarket blower kit), and some of the more affluent rod builders tried them at the dry lakes.

The first generally noted example of a Roots-type blower being fitted to a hot rod was in the late 1930s when the Spalding brothers somehow acquired a Mercedes-Benz blower and put it on their Ford V-8. After the war, Don Blair bought this blower from the Spaldings and adapted it to his "Goat" Unlimited–class roadster for the 1946 and 1947 seasons. Running alcohol through two Stromberg 48 carbs, and driving the blower with two V-belts, the car turned 141 mph.

Another Italian example, this '31 Alfa Romeo Zagato Model 1750 6C, mounts the Roots blower at the front, driven directly off the crank. Again, note fins on the blower, ducting, and manifold, as well as two small spring-loaded pop-off valves at either end of the duct connecting the blower to the intake.

The person usually credited with the first installation of a GMC diesel blower on a hot rod is Barney Navarro. Barney had been aware of blowers for some time, but they were scarce and expensive. Then one day in 1948, Kong Jackson showed up with a 3-71 GMC out of a World War II landing craft, and offered it to Navarro for $60. Barney was manufacturing his own line of Ford V-8 heads and intake manifolds at the time, so he modified one of his manifold patterns to accept the blower and cast an intake for it. He built his own drive using four V-belts and mounted four Stromberg 48 carbs on top of the blower to run alcohol. On a de-stroked, 176-ci V-8 in his 1927 T roadster, this early Jimmy setup pumped 16 pounds of boost and pushed the car to 146.9 mph. The only internal modification Barney made to the blower was to bore the case slightly larger for increased rotor-to-housing clearance for higher RPM use.

Barney not only ran the roadster at the dry lakes, but also raced it on the dirt circle tracks, possibly the only supercharged hot rod to do so. Although he never had any mechanical problems with the blower, he had plenty of trouble with the V-belts, especially on the tracks, since they tended to heat up and disintegrate.

Barney solved this problem by drilling a series of holes vertically and horizontally through the pulleys to cool the belts.

Tom Beatty, who worked for Navarro, built a similar system for his own lakes roadster, adapting a 4-71 GMC to an Oldsmobile OHV V-8 for his belly-tank Lakester. Beatty eventually manufactured manifolds and multi-V-belt drive "kits" for the GMCs based on the Navarro design, and helped promote the more widespread use of "Jimmies." In fact, back in the 1950s, Beatty stuffed one of his blown Olds race engines into his 1940 Ford sedan delivery to use as a street-driver and push truck at Bonneville.

Navarro was also one of the first to run a blower at the drag races, since he entered his roadster at the first Santa Ana drags in 1950. However, Barney did not pursue drag racing with his blown engine because, as he put it, "I broke too many quick-change rear ends."

Very likely the first use of a blower at the drags was a grudge race

CHAPTER 2

Barney Navarro pioneered the use of GMC 71-series diesel blowers on hot rod engines after the war. Using a modified 3-71 on a destroked 176-ci flathead V-8, this roadster turned 146 mph at the lakes in the 1940s, plus raced on circle tracks and at the drags. His one-time employee, Tom Beatty, machined the multi-V-belt drives and made GMC setups for engines such as Oldsmobiles for years.

at the first legal, regularly operating drag strip at the Goleta air strip in 1949. The contest was between Tom Cobbs, who was running a 3-71 GMC blown Ford flathead, and Edelbrock's Fran Hernandez, who was using a secret new fuel called nitromethane in his flathead-powered '32 coupe.

Hernandez won that round as Cobbs spun his tires at the start. But it was drag racing that really pushed the development of GMC blowers in hot rodding. This big Roots blower produced gobs of horsepower and torque in the low RPM ranges, which is exactly what dragsters needed to get off the line—unlike the lakes and Bonneville racers who went for top end speed. However, the Cobbs/Hernandez duel was also representative of another new element in rodding that affected both drag racing and blower development: nitro. Once the secret of nitro got out, rodders discovered that it gave them as much horsepower as superchargers did. But it was also very temperamental, literally explosive, stuff. Early experiments with blowers on alcohol or gasoline proved fairly reliable, but the combination of a blower with nitro often ended in disaster. Consequently, widespread use of GMC blowers in drag racing had to wait until the racers got the nitro situation sorted out.

This is not to say that some drag racers weren't using GMCs right away. One of the first was Ernie Hashim of Bakersfield, California, who mounted a 3-71 on top of a Ford V-8 as early as 1950 and was using it at the lakes as well as to race on airfields in the San Joaquin Valley, such as Maricopa and Famoso. He got his 3-71 from partner John Gilbert, who operated heavy equipment in the Northwest and had therefore become acquainted with GMC diesel blowers. By 1955, Hashim had adapted a front-mounted 4-71 GMC to a Chrysler Hemi with one of the first Hilborn 2-port injectors made for GMCs, which he ran in his '32 Ford roadster at Bonneville and in a rail at the drags. Shortly afterward, Hashim mounted a 6-71 on top of the Chrysler and fabricated one of the first Gilmer belt drives. About the same time Ed Iskenderian purchased a batch of 6-71 GMC superchargers and hired Hashim to rework them for use on dragsters, which involved reversing the rotors, milling the case, and resetting the clearances. In 1959, Isky introduced his "Forced Induction" blower drive kit, using a toothed Gilmer belt, for top-mounted 6-71s.

Prior to that time the most popular blower setup for drags at Bonneville was Chuck Potvin's front-drive for 6-71s. Early versions, introduced in the mid-1950s, were of a "U-Fab" variety; later models used cast-aluminum manifolds and drive housings. The big advantage of the front-drive blower, besides the fact that the lower profile was better for aerodynamics and gave the driver a better view, was that the direct drive from the crankshaft solved the persistent problem of drive-belt slippage when the blower was pumping substantial boost. The drawback was that this setup provided only a 1:1 blower/drive ratio. Toothed Gilmer belts with easily swapped drive pulleys solved both problems and led to the unanimous popularity of top-mounted blowers for drags, street, and most other applications.

Mickey Thompson probably gets credit for the first blown Chrysler Hemi. In 1953 he dropped one of the new hemi-head motors into Bill Burke's old streamlined Bantam coupe along with a more traditional 3-carb flathead V-8. To this strange marriage Thompson added a 4-71 GMC atop the Chrysler. The first year the blower melted two pistons in the Hemi; later the odd-coupled contraption went in excess of 190 mph at Bonneville. In 1954 Bruce Crower brought a 1949 Hudson to Bonneville powered by a blown Chrysler. It ran 157 mph, and he drove it on the street, as well. In 1956, Ernie Hashim and Tony Waters set the fastest speed ever for a stock-bodied roadster with their blown Hemi '32 at 189 mph. That same year Tom Cobbs switched the homemade front-mount 4-71 from the flathead in his '34 coupe to the brand-new Chevy 265 V-8, very probably the first GMC-blown Chevy small-block.

BLOWER BACKGROUND

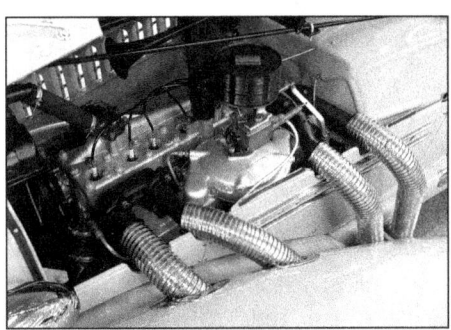

Americans preferred centrifugal blowers on the few production cars that had them. The '35 Auburn Speedster proclaimed its super-charged status on the hood, right above the big chromed pipes. This blower was shaft-driven with bevel-gears, and mounted a single carb on top.

next two meets. Other than developments in fuel injection systems, alloy blocks, and big-displacement blower cases (8-71s to 14-71s), the story in fuel drag racing has been essentially the same ever since.

Street Supercharging

As far as supercharging for street-driven, gasoline-burning automobiles goes, the history is relatively brief, though still developing. After the prestigious supercharged road cars of the 1920s and 1930s, the next appearance of blowers was a few bolt-on supercharger kits that suddenly appeared on the market about 1950. These included the McCulloch, the rare Frenzel, the more-plentiful S.Co.T./Italmeccanica, a few kits based on reworked GMC 3-71s and 4-71s such as the J.E.M., the Speed-O-Motive, Tom Beatty's, and a bit later the Judson and Latham. We will discuss these blowers in more detail in Chapter 4, but they were used primarily in street applications, rather than racing. Because such blower kits were quite expensive for the time, not many found their way onto hot rods when they were first introduced.

The next development came in the mid-1950s. After Chevrolet introduced its new small-block V-8 in 1955, Ford and other manufacturers suddenly found themselves playing catch-up. Since its new Y-Block was no match for the Chevy, Ford turned to supercharging as the one sure way to best the Chevys on NASCAR tracks, on the beach at Daytona, and at Pike's Peak. They had McCulloch design a special centrifugal blower for the racing Fords, and then offered a standard McCulloch variable-speed belt-driven blower as optional equipment on 1957 Fords and T-Birds. The same year Studebaker offered the McCulloch on their Golden Hawks

The top-of-the-line Duesenberg SJ was from the same family as the Auburn and Cord, and used a similar centrifugal blower. This special '35 SSJ, owned by Gary Cooper, was one of three modified at the factory with two updraft carbs adapted to the blower.

and on some of the last Packard models. As late as 1963, the McCulloch/Paxton was used as factory equipment on the Studebaker Avanti.

At about that same time, however, Detroit turned to turbocharging, starting with the Corvair and the Olds F-85, and then becoming much more prevalent on small 4-cylinder models (such as Chrysler K-cars and the Ford T-Bird). During the "gas crisis" and smog-controlled 1970s, the aim was to squeeze a modicum of performance from these engines while achieving fuel economy and emissions standards. Besides European models ranging from Porsches to Volvos, the most successful performance-oriented turbocharging application to come from Detroit during that period was the intercooled Buick turbo V-6. It wasn't until the late 1980s that Detroit began to use belt-driven, Roots-type superchargers on a few models, starting at Ford.

Primarily using various sizes and designs of Eaton blowers, the use of belt-driven superchargers continues to spread, both in the United Stastes and Europe, producing very healthy horsepower numbers in many cases. At the time of this writing, the 6.2-liter

Also in 1955, top dragster pilot Calvin Rice was getting a homemade front-drive GMC blown Chrysler Hemi to run faster than the fuel flathead that won the first NHRA Nationals in his slingshot rail. However, the 6-71 blown Hemi did not become the standard dragster powerplant until about 1959. That was the year of the first Bakersfield Fuel and Gas Championships, and the first trip to the West Coast for Don Garlits. When Garlits arrived he was running naturally aspirated on eight carburetors, but all of his California competitors had recently switched to the big GMC blowers. After that meet, but before his other two scheduled West Coast appearances, Garlits towed the dragster immediately to Isky's to have a 6-71 installed between the Hemi and the eight carbs. He won the

V-8 LS9 Corvette engine, producing nearly 650 factory street horsepower due to a water-intercooled 2.3L Eaton Roots-type supercharger producing 10.5 psi of boost, was the ultimate example.

Through the 1960s and early 1970s, there were isolated examples of supercharged street-driven hot rods, but most of these were considered phenomenal at the time. The sight and sound of a working GMC blower on the street, not to mention the potential power on tap, was awe-inspiring. But at that time GMC blowers were scarce (other than for big diesel applications), parts to adapt them to a street engine were nearly non-existent, and getting one to work right in traffic took lots of trial and error.

It wasn't until the late 1970s to early 1980s that companies such as Gary Dyer's Machine Service in the Chicago area and the Railsback's Blower Drive Service in Whittier, California, began, first, to adapt GMC blower mounting plates to existing aluminum intake manifolds for a variety of street-oriented V-8 and V-6 engines. Then they cast their own blower intakes for a similar range of engines with provisions for coolant inlet/thermostat housings and standard distributors. This led to a boom in street supercharging, mostly using 6-71 blowers with dual 4-barrel carburetors on top, in the growing street rodding and street machine/truck (quickly dubbed "Street Freak") arenas. They learned that this exceptionally effective method of gaining major attention while producing major horsepower was actually quite streetable.

Soon other drag-race or ski-boat blower builders, such as Don Hampton, Gene Mooneyham, Mike Kuhl, Mert Littlefield, and several others began retooling to produce intake manifolds, belt-drive systems, and other parts and accessories to adapt reworked GMC blowers—primarily 6-71s—to a variety of street performance applications. Some of these manufacturers had already been casting their own 6-71, 8-71, or larger, GMC-based blower cases and end plates, initially for improved strength, tolerances, and availability (for racing applications) over GM diesel-based units.

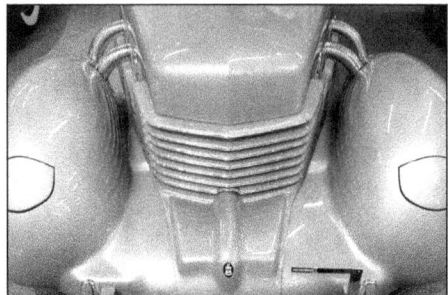

The classic coffin-nose Cord had the same chrome pipes, but mounted the centrifugal blower on top of the flathead V-8 engine, driven from the rear, as was the generator.

Then, in the mid-1980s, B&M Automotive, the venerable producer of "Hydro-Stick" and other performance automatic transmissions and accessories, introduced a freshly designed, relatively small (144-ci), low-profile, lightweight, and low-cost Roots-style supercharger and complete installation kit (including intake manifold), for small-block Chevys and Fords. Based on a 2-lobe rotor design similar in size and shape to the 53-series GMCs, but made of low-cost extruded aluminum and tipped with Teflon strips to reduce the need for tedious rotor-to-case clearance setting, these all-new superchargers became instantly successful—both in terms of sales and performance/reliability.

Soon B&M was adding larger blowers of similar design, and long-time aftermarket intake manifold producer Weiand jumped in with its own small, 2-lobe blowers in a similar design, followed by 3-lobe 6-71, 8-71 (and larger) blowers, manifolds, and drive kits in the GMC style. In just a few years, literally tens of thousands of these superchargers were sold, mostly for street applications. Quite surprisingly, however, both the B&M and Weiand supercharger lines (in fact, all of Weiand) were purchased by Holley in the late 1990s. Holley has been producing only a slightly downsized line of Weiand blower kits for street and marine applications since.

The 1980s were also the decade during which the automotive industry struggled to change from carburetors to electronic fuel injection. The first attempts with throttle body injectors (TBI), which basically bolted in place of carburetors, did not lend themselves well to supercharging. But by the time they got direct-port EFI sorted out, with a single throttle body incorporating an MAF sensor feeding into a common plenum manifold, with individual injectors located at each intake port, this new configuration was perfect for the relatively simple addition of a bolt-on, belt-driven, blow-through type of supercharger. The type of blower that fit this description was a centrifugal unit, such as the venerable McCulloch/Paxton, which could be mounted to the front of the engine with brackets like an alternator or A/C compressor, driven with a belt in similar fashion,

BLOWER BACKGROUND

During World War II, supercharger development progressed rapidly, but for airplane engines rather than for automobiles. The huge unit at the front of this Rolls-Royce Merlin V-12 is a 2-stage, crank-driven, centrifugal blower. Even today, little of this technology has been applied to cars.

with its outlet connected to the EFI inlet by a single large tube. We'll discuss details more fully in Chapter 5, but the EFI unit doesn't require external pressurization (like a carburetor did), and the MAF sensor reads the increase in airflow and automatically increases fuel delivery at the injectors. What could be simpler?

Further advantages of such a centrifugal supercharger installation are that it can be fit under the stock hood in most cases, and that its layout makes the incorporation of an intercooler relatively simple, especially an air-to-air type. Such a cooler can usually be mounted in front of the radiator, with the outlet tube from the blower attached to the cooler inlet, and a second tube running from its outlet to the EFI inlet. Simple. And such supercharger installations, with or without intercooling, do not require complicated, expensive, and heat-producing exhaust manifold rerouting that turbochargers do.

Thus the ball-drive Paxton blower from the 1950s got a new round of attention, but Paxton was quick to see that a more modern design, incorporating impeller refinements derived from years of turbocharger development, plus a more reliable gear-type step-up internal drive, were needed. Consequently, Paxton introduced its all-new Novi centrifugal supercharger in the 1990s. Not surprisingly, they were accompanied by a handful of all-new centrifugal supercharger manufacturers, including Vortech, ATI ProCharger, and Powerdyne.

Two other supercharging developments during this period largely made possible by computer-controlled design and machining included the use of a new, small, 3-lobe Roots-type compressor made by huge aftermarket supplier Eaton on 3.8L V-6 Thunderbirds in 1989. This was the first instance of any type of belt (or gear) driven blower as OEM (original equipment manufacturer) equipment on any new car since the 1950s. Soon several sizes of Eaton blowers were being added as optional, or even standard, equipment on a variety of new cars both in the United States and Europe. Given the availability of these new, smaller, yet more efficient and more precisely machined, Roots blowers, it was only natural that someone in the aftermarket would find ways to adapt them to other popular engines for street-driven hot rod applications. Jerry Magnuson, who had plenty of experience designing and building small, 3-lobe, Roots compressors with his previous Magna Chargers, was the first not only to employ the Eaton blowers for a full new Magna Charger line, but also initiate ongoing revisions to the Eaton to further increase its efficiency and capacity.

The other development during this period was the introduction of the first viable Lysholm screw-type compressor for automotive supercharging. Two companies, Whipple Industries and Kenne Bell Performance Products, both in California,

One of the first Roots blowers used on a hot rod was a Mercedes unit that Don Blair got from the Spalding Brothers, who ran it on an OHV-equipped Ford V-8. On the flathead V-8 in his Old Goat *modified roadster, it turned 141 mph in 1946.*

The only instance we've seen of dual-stage supercharging on a dragster was this configuration on Ted Rawleigh's 1960s Olds-powered rail that had a crank-driven 6-71 pumping into a belt-driven 4-71. It made 670 hp on gas, but the tires and chassis of the time couldn't put it to the ground, and it hasn't been tried since.

The year of the first Bakersfield Fuel and Gas Championships, 1959, was when the 6-71 GMC-blown fuel Chrysler Hemi came to rule drag racing, and things really haven't changed all that much since.

A COMPLETE GUIDE TO STREET SUPERCHARGING

CHAPTER 2

This Cadillac flathead V-8-powered "rail" seen at the first World Series of Drag Racing in 1954 appears to be topped with a 2-71 GMC blower fitted with two carbs on a handmade intake manifold. It was turning respectable 110-mph times.

The driver looking over his shoulder in this GMC-blown, GMC-6-powered Bantam roadster (with part of a 1939 Chevy hood) is none other than "Dyno" Don Nicholson, who cut his teeth on Jimmy sixes. The side-mounted 4-71 is chain-driven and mounts three 97 carbs.

In the late 1940s superchargers were hard to find, so enterprising hot rodders used what was available. This Roots-type blower is of undetermined origin, but the owner has made a neat, belt-driven installation, with two Stromberg carbs, on top of the Cadillac flathead V-8 in his dusty lakes roadster.

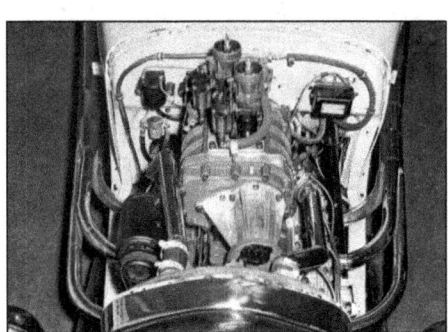
GMC-based street blowers were very rare in the 1950s, but this neat installation of a 3-71 with two 97 carbs on a flathead V-8 in a 1927 street roadster was done with a J.E.M. drive kit in 1950.

began making installation kits to adapt a fairly small, compact screw compressor made by Autorotor in Sweden to various engines, including both small- and big-block Chevys and Fords. (More on this in Chapter 7.)

Finally, given all these developments in new supercharger types and sizes, not to mention a large surge in turbocharger applications during the fairly short-lived import/compact tuner craze at the turn of the century, and the complete switch to electronic fuel injection on new cars, you'd probably surmise that the days of a big GMC blower on top of a V-8 engine (with a pair of 4-barrel carbs on top of that) are gone. Diminished? Yes. Supplanted by new compressors with electronic fuel/ignition management and possibly an intercooler on most new-car applications? Yes, definitely.

But there are a whole lot of older cars and trucks out there that people continue to fix up and hot rod. The vast majority of these vehicles, in reality, are driven only briefly and selectively. Therefore the thinking seems to go in many cases, "If we're going to put a big V-8 in this thing, why not go all out and stick a big blower on it, too?" The current price of gasoline has little effect on these weekend warriors. Whether mounted on early T-bucket roadsters, 1930s or 1940s street rods, jacked-up Gasser-style machines, modified 1960s muscle cars, sport trucks, or whatever they're calling the hot rodded vehicles you see at weekend events and in the magazines these days, you'll see plenty of big GMC-type blowers with either old-style carburetors on top, or something like Hilborn or Enderle fuel injection converted to EFI. The biggest difference is that there is little point in reworking an old, worn-out GMC unit today, as complete new 6-71 and 8-71 style units are now available, ready to bolt on, from companies such as Blower Drive Service, The Blower Shop, Weiand, and others.

And, wouldn't you know, old is new again. While a couple of prior attempts by small manufacturers to reproduce and improve vintage superchargers, such as the Latham, failed, the latest entry into this retro blower field is an exact and apparently successful all-new version of the old S.Co.T. Roots blower built by H&H Flatheads. We'll see what happens next as the history of street supercharging both advances and repeats itself.

CHAPTER 3

How Blowers Work

One of the first and most basic tenets of hot rodding is a strong distrust, or downright disbelief, in theory as opposed to practical application. The *modus operandi* of hot rod engineering is to look at what has worked best in the past, figure out a few practical tricks to make it work a little better, and then bolt it on the car and give it a try. If it doesn't work better, you go back to what you know through experience will work.

Although the field of automotive performance modification is becoming more and more sophisticated, hot rodders still believe in what they can feel when they get behind the wheel, or in what the timing slip says at the drag strip. The manufacturers of speed parts these days rely on flow benches, dynamometers, and computers to design and test new products, but the average rodder—as well as most racers—still assert that "you can't drive a dyno."

What these hot rodders know, and have known since the 1950s, is that superchargers work. You bolt one on an engine and it makes horsepower. Spin it faster or bolt on a bigger one, and it'll make even more horsepower. Go too far and you'll

The only way to truly measure how much horsepower a supercharger adds to an engine is to test it on a good dyno, and several blower manufacturers have well-equipped dynos today. At Magnuson Products they have a chassis (rear wheel) and an engine dyno, and this is Jerry Kugel's LS Chevy on the latter being fine-tuned with a new MP 2300 TVS blower. It measured 875 hp at the flywheel at 16 psi on gasoline, then ran 201 mph at Bonneville in Jerry's regularly street-driven 1932 Ford roadster. A well-instrumented dyno can measure blower efficiencies, as well.

blow head gaskets or melt pistons. Hot rodders have also learned that, although turbochargers are somehow supposed to be "better" than belt-driven blowers, they just don't deliver the same instant horsepower on the street or at the drag strip, plus they're much more complicated and temperamental to set up right.

Unfortunately, this quixotic practicality common to hot rodders can be both commendable and misleading. Hot rodders have done things with cars and engines that have left

---

A COMPLETE GUIDE TO STREET SUPERCHARGING 29

the theoretical engineers flabbergasted. Rodders have often succeeded where a highly educated engineer would never have attempted a project, just because the rodder didn't know that it wasn't supposed to work. If a perpetual-motion machine or a perfectly efficient internal-combustion engine could be built, it would be a hot rodder who would figure out how, through sheer perseverance and enthusiasm.

But the harsh reality is that a perpetual-motion machine will remain an impossibility, and even the best internal combustion engine will be far from perfect. The laws of the conservation of mass and energy are true: you cannot get more out of a system than you put into it. Also, and more important, a law called entropy applies: you can't even get *as much* energy or work out of a system as you put into it when you are converting matter to energy and energy to work, as you are in an engine.

This is all very pertinent to supercharging because a blower can increase the volumetric efficiency of an engine above 100 percent. And, although a belt-driven blower uses up a certain percentage of the engine's horsepower in order to run, it produces much more power in the engine than it takes. These facts can fool us into thinking that a supercharger is some magical apparatus that can defy the laws of physics. It can't.

The reason why a blower seems to work miracles on an internal combustion engine is because the engine is so inefficient to begin with. A good gasoline engine is lucky if it can convert 30 percent of the energy contained in the fuel into actual work. The addition of a supercharger, in most cases, actually lowers this figure because it requires a greater percentage of fuel to make more power in the motor (I'll explain

This is Whipple Superchargers' tidy and well-instrumented dyno cell, where a ZZ4 Chevy with full street accessories is being tested with a carbureted Whipple screw compressor.

in a minute). Further, all superchargers are less than 100-percent efficient in terms of the amount of energy they consume compared to the amount of air they pump, and in terms of the mass of air they pump compared to the size of the blower and its volume.

We will not be able to fully explore the intricacies of supercharger design and efficiency here. In fact, a surprisingly small amount of research has actually been compiled on superchargers. What I want to do in this chapter is give you enough engineering background to understand what blowers can do and what they can't, to dispel some myths about superchargers, and to give you a more solid basis from which to choose the type of blower system that will be best for your vehicle and the way you drive it.

Density, Volume and Pressure

Myth number one is that a blower's primary function is to increase the volume or the pressure

What size blower do you use on what size engine? While logic tells you a bigger engine needs a bigger blower, "sizing" a belt-driven supercharger, especially a positive-displacement type, is less critical than you might think. The relatively small MP 122 Magna Charger with three large 2-barrel carbs on top can feed a 350 Chevy by spinning it with faster-ratio pulleys, since it maintains good efficiencies at higher RPM. We don't know how big the Rat Motor is, but the 10-71 Kuhl blower with twin double pumpers is probably more than it needs (especially with that small pulley on top). But, in general, it's usually better to run a big blower too slow than a small one too fast, in terms of efficiencies and being able to turn up the boost when you want.

of the air in the intake system of the engine. The real purpose of the supercharger is to increase the *density* of that air.

Density is the mass, or weight, of a substance in a given volume. For most solids or liquids, weight is nearly proportional to volume—increase the volume, and you increase the weight by a proportional amount. In other words, the density of a given solid or liquid does not change very much under normal conditions. Consequently, we tend to think of an increase in volume of a substance as an equal increase in the amount (mass) of that substance.

But this thinking is never wholly correct, and it certainly does not apply to gases. The density of a gas such as air changes considerably as its temperature or pressure changes. Increase the temperature and the density of the gas decreases (if it's not in a closed container) because the gas expands. Increase the pressure and the density will usually increase because a greater amount (mass) of the gas will be compressed into a small space (volume). I say "usually" because we are dealing with more than one variable at the same time when we are dealing with the state of a gas. If a gas is both compressed (which should increase its density) and heated (which should decrease its density) concurrently, the net result could be an increase, a decrease, or no change at all in the density of the gas.

These facts are extremely important to an understanding of supercharging because a supercharger does in fact both compress and heat the air entering the engine, in addition to increasing the volume of air passing through the intake system.

The Gas Law

Before we go any further, let's take a quick look at the basic law that describes the relationship between the pressure, volume, weight, and temperature of a gas. Known as the Ideal Gas Equation, or just the Gas Law, it is usually expressed by the equation:

$$PV = nRT$$

If your engine's out in the wind, like this, or the blower is sticking through the hood—and has a big scoop on it—it'll have no problem sucking in as much air as it needs at the coolest ambient temperature.

Here, P is pressure, V is volume, n is the weight of the gas in moles, R is a constant (called the Molar Gas Constant, which has different values depending on the units used for the other quantities), and T is the temperature.

It is not within the scope of this book to fully explore how this equation can be used, or how gases act in general—you can find an explanation of the Gas Law, how to work it, and values for R, in any thermodynamics textbook. What this equation should immediately show you, assuming you have a basic familiarity with algebra, is the relationship between the pressure, volume, temperature, and weight of a given gas.

If we are discussing a given amount of gas, in moles (that is, a certain weight of the gas; or a certain number of molecules), then both n and R in the Gas Law would be constant, and we could write the equation thus:

$$\frac{PV}{T} = \text{Constant}$$

What this tells us is: that for a given amount (weight) of gas, increasing the pressure and keeping the volume the same will increase the temperature proportionally; increasing the temperature and keeping the volume the same will increase the pressure proportionally; increasing the volume and keeping the pressure the same increases the temperature; and so on.

In relation to supercharging, the significant things the Gas Law tells us is that increasing the pressure increases the temperature, and vice versa; that a temperature rise at a given pressure will increase the volume, which means a decrease in density; and that both the pressure and the temperature could be increased without increasing the density at all. Remember, increasing the *density* of the air entering the engine is what we want the blower to do.

The Problem of Heat

The thorn in the side of supercharging is heat, which is a common

A Hilborn 4-port injector converted to EFI is not only slick on a 6-71 blower, but will feed it all the air and fuel it can use. That low-profile air cleaner, however, probably can't flow as much air as the blower and injector can, plus it's drawing in hot underhood air.

and easily manifested form of energy—a very easily wasted form of energy—that is a typical by-product of work being done. In supercharging, heat is a multiple detriment. In the first place, the act of compressing air heats it, as we saw above. Second, much of the engine horsepower used to turn the supercharger and compress the air eventually is converted to more heat, which is transferred to the air. Most blowers, especially Roots types, literally *beat* the air, which heats it considerably; plus friction between the air and stationary and moving surfaces, as well as the friction of air turbulence, all combine to heat the air further. The heat tends to expand the air (increase its volume), which raises the pressure, but does not increase the density.

To give you a practical example of what could be taking place in a supercharger, imagine a closed box full of air at room temperature and at atmospheric pressure. Let's say the box measures 1 foot per side, so that its volume is 1 cubic foot. The volume of air in the box, 1 cubic foot, cannot change, since no air can get in or out. Likewise, the density of that air—the amount of weight, or the number of molecules, of the air—cannot change. If we insert a pressure gauge in one of the walls of the box, it will read 0 psi, since both the pressure and temperature of the air inside the box is the same as that outside.

Now let's take our box of air and put it on the stove. As the air inside is heated it tries to expand, but cannot because it is contained in the closed box. The result? The pressure increases. We will actually see "boost" on the pressure gauge even though the air is not being compressed, and the density remains exactly the same. In other words, we see a boost reading on the gauge even though the amount of air in the box has not increased at all. The same thing happens, to more or less degree, in the manifold of a supercharged engine. If a blower heats the air drastically, instead of pumping it efficiently, it could show a boost reading on the gauge—simply by heating and expanding the air—without causing any *increase* in air (or power) being pumped into the engine.

To see how this could happen, we use the Gas Law in its simplified form:

$$\frac{P_1 V_1}{T_1} = \frac{P_2 V_2}{T_2} = \text{Constant}$$

Knowing that the volume is constant in both cases, we can figure the pressure rise by using the proportion:

$$\frac{P_1}{T_1} = \frac{P_2}{T_2}$$

Temperature must be figured in degrees Rankine (absolute temperature, which equals degrees Fahrenheit plus 460), and pressure in psi absolute (psia). Using this simple equation, we find that if our box of air starts out at a typical atmospheric temperature and pressure of 60 degrees F and 0 psi (520R and 14.7 psia) and is then heated to 240 degrees F, we will see a "boost" reading on our pressure gauge of 5.1 psi. Remember, we have neither compressed the air nor increased its density. We have simply heated it. And we have 5 pounds of boost on our gauge!

Now, although a blower manifold is not a closed box, nor is real air an ideal gas, the above example still gives a good approximation of what could happen in a blown motor. If you were getting a 200 degrees F temperature rise in the manifold at 5 pounds of boost, your supercharger would be giving you *no increase* in air charge density at all, and would be robbing you of engine horsepower (by driving the blower), at the same time that the increase in intake temperature could promote detonation and other engine damage. Fortunately, most superchargers

In this case we have a large Paxton Novi centrifugal blower drawing air inside a cramped, hot engine compartment. However, note the very large, low-restriction air cleaner. Better yet, those two large tubes feed the compressed air to a large air-to-air intercooler mounted behind the grille, before feeding it through a bonnet into the 4-barrel carb. Also note the pressure-relief valve on the bonnet to guard against overboosting.

Centrifugal blowers are particularly sensitive to airflow restrictions (including tight bends in ducting) on the inlet side. On this big Viper V-10, an equally large Paxton draws plenty of air directly from a huge air cleaner mounted in an enclosure that draws fresh air from the front of the car. What you can't see is the blower outlet, which feeds through an air-to-water charge cooler (with small black cap) before being ducted directly into the EFI throttle body.

(especially today's modern types) work considerably better than this example, but all sacrifice a good percentage of their potential benefit to the demon of heat.

Blower Efficiency

Since machines such as engines and superchargers do not operate perfectly in the real world, we use the term "efficiency" to compare how well they do work to how well they would work in a theoretically perfect environment. Many blower manufacturers or salesmen refer to a single "blower efficiency" figure, but this is very misleading. Like the internal combustion engine, which can be measured for volumetric, thermal, mechanical, and other efficiency ratings, the supercharger likewise must be tested for efficiency in terms of different functions. Although the adiabatic, volumetric, and mechanical efficiency ratings of a supercharger all do influence one another to some degree, it is not really practical to try to lump them all together into one comprehensive blower efficiency figure. One big problem is that the mechanical and volumetric efficiencies of a supercharger operating on a real engine are very difficult to measure practically or accurately. Consequently, and because it has the greatest bearing on supercharger performance, the figure usually cited for superchargers is the adiabatic efficiency, which can be readily calculated. However, if someone gives you a blower efficiency figure for a given supercharger, ask what sort of efficiency was measured and how it was determined.

Adiabatic Efficiency (A.E.)

If you are not familiar with thermodynamics, the term adiabatic efficiency might sound scary or

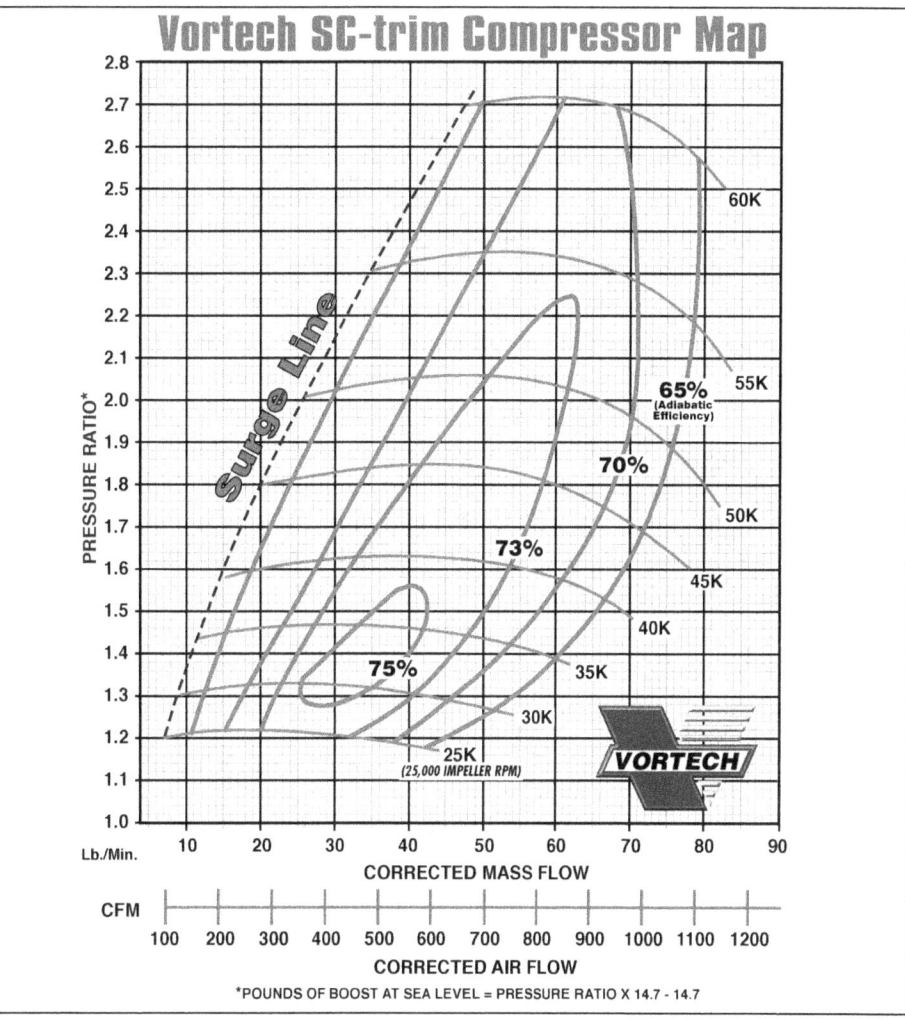

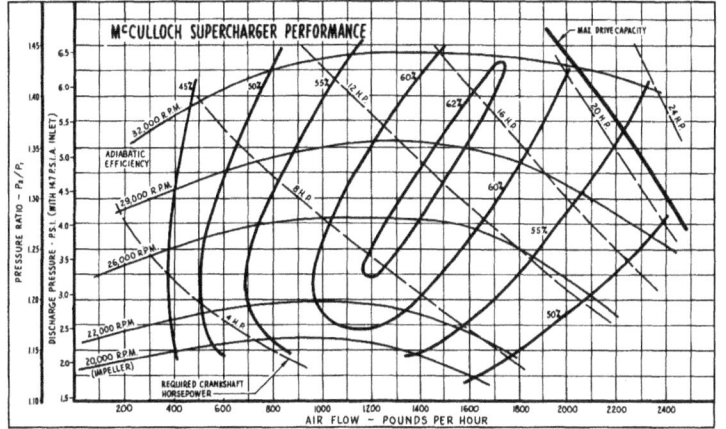

Compressor "flow map" charts, used mostly for centrifugal blowers, look daunting to an untrained eye. Primarily they show adiabatic efficiency, given blower RPM, airflow, and boost (given as "pressure ratio" on the left; a ratio of 2.0 would be 14.7 psig). These charts are for a 1950s McCulloch and a new V-1 Vortech with an M-trim impeller. Adiabatic efficiency is given in percentage, with the oval (called the "island") being the area of highest efficiency. To accurately compare the charts, look at them between pressure ratios 1.0–1.6. The newer blower has a larger island there, with a maximum A.E. of 75 percent (compared to 62 percent for the old one), and it holds 70 percent A.E. to nearly 25 pounds of boost. Also note the horsepower required to turn the blower on the older chart.

CHAPTER 3

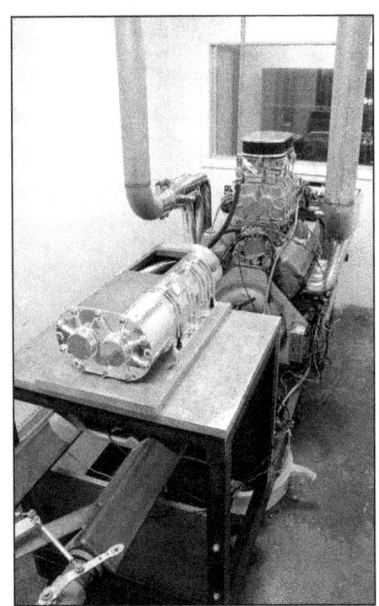

Larry Bowers built one of the first "blower dynos," powered by a 351 Ford, to measure how much HP it took to drive a big Jimmy blower. Here's what his successors, The Blower Shop, have rigged up to spin and test up to 14-71 race blowers. Yes, the big-block with the blower and dual quads is just to turn the 14-71 on the other stand, against pressure which can be regulated with valves seen in the foreground. Like any modern dyno cell, it's computerized to read pressure, temperature, horsepower, RPM, and other variables, while holding one or more constant.

complicated, but it's really quite simple. The term "adiabatic" simply means a thermodynamic process in which no heat is gained from, or lost to, sources outside the system. The problem is that many self-appointed blower experts have used the term without fully understanding its meaning or its computation, and have therefore spread some confusion about it. To the non-theoretical blower builder or user, adiabatic efficiency is a measure of how much the blower heats the air that it is pumping. The less it heats the air, the more efficient it is.

As we have seen, and will discuss further in a moment, the amount that a blower heats the air charge has a large (negative) effect on the amount of power it will produce in the engine. Plus, it is a good indicator of how well the blower is doing the job of pumping (that is, it reflects the mechanical and volumetric efficiency losses), since extraneous work done on the air by the blower will be converted to heat.

The temperature rise across the blower (the difference between inlet air temperature and outlet, or manifold, air temperature) is easy to measure. Consequently, it is easy to compare the temperature rise with one blower at a given boost pressure on a given engine to that of a different blower at the same boost pressure on the same engine. Such a comparison will certainly give us an approximation of the relative adiabatic efficiencies of the two blowers, but it won't give us a correct percentage figure.

One book on superchargers states that a blower that draws in air at 70 degrees F, compresses it to 1.5 atmospheres (about 7 psi of boost), and discharges it at a temperature of 70 degrees F would have 100-percent adiabatic efficiency. As we saw from the Gas Law, this is impossible unless we incorporate a very effective cooling device into the supercharger. The act of compressing air heats it (because we must do work on that air to compress it, and the air absorbs the energy of that work as heat).

If we could compress a gas by some physical means without adding any more heat to it than the heat generated by the act of compression, and we did not let any of that heat escape, we would have perfect adiabatic compression, or 100-percent adiabatic efficiency. Although perfect adiabatic compression is impossible in the real world, we can calculate the heat of perfect adiabatic compression by the following formula:

$$T_2 = T_1 \left[\frac{P_2}{P_1}\right]^{.283}$$

In this formula, T_1 is the inlet (or ambient) air temperature, P_1 is the ambient air pressure, P_2 is the outlet (or manifold) pressure, and T_2 is the new temperature to which the act of compression will raise that air. Temperature is figured in degrees Rankine and pressures are absolute. To get T_2 in degrees F, subtract 460.

Raising a number to the .283 power is a bit difficult, but the pressure ratio (P_2/P_1), raised to this power, can be quickly figured from "Y-tables" for air in some thermodynamic textbooks or handbooks. Once you have figured the ratio of P_2/P_1, the Y-table will give you a value of Y for this amount. For instance, if P_2/P_1 is 1.5, or about 7.4 pounds of boost, the value of Y is .12159. Then, using the simpler formula:

$$\Delta T(\text{ideal}) = T_1 \times Y$$

You can figure the ideal temperature increase, in degrees F, for a compressor at 100-percent adiabatic efficiency.

To show how the equation works, let's say that the ambient air temperature is 68 degrees F. This is the blower inlet temperature, or T_1, which converts to 528 degrees R. Ambient air pressure, P_1, is one atmosphere, or 14.7 psia (psi absolute). Let's say the blower is making 7.4 pounds of boost in the manifold, so P_2 is 22.1 psia. If our blower were a perfect compressor, the formula shows us that it would heat the air 63.36 degrees F, or raise T_2 to 131.36 degrees F. If we raise blower boost to 14.7 psi (29.4 psia), T_2 would go up to 182.42 degrees F. This would be the temperature rise in the manifold if the blower had 100-percent adiabatic efficiency. But, of course, no supercharger can have 100-percent adiabatic efficiency because several other factors in a real mechanical pump contribute to heating the air: friction of air against blower parts, friction of air against air (turbulence), friction of mechanical parts, air leakage, and so on.

To figure the adiabatic efficiency of a given supercharger, use the equation:

$$\text{Adiabatic Efficiency} = \frac{(T_2 - T_1) \text{ Ideal}}{(T_2 - T_1) \text{ Actual}}$$

This is the ratio of the perfect (adiabatic) temperature increase figured from the previous equation, to the actual temperature increase observed across the supercharger.

For instance, if we use the example above of the blower making 7.4 pounds of boost with an inlet air temperature of 68 degrees F, the ideal heat rise (T_2-T_1 ideal), or the heat rise at 100-percent adiabatic efficiency, should be approximately 63 degrees F (to 131 degrees F total). But let's say that the actual temperature in the manifold is 194 degrees F. This would give us an actual of 126 degrees (T_2-T_1 or 194–68).

Our adiabatic efficiency ratio would therefore be 63/126, or .50. Expressed in percentage, the adiabatic efficiency of this supercharger would be 50 percent. Given the same inlet temperature and manifold pressure, if the actual manifold temperature were only 152 degrees F, the blower's adiabatic efficiency would be 75 percent.

Hardly any superchargers have an adiabatic efficiency of 75 percent, even today. High 60s to low 70s are about as good as the significantly improved centrifugal, Lysholm screw, and the continuously developing Eaton Roots-type blowers can produce. The older Roots-types blowers, such as GMCs, are doing well if they can reach 50-percent adiabatic efficiency.

Mechanical Efficiency

In this book we are dealing specifically with superchargers that are driven mechanically by the engine, as opposed to turbochargers that are driven by exhaust heat and pressure, or even superchargers driven by some other remote source (such as an electric motor—one of these was actually advertised in magazines in the 1950s). Consequently all of the blowers we will be discussing consume a certain percentage of the engine's power in order to make more power. If superchargers didn't make a lot more power than they consumed, we wouldn't use them. But you might be surprised to find out how much horsepower it takes to turn something like a 6-71 GMC making 15 to 20 pounds of boost.

The mechanical efficiency of a supercharger is a measure of the amount of engine horsepower the blower actually consumes to produce

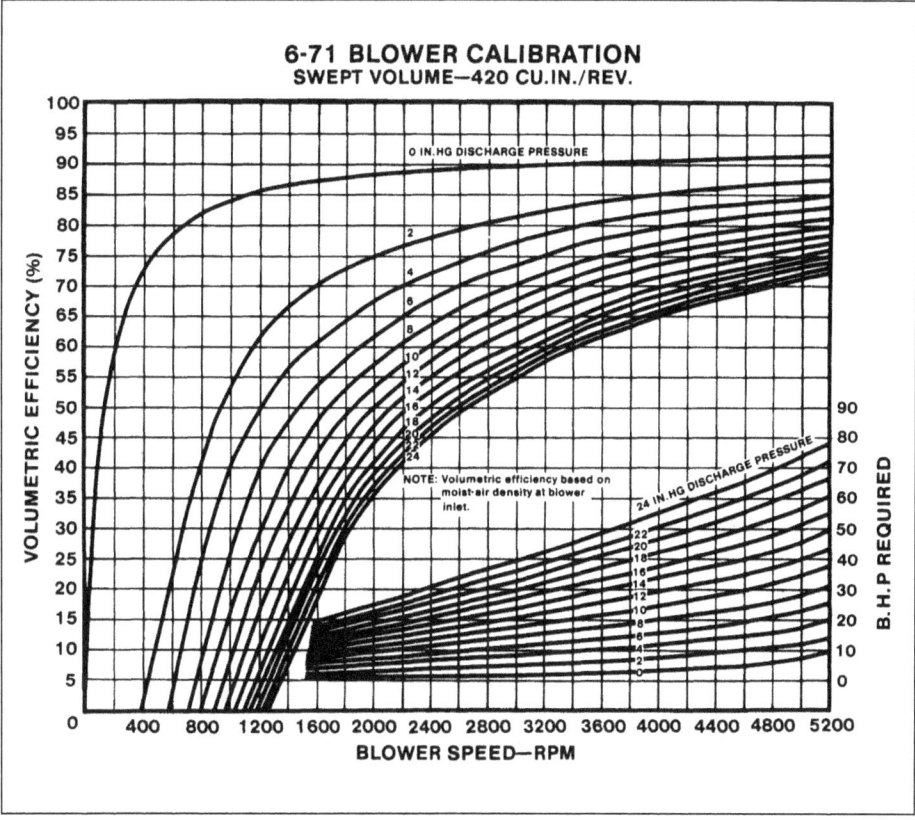

Although GMC blowers weren't designed to make boost, Detroit Diesel engineers had the equipment—and obviously the curiosity—to test them under such conditions. This chart, made sometime in the 1950s or 1960s, shows the volumetric efficiency and the mechanical efficiency ("B.H.P. Required") of a 6-71 blower set to factory clearances and run from 0 to 5,200 rpm. The successive curves show results at increasing boost pressures, from 0 to 24 inches of mercury (30 inches of mercury is roughly 1 atmosphere, or 14.7 psi; 20 in. hg. would be about 9.8 psi at the blower outlet).

CHAPTER 3

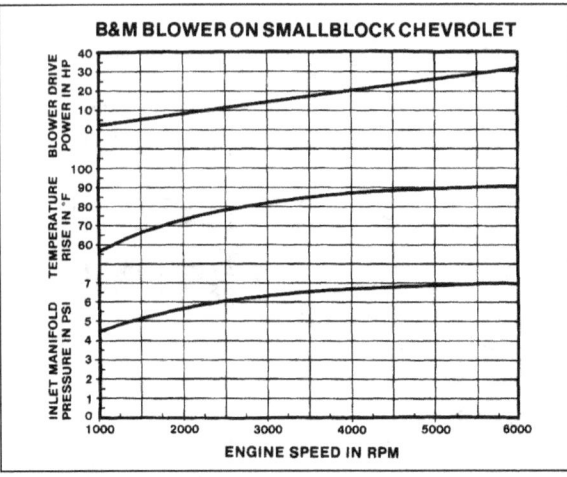

This composite chart was calculated by B&M for its 144-ci 2-lobe blower tested on a 350-ci Chevy V-8. The bottom line shows the blower making 5 to 7 psi of boost, increasing with engine speed. The middle curve shows heat rise across the blower, which roughly parallels the boost curve. And the top line shows horsepower required to drive the blower, which increases linearly with speed. These are interesting figures for a relatively inefficient, low-boost blower on a relatively large engine.

a certain amount of boost at a given speed, compared to the amount of power it would take to compress air at the same rate under ideal conditions.

From readily available thermodynamic equations, we could calculate the amount of horsepower it would take to turn a supercharger of a given displacement, at a certain RPM, to make a certain amount of boost under ideal conditions—that is, without any mechanical losses due to friction, turbulence, leakage, or other real-world conditions. The ratio of this figure to the actual horsepower a real supercharger consumes to produce the same amount of boost would give us the mechanical efficiency percentage of the blower.

However, a practical and reliable method for measuring the actual horsepower drag of a blower on a real running engine is difficult to devise. A few blower builders or racers in the past have tried to devise various types of "blower dynos" to measure the power it takes to turn a supercharger such as a 6-71 or 8-71 GMC by simply pumping air into a container with a regulated outlet, but they have found: 1) that the amount of power it took to drive the blower (especially in a dry state) was staggering, and 2) that controlling and making repeated tests on such devices was very difficult. It has taken the resources of a large company like Eaton, with access to the type of sophisticated mechanical and electronic testing equipment available in Detroit, let alone the engineers and budgets to operate it, to be able to do accurate supercharger mechanical-efficiency testing.

However, since most of the mechanical losses in the blower show up in the form of heat, we can figure an approximation of the mechanical efficiency of a blower by converting the measurable extra heat energy gain (above 100-percent adiabatic efficiency) into work energy units (horsepower). However, this would still be a rough approximation involving too many variables. And it further shows that the adiabatic efficiency figure, which is easier to calculate, is more meaningful; doubly so, since it partially reflects mechanical efficiency as well. So we will not delve into formula here for figuring mechanical blower efficiency.

Volumetric Efficiency

A third measure of blower performance is volumetric efficiency (VE). Blower VE is very similar to engine VE, and it is actually measured in the same way. Specifically, the volumetric efficiency of a supercharger is the ratio of the actual volume of air it pumps per revolution, compared to its internal displacement per revolution.

While it sounds simple, supercharger VE is perhaps the least understood, or just the most difficult to pin down, of blower ratings. In the first place, the internal capacity of a positive-displacement blower, such as a Roots, is easy to calculate, since there is a measurable swept volume per revolution. For instance, the displacement of a 4-71 GMC is 274 ci and that of a 6-71 is 411 ci. However, the static internal volume of non-positive-displacement blowers such as centrifugal types is nearly impossible to figure, especially for the purpose of deriving a volumetric efficiency number.

The volume of air being drawn into a supercharger can be measured in cubic feet per minute (cfm) with a manometer-type airflow gauge as used to measure airflow through the intake of a test engine on a dynamometer. Whether we measure the

For decades little thought was given to improving the volumetric efficiency of any type of blower. One of the first to experiment with inlet/outlet shape and size to improve blower VE was Jerry Magnuson on his first Magna Charger in the 1970s. This lineup of modern, Eaton-based Magna Chargers graphically demonstrates his continuing quest to improve the quantity and quality of airflow through the blower, showing just the inlet side, beginning with the oldest on the right and newest on the left.

air going into the blower or the air coming out, we could get figures to compare the pumping efficiency of a given blower under varying conditions, or of different blowers under the same conditions. But trying to determine a numerical volumetric efficiency for any one supercharger, especially compared to other types, is difficult and often misleading.

The problem is, once again, that we have several variables operating at the same time. Most textbooks contend that the volumetric efficiency of a Roots-type blower increases with its rotational speed. They base this assertion on the observation that air leakage around the rotors is the primary volumetric loss in the supercharger. Since the amount of air that can leak past clearances around the rotors is a function of time (it takes a certain amount of time for the air to leak through the clearances), the faster the rotors turn, the less leakage can occur per revolution; consequently, the higher the blower RPM, the higher the volumetric efficiency.

On the other hand, with any type of supercharger, as manifold pressure increases with blower speed, volumetric efficiency will decrease because of back pressure, which causes increased leakage (or "back-up" of airflow in a centrifugal-type).

Perhaps more obviously, the volumetric efficiency of a supercharger—which actually is an air pump—is similar to that of an internal combustion engine in terms of getting air in and getting it out. Like an engine, any blower has a given size and shape of intake and an exhaust port that air must flow through. We put a supercharger on the engine to force-feed air through its intake passages. But we still have only atmospheric pressure to feed air into the blower's intake. As the rotors in a Roots blower, for instance, turn past the inlet opening, there is only a given amount of time for the atmosphere to push air into the rotor cavity before it closes (turns past the opening to seal against the case). The faster the rotors turn, the less time they will have to fill completely with air, and the lower the blower's volumetric efficiency will be.

The problem is to determine accurately, under actual operating conditions, which of several factors affecting blower volumetric efficiency is predominant, or how they combine for a net VE under various conditions. This might be more important than it seems at first. Jerry Magnuson, back in the days when he was developing his original, small, 3-lobe Roots-type Magna Chargers (in the 1960s and 1970s), designed them around the assumption that volumetric efficiency is the major design criterion, and that—besides efficient inlet and outlet "ports"—blower VE is predominantly a function of air leakage around rotor clearances, at least in street-boost ranges up to 10 psi. Given this assumption, the conclusion is to use as small a blower as possible on an engine for two reasons: 1) because you want the blower to run as fast as possible to make a given boost, and 2) because air leakage is not only a function of time, but also of total clearance surface area. Making the blower smaller will reduce the size of the air leakage paths, and therefore improve volumetric efficiency. Turning this smaller blower faster, in relation to engine speed, will give you the boost you want, more efficiently. Magnuson still ascribes to this theory, in fact emphatically, with the Eaton blowers he uses for his current Magna Charger applications.

However, consider the logic that could apply to larger, GMC-type blowers. Proponents say that a larger blower, turned at a slower speed, with tighter rotor clearances, would be the better choice. The slower blower RPM would allow setting the rotor clearances closer, since there would be less rotor growth and, in GMCs, less rotor "untwist." If the blower turned slower relative to engine speed to make the same boost, it would be beating the air less, or doing less extraneous work on it, which would heat the air less (that is, raise the adiabatic efficiency). This is not only desirable in itself, but it would also heat the blower parts less, reducing expansion and allowing tighter clearances for better VE. Further, although tighter clearances will slightly increase the power needed to turn the blower, a longer blower turned at a slower speed (such as a 6-71 rather than a 4-71) will produce more boost with the same, or less, drag from gears, pulleys, belt, and so on.

Isentropic Efficiency

A new type of blower efficiency, called "Isentropic," has become the latest catch-all measurement of overall blower efficiency. Apparently first derived in the steam engine field, and made possible to measure by highly advanced testing methods and data-gathering equipment now employed by large supercharger manufacturers such as Eaton in the United States and certain screw compressor builders in Europe, it is based on the concept of entropy in a thermodynamic system. We're not about to explain this phenomenon here. In fact, in reviewing the topic in one of my college physics textbooks, I was surprised to read that the opening statement in the chapter on entropy begins: "There is no concept in the whole field of physics which is more difficult to understand than is the concept of entropy, nor is there one

It's difficult to show an air-to-air intercooler installed in a vehicle, but this display stand with a Paxton Novi 2000 blowing into the factory EFI unit on a Shelby Ford engine shows its simple layout quite plainly. The compressed, heated air from the blower is routed into the aluminum heat exchanger (just like water through a radiator), where it is cooled by ambient air passing over the fins, and is then routed by tubing to the engine's intake system.

which is more fundamental." Defined very, very basically: Entropy is the necessary corollary to the law of conservation of energy, which says that in a system where a certain amount of matter is converted to energy and/or energy is converted to work, there is a certain percentage of inevitable loss. Often this loss is manifest as heat, but also in other forms.

Again, speaking very basically, the calculation of isentropic efficiency contrasts the actual various losses in the supercharging process to those that would be lost to entropy alone. In other words, it is similar to the calculation of adiabatic efficiency, but takes into consideration more variables than just heat. In fact, isentropic efficiency is plotted on compressor maps similar to those for adiabatic efficiency, showing "islands" of isentropic efficiency percentages.

We're not going to say anything further here, because it gets complicated quickly. If you want to delve into it further, we suggest you Google isentropic efficiency, or perhaps better, look it up on Ask.com, where you'll find as much technical information as you could want.

The purpose of the preceding discussions is two-fold. First, they demonstrate that the science of blower technology requires a close examination and evaluation of many variables before accurate assumptions can be made. Because so many variables are involved, it is often difficult to determine exactly what change, or what side effect of a change, led to an observed increase or decrease in blower performance. Second, it indicates that a good formula or rule of thumb for choosing the proper size supercharger for a given engine will be impossible to give.

I was hoping that I would be able to devise some sort of table or equation that would immediately tell you how large the optimum blower should be for a given-displacement engine. But once again, a broad array of variables has thwarted me. In a practical sense, the sizing of a supercharger to an engine is not as critical as one might think—certainly not as critical as the sizing of a turbocharger. The mechanical drive of the blower can be stepped up or down easily to help regulate the output to the engine's needs. The sizing of a centrifugal supercharger is a bit more complicated because it involves different impeller designs in a given case, as well as different-sized cases and drive ratios. Also, the correct sizing of a centrifugal blower to a given engine is more critical because boost increase is not linear with blower speed. Put too big a centrifugal blower on an engine, or drive it too fast, and you can get into parts-breakage boost in a hurry (though "waste gate"-type boost-control valves can be incorporated, even in street setups, to guard against this).

In practical terms, current supercharger manufacturers—centrifugal or positive displacement—have tested their units and designed kits for specific installations. They can usually tell you which blower will make what amount of boost, at what RPM, on a given engine. If they can't, be wary.

The Air Density Ratio

The biggest problem with using blower volumetric efficiency as a guide in designing or sizing a supercharger is the same problem described earlier about confusing air volume with air density. Even if we could accurately measure the volume of air being pumped out of the blower, this is not really an accurate measure of the increase in the air the blower is supplying to the engine. Why? Because air (as we saw earlier) is elastic. Differences in temperature or pressure will change the volume of a given amount of air, and this is exactly what happens on the outlet side of a supercharger.

It is not the increase in volume, but an increase in *density* of intake air that increases power in an engine. Have we repeated this enough times for it to sink in yet? We want to pack more molecules of air into the cylinders so that: 1) we will have more molecules of oxygen to burn with more molecules of fuel, but more importantly, 2) to get more molecules of air (matter per volume) into the cylinder to expand and exert pressure on the piston after combustion. We measure the number of molecules of a gas in a given volume by

$$\text{Density Ratio} = \frac{\text{Inlet Temperature Absolute}}{\text{Outlet Temperature Absolute}} \times \frac{\text{Outlet Pressure Absolute}}{\text{Inlet Pressure Absolute}}$$

the weight of the gas per volume, and this is called density.

As we saw from the Gas Law, the density of a gas depends on both its pressure and its temperature. Since these are quantities we can readily measure for the intake charge, with temperature and pressure gauges, we can figure the actual air density increase being produced by the supercharger in the intake manifold. Although the air density ratio is a term not often mentioned in relation to superchargers, I feel it is a much more meaningful (not to mention more easily calculated) measurement than the blower's adiabatic or volumetric efficiency. The formula for calculating the air density ratio is shown on this page. If we use the previous example of a supercharged engine operating at an ambient temperature of 68 degrees F and standard atmospheric pressure (14.7 psia), making 7.4 pounds of boost and recording a temperature in the manifold of 131 degrees F, we can plug in these figures and figure the density ratio:

$$\text{Density Ratio} = \frac{68 + 460}{131 + 460} \times \frac{7.4 + 14.7}{14.7}$$

$$\text{Density Ratio} = \frac{528}{591} \times \frac{22.1}{14.7}$$

$$\text{Density Ratio} = .8934 \times 1.5$$

$$\text{Density Ratio} = 1.34$$

The air density ratio measured across the supercharger for this engine is 1.34:1, or a 34-percent increase. The beauty of this equation is that it takes into consideration most of the real factors operating on the intake charge, such as the cooling effect of evaporating fuel in the air, or, more significantly, the effect of an intercooler in the system. (See above)

You can figure the air density ratio in your engine by installing a manifold boost pressure gauge and a manifold air temperature gauge in your car. Blower boost gauges are common and available from most gauge or supercharger suppliers. Unfortunately, manifold temperature gauges are not. A typical capillary-bulb temperature gauge, as used for water or oil, is much too slow acting. In back-to-back tests of 6-71 blowers we did for *Hot Rod* magazine in 1984 at the Keith Black dyno, we used a fast-acting, needle-type thermocouple sensor inserted into the blower manifold, with an electronic digital readout meter, which gave fast, usable readings. Unfortunately, we found that this type of sensor was affected by its exact placement in the manifold, with readings changing given where it was located in relation to the air/fuel stream under the blower. Given the types of spot-reading temperature gauges available today, the industry needs to develop a good, available, manifold temperature sensor and gauge, which should then be a requisite component of any supercharger installation.

With good manifold boost and temperature gauges, you also need to know the ambient air temperature and pressure. Most new cars include an outside air temperature readout as part of the standard gauge package, which can vary significantly, but barometric pressure can be calculated at 14.5 to 14.7 psi in nearly any application.

The point is that if you only have the usual manifold boost gauge, it doesn't tell you how much usable power the blower is adding to your engine. Engine power is proportional to intake air *density*, not pressure, and the blower air density ratio will tell you how much increase in horsepower the supercharger is providing, minus the horsepower consumed by the blower to operate.

For instance, if the engine in the previous example made 200 hp unblown, the blower would increase horsepower 34 percent to 268 hp, minus, let's say, 15 hp to run the blower, for a net horsepower of 253, or a net power gain of 26.5 percent. These figures were not taken from any real engine; they are simply examples to show how the calculations work. The point is that anybody can tell you a given blower will double or triple your horsepower, but you don't know what it is really doing unless you put the engine on a dyno or, much more simply, install boost and temperature gauges and figure the above calculations.

The Limits of Supercharging

What the blower density ratio tells us is that you can pump more horsepower into your engine in direct proportion to the increased amount of air you pump into it. Remember, that engine runs on air, and the more air you can get in it, the more power it makes. That's the undeniable beauty of supercharging. It overcomes the natural limits imposed by a naturally aspirated engine's volumetric efficiency. But there are obviously limits to the amount of power we can pump into a motor with a blower. If there weren't, we would use small, compact engines in all of our cars and supercharge them to make hundreds of horsepower.

There are three basic limits to supercharging. First is the point of diminishing returns of the blower itself, which is determined by its overall efficiency. At some point the blower will not be able to make any more boost because of pumping losses, or it will heat the air more than it compresses it, or it might even reach the point of consuming more engine horsepower than it is providing. Some of these problems become factors in blown competition engines but they rarely affect street supercharging, where boost levels will normally be less than 10 pounds. The only exception would be trying to supercharge a large-displacement engine with a much-too-small blower.

Second, the amount of boost you can pump into the engine, and the resulting increase in cylinder pressure, will be limited by the physical strengths of engine components. It does no good to raise boost beyond the point where you blow gaskets, burn pistons, or break cylinder walls. In a competition engine, you can increase the strengths of these components to a point to withstand greater pressures or temperatures. But, again, most street supercharging applications do not even reach the physical limits of stock engine components.

Third, for street supercharging, the practical limit to horsepower gain is detonation. Once an engine begins to detonate (knock), its horsepower curve stops climbing. And not only does the detonation point of an engine limit power output beyond that point, but serious detonation in the cylinders will also quickly destroy engine components such as pistons, rings, and spark plugs.

Two primary factors determine the point at which an engine will detonate: the effective compression ratio (or peak cylinder pressure) and the octane rating of the fuel used. In a street supercharged engine, the fuel will be pump gasoline, which comes in dismal octanes these days. (The octane number of a fuel is simply and

The advantage of a water-to-air intercooler, as seen by this example of a Vortech blower on an LS GM V-8, is that the compressed air has a much more direct path to the engine's inlet, passing through a compact cooler housing a finned "heat absorber" filled with water cooled by a larger radiator mounted at the front of the car.

literally a measure of the point at which it begins to detonate in a special test engine with a variable compression ratio. The higher the octane number, the higher the compression before it knocks.)

Since part of the reason for adding a supercharger to an engine is to increase the effective compression ratio, and since the blower will also raise the temperature of the charge in the cylinder, which also abets detonation, other means may have to be taken to control detonation if the supercharger is used to raise compression to a significant level.

Most of today's blower systems designed for real street driving use efficient compressors at safe boost levels, possibly with an intercooler, all of which contribute to significant power increases on available pump gasoline. If you're using a bigger, older-style blower for serious horsepower gains (or just for showing off), or if your supercharger system does encounter audible "pinging" on pump gas under boost, there are a few things you can do.

First of all, naturally, you want to use the highest-octane gasoline available. Unfortunately, these days, that means about 92-octane unleaded at best. If your supercharged vehicle is a weekend toy, you can use octane boosters readily available in a can. A few places have high-octane "race gas" available at the pump, or in containers. Or you might even consider running your car on methanol (just remember you use twice as much alky as gas). As this is written, certain areas are serving ethanol blends (up to E85) at the pump, and other types of alternative fuels are being tried. We'll have to see what's available at the pump in the near future, and what its octane rating might be (including how that rating is figured). The rule of thumb is: if it knocks or pings, you will eventually hurt your engine and you need a higher-octane fuel (or other measures to control detonation).

Other tricks that help control detonation in street engines include richening the fuel mixture (or getting it right—remember, blowers tend to lean the ratio) to cool the intake charge, retarding the ignition, or injecting water or alcohol into the intake airstream. Each of these methods is practical and effective on a blown streeter, but you should realize that each is a compromise. With any of these "Band-Aids" you will be getting more power than you could if the engine goes into detonation, but not as much as you would if the engine did not otherwise detonate at that point (for instance, if the fuel octane were higher, or the intake air temperature were cooler). Obviously, correcting a lean air/fuel mixture (which significantly increases cylinder temperature), or adding an intercooler to the system, are not Band-Aids, but effective means for making a street blower operate on available pump gas.

The point is that on a street

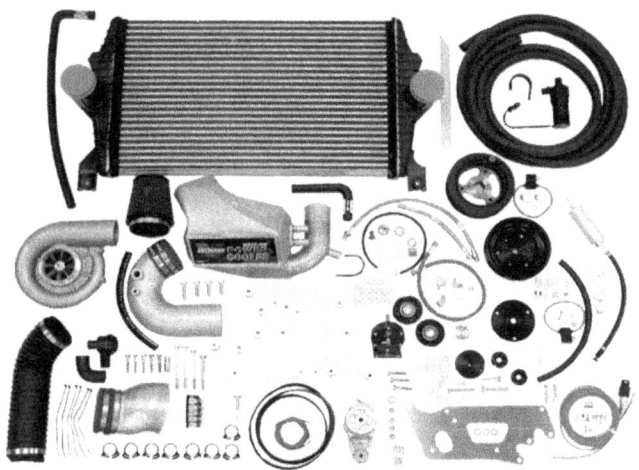

This complete Vortech bolt-on supercharger kit, including a water-to-air Super Cooler, shows an example of a good-sized front-of-the-vehicle water cooler, plus the electric pump and hose to circulate the cooled water to the unit mounted between the blower and the engine intake. Both systems rely on ambient air temperature to cool the supercharged air; however, ice can be added to a reservoir in a water system for short-distance racing.

blown motor running on gasoline (as opposed to race motors running on large quantities of cooler or higher-octane fuels like alcohol, race gas, or nitro), the primary factor limiting the amount of boost you can pump in with a supercharger will be the octane rating of available gas rather than the melting or breaking points of engine parts.

As a matter of fact, one seldom-mentioned benefit of supercharging pointed out by L.J.K. Setright in a book on turbocharging and supercharging is that the Mean Effective Pressure (MEP) in the cylinder of a supercharged engine is considerably higher than that of an unblown motor (it has to be for the engine to make more power, since engine power is a function of MEP), but the peak cylinder pressure allowable in either engine cannot exceed the physical strength limits of the engine parts (or the knock limit of the fuel). This, first of all, demonstrates why a supercharged engine can make more power than a naturally aspirated engine of the same effective compression ratio. So why is it better to lower the static compression ratio and add a supercharger rather than to use high-compression pistons to achieve the same effective compression in the cylinder? The answer is that the blower produces more pressure in the cylinder throughout the power stroke, whereas the high compression piston produces a high initial (peak) pressure above the piston at combustion, but proportionally less pressure as the piston travels down the bore.

Setright's point is that the higher continuous pressure in the cylinder of a blown engine produces a more constant loading on the piston, rod, and crank during the power stroke than that in an unblown engine. The same is true during the intake stroke when the blower is helping to pump air into the cylinder. Consequently, the supercharger actually helps reduce mechanical stresses on engine parts by "cushioning" inertia loads. Further, since the blower makes more power at given RPM levels, this means that a blown engine does not have to spin as tight to make the same power as an unblown engine, thus further reducing stress on engine parts.

Expansion Ratio and Thermal Efficiency

A negative effect of the lowered static compression ratio necessary in a supercharged engine is a consequent lowering of the expansion ratio and thermal efficiency of the engine. The expansion ratio in a cylinder is a measure of how much the compressed air/fuel mixture in the combustion chamber can expand (and therefore exert pressure on the piston) before the exhaust valve opens somewhere near BDC on the power stroke and "blows down" the cylinder. It is the expansion of the heated gases (air) in the cylinder that does the work to run the engine, so the expansion ratio obviously has a direct bearing on engine power.

If valve timing remains the same,

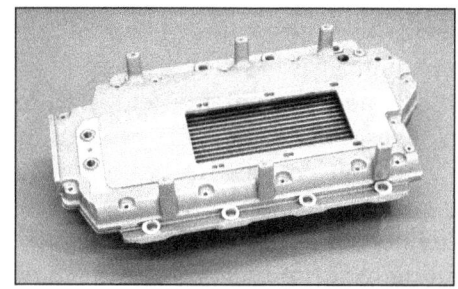

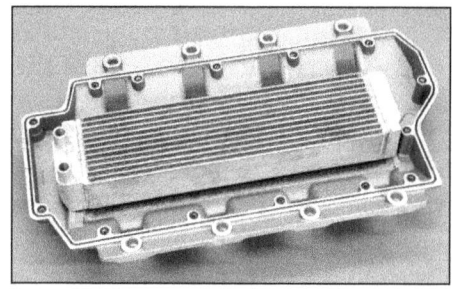

Adding an intercooler between a large Roots blower and an intake manifold is difficult, but today's smaller, more efficient blowers, plus electronic fuel injectors placed at intake ports, make water-to-air coolers more feasible. This Magna Charger intake manifold for an LS Corvette engine incorporates a water-to-air charge cooler, as seen. The blower's charge is forced through the cooler before being directed to the ports, while cool water is pumped to the cooler's tubes through the small, round openings at the front.

the expansion ratio in an engine is proportional to the geometric (static) compression ratio. By lowering the compression ratio in a supercharged engine (that is, by enlarging the combustion chamber volume), we can get a larger quantity of air and fuel into the cylinder, which will expand with a proportionally greater force once it is burned (heated). However, considering that the cylinder is still the same size, this heated charge of gas will still have only the same distance to push the piston, and the same piston top area on which to push. In other words, although we have greatly increased the force pushing on the piston for the entire length of the power stroke, the piston reaches the bottom of that stroke well before the power of the expanding gas has been used up.

Remember that the temperature of a gas drops as that gas expands in volume. In an engine cylinder, the heat that makes the gas expand in the first place comes from the energy content of the fuel (energy that can be converted to heat, and can be measured in British thermal unit(s) (BTU). The thermal efficiency of the engine is a measure of the percentage of the potential heat energy in the fuel that is actually converted to work in the cylinders. Without going into a lengthy explanation of all these processes, I hope you begin to understand how the static compression ratio, expansion ratio, thermal efficiency and, ultimately, the fuel economy of an engine are all closely related. In terms of supercharging, the results are that, for a large increase in power, we must waste some of the potential power available, which means wasting some fuel, and this wasted power will show up as an increase in exhaust heat and/or water temperatures.

In a street supercharged engine the expansion ratio can be increased somewhat by retarding the exhaust valve opening timing and reducing intake and exhaust valve timing overlap. The extra pressure (heat) of the burned gases in the supercharged engine at the end of the power stroke will help push the exhaust through the valve and out the port.

Let's Get Practical

The reason we've spent so much time discussing blower and engine theory is to answer some questions about what makes things tick and why. Such questions are far too seldom asked about superchargers, and supercharging theory in general has progressed little since the 1940s. We would also like to dispel certain misbeliefs about blowers.

But in this book and in hot rodding in general, we are much more interested in practical application than we are in detached theory.

We know from practical experience that blowers work. We have given several reasons why they are not perfect, and we have shown some ways in which they can be improved. But in most cases, the blower gives much more than it takes. In typical

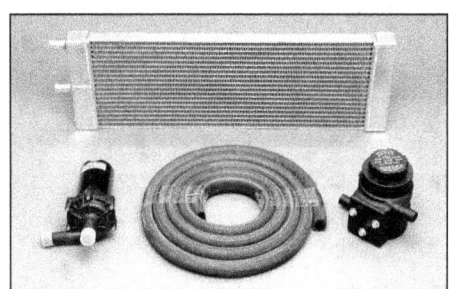

This is the rest of the Magna Charger water-to-air intercooling system. A small rotary electric pump (at left) circulates water, via a rubber heater-size hose, through the aluminum heat exchanger (or "radiator") mounted in fresh air at the front of the vehicle. The part at right is simply a cap to fill the system with water.

installations, a supercharger gives more power per cubic inch, more power per RPM, and more power per dollar spent than all other standard unblown engine modifications.

We have seen that the major problem associated with a street blower is heat. When the blower is making boost, it will be making more heat in the engine, and this means that you have to increase the capacity of the cooling system to carry away this heat before it damages engine parts. The heat carried away by coolant, or blown out the exhaust, is power wasted. Likewise, the more the blower heats the air in the intake manifold, the less efficient it is, the less potential power it will be pumping into the engine, and the more power it will be taking from the engine to operate.

Therefore, the most important and effective thing you can do to improve blower performance and efficiency is to keep the intake charge as cool as possible. This means drawing cool air into the blower, using as efficient a blower as possible to keep manifold temperature down, and thereby lowering combustion temperature so that more of the power of the expanding gases can be extracted in the cylinder. Since we cannot very well raise the operating temperature of the engine (especially on a street motor), this means that the only way to maximize engine power and efficiency, from a thermodynamic standpoint, is to lower the temperature of all processes down the line ahead of the exhaust stroke. Lowering the intake and combustion temperatures will also lessen the tendency of the engine to knock on available pump gasoline.

Today there are two obvious methods that can, and are, being used to accomplish this goal. The first is to use a modern, more efficient type of supercharger that doesn't heat the air charge as much in the first place. And the second, often in conjunction with the first, is to add an intercooler of some sort to the system. In fact, the only practical reasons for not using an intercooler to maximize the efficiency of a street blower are, first, the extra cost and, second, the problem of physically fitting (or "packaging") an intercooler into certain types of blower systems. These are the types of concerns that worry new car manufacturers—more and more of whom are finally learning that mechanically driven superchargers are not only practical and reliable in themselves for daily driven vehicles, but can make smaller, lighter, more efficient engines (and cars) act like bigger, more powerful ones.

These are also concerns of several of today's aftermarket supercharger manufacturers, who want to sell packaged kits to bolt onto (and into) today's modern vehicles. Fortunately, cost is not as critical a factor in the aftermarket, and including an intercooler in these kits is possible and wise. For these reasons, adding a supercharger to a vehicle that will actually see day-to-day driving is becoming much more common—and practical—than it once was.

However, one other thing we should consider that differentiates street supercharging from competition blowers is that a street machine is driven at part throttle the vast majority of the time. A gasoline engine is terribly inefficient in the first place, but it's considerably worse at anything less than wide-open throttle. At part throttle, the blower is basically a parasite on the engine (not to mention that a big blower, especially something like a GMC, with drive and carbs or injection, adds at least 100 pounds—or more—to overall vehicle weight that the engine must pull). Since it isn't making boost, or actually pumping air, a

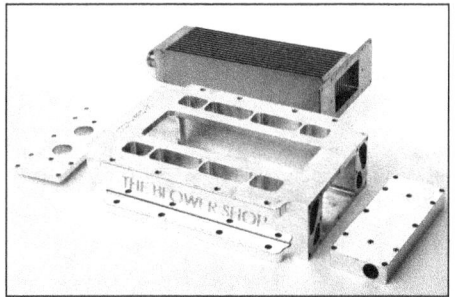

People have tried many ways to intercool big GMC blowers over the years, but the two main problems have been a large- and cold-enough source of water to effectively cool one, and an exchanger that wouldn't compromise airflow or actually collapse under high-boost pressure. This billet aluminum unit from The Blower Shop is designed for marine applications, where there's abundant cold water to pump through it, and uses a copper/brass core that has been tested to 900 hp at 7.6 pounds of boost.

blower will take much less horsepower to run at part throttle than it will at full throttle. Plus, manifold vacuum can actually spin most superchargers (especially a Roots type) like a windmill. But at part throttle a supercharger will very likely be taking more power than it is giving—not much, but some.

Partly for this reason (so you can readily see when the blower is working—making boost—and when it's "sucking" with vacuum in the manifold), we strongly recommend that any supercharged vehicle be fitted with a good, readily available boost gauge, any of which made for such applications will read both boost or vacuum in the manifold. Plus, though it may still be difficult to find an available, effective one, we equally recommend a fast-reading manifold temperature gauge. If you're the type of person who's interested in the mechanics and thermodynamics of supercharging as discussed in this chapter, these two gauges will let you immediately see what, and how well, your blower is doing. And they will give you the information to figure any of the calculations discussed here.

That said, we must admit that a large percentage of those contemplating the addition of a supercharger to their favorite vehicle—those of you reading this book—neither intend to drive this car daily, nor want to hide the fact that it is supercharged. Plenty of you still want that big, polished, whining 6-71 (or bigger) GMC-type blower sprouting from an equally brawny engine through the hood (if you have one). Others will be perfectly happy with the whoosh and obvious surge of power available any time you mash the throttle.

The newer, smaller, more efficient superchargers, coupled with EFI and intercooling are the true beauty of street supercharging today. You can have it any way you want it—even as warranted factory equipment on more and more new cars. Put one of these smaller, efficient blowers on a small engine in a light car, and you will actually be increasing fuel economy—perhaps significantly—over a larger engine/vehicle producing the same power unblown (that is, inefficiently). The parasitic loss of these blowers is proportionally small when you're cruising at part throttle, so you can think of these superchargers as ready power on demand—any time you hit the throttle. And if you want more power, just turn up the boost. Belt-driven blowers are readily adjustable with a quick change of pulley ratios. And if that isn't enough, get a bigger blower. Still not enough? Turn up the boost on that! As we've said, bolting a blower on your engine is one of the simplest modifications you can make to it, and it can increase engine power far more than all other non-blown

CHAPTER 4

VINTAGE SUPERCHARGERS

In previous editions of this book, we called this chapter "Swap Meet Gems" and focused on the fact that there were several types of aftermarket supercharger kits made for automobiles from the 1950s on, and that many of these were usually available at swap meets for very affordable prices. Further, since most of these superchargers have only one or two primary moving parts—which should never touch, rub, or wear—finding a good, usable (or easily rebuildable) older supercharger was a practical proposition. Today, it must be remembered that many of these older blowers were less than efficient, if not downright crude, plus most were made for relatively small engines, so they aren't your best choice in a power adder for a modern engine. On the other hand, several still work surprisingly well. Either way, there are a lot of used superchargers out there. Some are old, cool, and collectible; some are rare, funky, or just odd; and others are good blowers that have fallen out of production for one reason or another.

In the case of the older, rarer blowers and adaption kits, we now have two categories: those that are deemed "collectible," and have there-

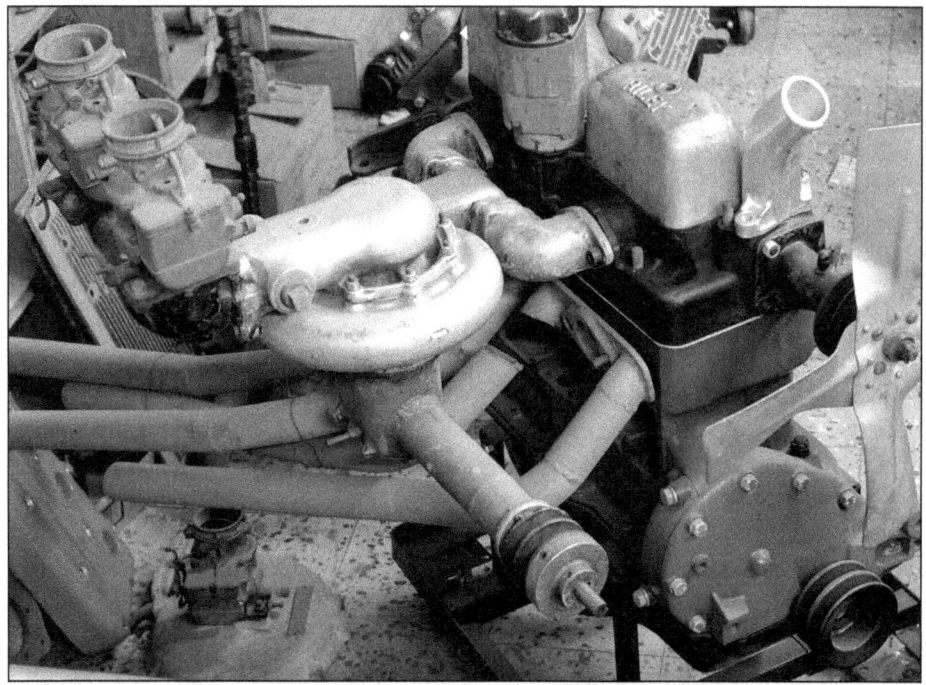

What is this blower? It's one of the late Gene Scott's many oddities and antiquities on display at Antique Ford Parts in Rosemead, California, and even current custodian Jim Gordon has no idea what it is. It's probably an automotive supercharger from a 1920s production or race car, and some enterprising hot rodder did a lot of work adapting it, and two 97 carbs, to his Riley-head Model-B engine. The blower on the floor below it looks like one from a 1930s Graham.

fore shot up in value (such as an original Italmeccanica or Frenzel), and those that are now just deemed weird or funky (such as a Judson or Latham) and should be available at good prices. Certain older blowers, such as specific ball-drive McCullochs that were used as optional factory

This unit, seen at a swap meet, is more likely one of hundreds of types of "blowers" or pumps used for a wide variety of industrial purposes. Is it worth the $50 asking price? Not to adapt to your automotive engine.

equipment on mid-1950s Fords and other cars, can command high prices in that restorer market; at the same time, this has also generated new sources for hard-to-find parts and rebuilding for these blowers.

Either way, given a revived and growing interest in all things vintage in the hot rod world, mounting one of these older, rarer blowers on your engine can have plenty of "wow" factor—with or without a substantial boost in horsepower, and for a high or low price tag. In fact, at least one company, H&H Flatheads, considers the vintage market strong enough that they have tooled up to build a brand-new, exact-duplicate version of the venerable S.Co.T. blower, with kits to mount it on flathead Ford engines. But it's neither funky nor cheap.

Finally, as mentioned, there are literally tens of thousands of superchargers out there, produced in the past decade or two, that have become "vintage" because their manufacturers either went out of business, sold the supercharger line, ceased production of one type of blower to concentrate on another—whatever. These would include the enormous B&M blower line, early-style Magna Chargers, other smaller Roots-type blowers, and several companies that made street blower kits based on GMC blowers that have come and gone over the years. We'll look at all of these, briefly, here and give some tips on how to assess the condition and usability of such used superchargers today.

Early McCulloch Blowers

As far as I can determine, the first aftermarket blower kit made in America was a centrifugal supercharger made by Robert Paxton McCulloch in the late 1930s. This initial McCulloch blower was designed to bolt onto the manifold of a Ford V-8 and was driven by a pair of V-belts from the crankshaft. The impeller and scroll housing of the blower mounted horizontally above the intake manifold, the impeller being driven by a bevel gear from the belt-driven shaft. A single Ford 2-barrel carb mounted on top of the blower housing, was made of aluminum.

This initial McCulloch blower, made in Milwaukee, was similar to the centrifugal superchargers used on Duesenberg SJs, Auburns, and Grahams. McCulloch was a Stanford engineering graduate who was building racing engines for boats in the Milwaukee area in the 1930s. He would later develop superchargers for the army during WWII, and move to California to establish the McCulloch Corporation, which made, among other things, McCulloch/Paxton superchargers, small gasoline engines, go-karts, and chain saws.

These early McCulloch centrifugal blowers reportedly showed up on a few prewar lakes racers. The Granatelli brothers were using them on their own hot rods in Chicago as early as 1938, and became a distributor for them (they eventually bought the Paxton blower division from McCulloch

The first commonly known aftermarket automotive supercharger was this centrifugal McCulloch. The large horizontal impeller was driven by right-angle, step-up bevel gears turned by a shaft belt-driven from the crank. Designed for V-8 Fords in the 1930s, the blower bolted to (and blew into) the stock intake manifold, with a flange for the stock 2-barrel carb on top. Quite a few of these early McCullochs exist; this recent example mounts two carbs on an Almquist Y-adapter.

in 1959). But very few of these early flathead McCullochs exist today. Consider them strictly a collector's item.

The next generation McCulloch/Paxton centrifugal superchargers was introduced in 1953. These belt-driven blowers, adaptable to a wide variety of engines, were characterized by an ingenious and unique method of internal step-up "gearing" accomplished by a planetary drive using five large steel ball bearings. Consequently, these early-style Paxtons, which remained in production (with several revisions) through the 1990s, are commonly referred to as the "ball-drive" units.

While the planetary ball-drive inside the housing stepped-up impeller speed at a 4.4:1 ratio to make

CHAPTER 4

Another current example of an early McCulloch on a flathead V-8 mounts a single 97 carb as intended, but has been modified for a rear pulley to drive an alternator in a unique location.

This is an original McCulloch VS-57 centrifugal supercharger, plenty of which were sold in kits to fit various 1950s engines, while smaller numbers were fitted to certain Kaisers, Studebakers, and Packards between 1954 and 1958. VS stood for Variable Speed, controlled by the movable width of the drive pulley, which changed its effective diameter (and ratio).

In this cutaway of a VS-57, the impeller (which is missing) and scroll housing are on the left, with the air inlet in the middle and outlet at the top. Five large steel planetary balls, which step up impeller speed 4.4:1 times input shaft speed, are inside the clutch-like housing with several springs. The rest of the unit, with the large spring, bearings, and air-pressure-activated solenoid, moves the inner flange of the drive pulley in or out. When the pulley is "closed," as shown, the V-belt rides high in the groove, driving the blower slower. When it "opens," the belt drops down to a smaller diameter, thus increasing the drive ratio and spinning the blower faster. Later SN models kept the ball-drive and the housing, but eliminated the variable-pulley mechanism.

this centrifugal blower quite effective at higher engine speeds, the original models also incorporated a variable-ratio drive pulley on the blower to increase blower speed at lower engine RPM, and therefore compensate for the centrifugal blower's intrinsic lack of low-RPM boost. This was done by using a wide V-belt and pulley to drive the blower from the crankshaft, with the driven pulley on the blower having a variable width, controlled by a vacuum diaphragm inside the blower. This diaphragm could move one flange of the blower pulley in or out, thus making its effective driven diameter larger or smaller, and thus increasing blower drive speed at lower engine RPM, to increase boost in those ranges.

As far as we know, it is the only centrifugal (or any other type) blower to employ this logical device but, though it was relatively effective (when all the components worked properly), it added to the complexity of an already complicated (and expensive to make) supercharger design. Thus, this initial VS-57-series (for Variable Speed) was quickly discontinued by 1958 or 1959. It was replaced by the "SN-60" model (which stood for "Short Nose"), which used the same blower housing, but deleted the variable-ratio pulley and the internal diaphragm, spring, and other parts to operate it. The SN series, used for years, looked essentially the same externally as the VS Paxtons, including the wide, single V-belt drive with a large idler pulley and tensioner spring.

Neither of these should be confused with the VR-series Paxtons, which were made exclusively for Ford in 1957 for use as an option in T-Birds and some sedans. These blowers, which had a readily recognizable finned housing, were completely different, with an internal mechanism to move the ball-drive races, thus internally varying the step-up ratio with engine (and blower) speed. In this case, "VR" stood for Variable Ratio. Those who know say that only a couple hundred of these blowers were made. And since Ford owned the tooling and didn't want to deal with warranty issues down the road, it was probably destroyed.

To further complicate this issue, the Paxton blower actually used by Ford in its NASCAR and other racing ventures in 1957 was a similar but slightly larger unit known as the Phase 1. Plus, Paxton "blowers," made for a variety of industrial purposes (ventilation, fruit drying, pressurizing) through the 1980s or 1990s, used a housing similar to the Ford VR units, with a "Paxton" emblem. Some of these show up on eBay and other places for sale as rare Ford parts, but they aren't, nor are they intended for automotive supercharging.

To back up a bit, McCulloch was the first U.S. aftermarket blower manufacturer to secure contracts to fit his superchargers to new cars as optional OEM equipment. As said, the first ball-drive units were manufactured in 1953, and were sold in kits to fit (in a blow-through arrangement, with a pressure housing, or bonnet, on the stock carb/manifold) Fords, Cadillacs, Oldsmobiles, Buicks, and so on. These early units carried a McCulloch emblem on the case.

The first OEM contract was with Kaiser in 1954, and these blowers were installed on all Kaiser Manhattans that year; the next year Kaiser went out of business. Next came the contract with Ford in 1957, followed quickly by one with Studebaker, which had merged with short-lived Packard, both of which used McCulloch/Paxton blowers as optional equipment. After the company was acquired by the Granatellis in the late 1950s, the blowers were famously fitted to R-3 Avantis, as well as certain Shelby Mustang/Cobra optional packages. Sometime in this period the badging on the blower was changed from McCulloch to Paxton. During this period Paxton continued to sell kits to adapt this SN-60 blower to a variety of engines, as well.

We should note that the unique Paxton ball-drive served a few different purposes. First, it was considerably quieter than the straight-cut spur or bevel drive gears used in other blowers. Most people don't realize that the characteristic whine of a big, belt-driven GMC blower on a hot rod engine does not come from the rotors, the belt, or the air pumped through it—it comes from the two, small, drive gears in the front housing that turn the rotors. And, unlike hot rodders, new-car manufacturers (and buyers) didn't want a noisy supercharger.

Second, the ball-drive takes less energy to drive than step-up spur gears would. But most important, this

For 1957, Ford used these different VR-57 ball-drive McCulloch superchargers, identified by their finned housings. The one on the left was for NASCAR (until it was outlawed) and other racing such as Pike's Peak, while the one on the right was fitted to 211 "Blower Bird" Thunderbirds as factory equipment.

From 1966 to 1968 Carroll Shelby added an SN-60 blower, with its name changed from McCulloch to Paxton, with a Holley 4-barrel mounted inside a pressure box, to his namesake GT 350 Mustangs as an option to increase the power of the Hi-Po 289 to 375 hp. It was also offered as a Ford dealer-installed option through 1970. Today an identical kit, as shown, is available from Craig Conley of Paradise Wheels, Inc., of San Marcos, California. Conley acquired the rights, patterns, and existing spare parts for the ball-drive Paxtons, and not only has installation kits to fit other engines, but can also rebuild the older Paxton/McCulloch blowers.

CHAPTER 4

While the Frenzel blower made the cover of Hot Rod *magazine in 1952, very few of these centrifugal blowers were made. Designed to mount directly on a stock Ford V-8 manifold its vertically mounted impeller was driven by large, square-cut step-up gears in the aluminum housing in front of the scroll. The bolt-on Y-type mount for two 2-barrel Ford-type carbs was part of the package.*

planetary ball-drive design eliminated the major failure of previous centrifugal blowers for high-performance automotive engines—the fact that rapid acceleration or deceleration would strip the teeth off of conventional drive gears, due to the high rotational velocity of the impeller and its consequent momentum. This feature, coupled with the relatively small diameter/low inertia of the Paxton impeller, made the blower bulletproof in this regard (as well as quiet).

The only problem was that the five ball bearings had to be perfectly round and exactly the same size, with races machined to similar tolerances, for the system to work for any length of time before beginning to wear. As you can imagine, this problem was exacerbated when the blower was fitted to much-higher-revving engines. After a hiatus during the performance doldrums of the 1970s, the Granatellis addressed this problem with improved machining capabilities as well as bearing materials, and several improved iterations of the blower were introduced: the SN-89, SN-90, SN-92, SN-93, and SN-2000 (relating, roughly, to the year introduced).

However, during this period (the 1990s) Paxton developed a completely new, bevel-gear-driven blower, underwent a change of ownership, and ultimately merged with Vortech, which will be covered later. Consequently the ball-drive Paxton blowers were discontinued by Paxton in approximately 2000. The good news for owners, or buyers, of these older Paxtons is that Craig Conley of Paradise Wheels in San Marcos, California, bought the rights, all existing inventory, as well as patterns, tooling, and test equipment for these blowers at that time. He can not only service or rebuild recent Paxton SN blowers, but he can also retrofit older models with newer, high-tolerance ball-drives, and he can even assemble complete new units for specific applications.

The Frenzel

Another early centrifugal supercharger, introduced in 1950 as a bolt-on for Ford V-8s, was the Frenzel. Manufactured in Denver, Colorado, it was similar in design to the initial McCulloch, except that it bolted to the stock intake manifold with the impeller and scroll in a vertical position rather than horizontal, and it accepted two 2-barrel carbs instead of one. A spur-gear housing in front of the 7½-inch impeller ran the blower at 5.9 times crank speed. This blower was rated at 6 pounds boost at 4,200 rpm on the flathead, which would reportedly increase horsepower 50-percent over stock.

To give a good idea of how well these early blowers worked on production cars at the time, a stock Ford coupe was fitted with a Frenzel blower and tested at El Mirage dry lake in 1950. Without the blower, it ran 84.6 mph top speed and accelerated from 0 to 60 mph in 16.3 seconds. With the blower, it did 100.05 mph and 0 to 60 in 11 seconds. This was a substantial improvement for a single piece of bolt-on speed equipment, and helped justify the $175 price tag (which was also substantial in 1950). However, Frenzel blowers are extremely rare today. Apparently very few of them were produced.

The S.Co.T./Italmeccanica

By far the most popular, and apparently the most plentiful, of

VINTAGE SUPERCHARGERS

This polished Frenzel is the only one we've actually seen mounted and operating. The flathead, with dual mags and Elco Twin Plug heads, is a showcase of rare vintage speed equipment.

The S.Co.T./Italmeccanica Roots blower, by contrast, was made (in Turin, Italy) and sold in large numbers despite a high price for the early 1950s. This flathead Ford Italmeccanica came with its own manifold (with pop-off valve), and mounts/inlets for two Ford-type carbs on top. Smaller versions had one round inlet and a pad to accept various types of 1-barrels. The straight, 2-lobe, hollow rotors were cast aluminum.

This is a fine example of a polished and detailed S.Co.T. mounted on a flathead Ford with original kit components, driven by two V-belts and mounting two 97 carbs.

Dave Lukkari made or modified the intake manifold to mount the V-8-size S.Co.T. on his Ardun-head Ford. As a testament to the blower's practicality, this one has logged tens (if not hundreds) of thousands of miles without problem.

early blowers is the Italmeccanica/S.Co.T. This relatively small, good-looking, 2-lobe, Roots-type supercharger was first produced in Italy as the Italmeccanica and was imported as late as 1951 in complete kits for American cars such as Ford and Merc flathead V-8s, Chevy 6s, Crosleys, and Studebakers. These blowers were made in different sizes for different engines (they were also made to fit several European cars), but the most popular unit was that for the flathead V-8. The kit included a new manifold to accept the blower, with a pop-off valve, plus all necessary pulleys, generator relocation mount, and belts. The top of the V-8 blower case mounted two Ford 2-barrel carbs. The "I.T." blower, as it was often called, produced 6 to 8 pounds boost and increased horsepower on a stock 59A Ford V-8 from 82 to 150 at 4,000 rpm in one reported dyno test.

Later, American versions of this blower were assembled in New Jersey, using American thread and bearing sizes (though some I.T. blowers were fitted with S.A.E., as well as metric, fasteners) and were called the S.Co.T. (possibly for Supercharger Co. of Turin). Larger versions of the S.Co.T. were subsequently made for Cadillac and Oldsmobile V-8s in the early 1950s. However, as of 1952, a flathead V-8 S.Co.T. kit listed for $467.50, and the Cad/Olds kits were close to $800. That's considerably more than a whole new engine back then.

Early GMC Kits

As we have already discussed, rodders had begun to discover the GMC Roots-type blower by the late 1940s. One of the first to offer automotive adaptation kits for 3-71 and 4-71 Jimmies was Tom Beatty, first for flathead V-8s, and later for Oldsmobile overheads. Beatty made a manifold for the Olds that has his name on it. GMC pioneer Barney Navarro, with whom Beatty worked, produced

CHAPTER 4

Real hot rodders don't need kits. They make their own parts, as demonstrated by this 3-71 GMC blower adapted to an early Oldsmobile engine. A carburetor manifold was modified to mount the blower, the V-belt drive was handmade, and a simple plate adapts three Holley carbs on top—all apparently done long ago.

A rare 1950s Tom Beatty 6-71 intake manifold for an Olds V-8 was spotted at a swap meet. The blower had to be "pruned" of its mounting flanges, drilled and tapped around the outlet to match the manifold's pattern, then attached with bolts from the bottom up. Beatty's drives used four or five V-belts.

Most early manifolds to mount GMC blowers on overhead V-8s were made for racing, and didn't include provisions for coolant/thermostat or belt-driven accessories. One of the first complete "blower kits" for small-block Chevys was made by Cragar, using a manifold like this (from Offenhauser), which retained the stock water neck and distributor mount. The Cragar kit added a blower snout and driveshaft, idler pulley and bracket, rear blower cover, carb adapter plate, and drive pulleys for three V-belts. All you needed to add was a 4-71 blower.

a flathead blower manifold under his own brand, but we're not sure when it was offered to the public. Chuck Potvin made front-drive GMC kits beginning in the mid-1950s, and Isky finally came out with a complete top-mount 6-71 Gilmer-belt-drive and manifold kit for Chryslers and Chevys in the late 1950s. However, these and a few other GMC 6-71 blower kits were designed for competition, not street (with no provision for water pump, thermostat, etc.).

In about 1951 or 1952, both Speed-O-Motive and a short-lived company called J.E.M. (Jack and Ernie McAfee) tooled up intake manifolds, blower covers and snouts, and multi-V-belt drives to mount 3-71 and 4-71 GMCs on Ford flatheads, Cadillacs, and possibly other engines. These are quite rare.

The first really complete and widely marketed kit for adapting a 3-71 or 4-71 GMC to a street engine was Cragar's V-belt-drive setup introduced in about 1959. This kit included an intake manifold (which would accept either a 3-71 or 4-71) with a stock-type water neck, a drive snout and shaft for the front of the blower, a thin rear cover, a 4-barrel-carb intake, and a triple-V-belt-drive system. You had to supply your own blower, carburetor, and linkage. This kit was intended primarily for street applications and tons of them were sold, mostly for small-block Chevys (although advertising states they were available for "most popular V-8s"). Andy Brizio, former owner of Champion Speed Shop and builder of Andy's Instant T roadsters, bought the kit from Cragar in the late 1960s, marketing it for a time with the name "Andy's" embossed on the manifold (kits were available for small-block Chevys and Fords).

In the 1960s, as drag racers began using GMC blowers in great numbers, several speed-parts manufacturers, racers, and machinists produced competition-style blower drives, cases, end plates, manifolds, and various accessories under names such as Pete Robinson, Mickey Thompson (M/T), Delta, Van Luven, Danekas, Bowers, and many others that have come and gone.

Other Roots Blowers

Since we're partly discussing strange superchargers you might find on eBay or at a swap meet, we should point out that a wide assortment of Roots-type blowers, and blowers of other designs, have been produced in the United States for a variety of purposes (from scavenging or supercharging diesel engines, to pressurizing airplane or submarine cabins, to pumping molasses or flour). For instance, McCulloch built thousands of Roots-type superchargers for military landing craft powered by small engines during World War II. He later sold the design to Melee-Dexter, which was still producing it in the 1990s. In the early 1960s, Dick Jones of Champion Spark Plugs used a Melee-Dexter

VINTAGE SUPERCHARGERS

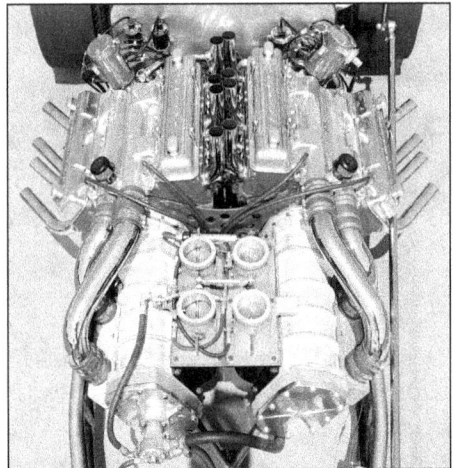

How about twin Potvin front-mount blower systems for twin Chevys? This is, of course, the Dragmasters' Two Thing dragster from the early 1960s, and these are the first-design (non-finned) Potvin manifolds.

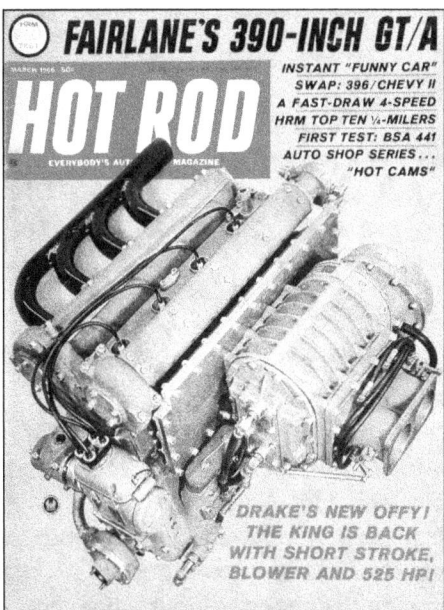

The Melee-Dexter was just one common type of small Roots blower used for a variety of industrial purposes. They weren't designed for performance automotive use (though neither were GMCs). In 1966, this one was fitted to a Drake Offy with Hilborn injection. It made the cover of Hot Rod, *but it didn't make it at Indy.*

The unique thing about Ray Fageol's KF superchargers was that both the 3-lobe rotors and the cases were made of extruded aluminum and could be cut to any length. However, even the Max 25 (shown), one of the largest, displaced only 63 cubic inches. They were offered with installation kits for Toyota 4-cylinders and GM 60-degree V-6s.

blower to supercharge the Offy Indy motor for an attempted comeback. It made the cover of *Hot Rod* magazine, but didn't do well in the race. Other Roots-type blowers have been made by Schwitzer-Cummins, the Pesco Division of Borg-Warner, and the original Roots company, to name a few.

The above examples might be considered "industrial" blowers (or pumps), certainly not intended for performance use on automotive engines—though many have been made to work in such a capacity in the past by ingenious hot rodders. As you might expect, though, there have also been several Roots-type blowers designed and built by enterprising aftermarket manufacturers over the years as bolt-on performance enhancements for street or competition cars that have come and gone.

One of the first of these was the small Pepco, made by the Fageol family, who not only made trucks, buses, and products for them, but also imported the first VW "Bugs" to the United States as early as 1950. Lou Fageol had been very active in race engine development for both cars and boats, and drove in three Indy 500s in the 1940s, including a twin-Offy powered, 4-71 GMC supercharged car! They also owned an early Porsche dealership involved in East Coast racing, which led to the development of the Pepco blower, which was first shown at Watkins Glen in 1950. It was a small Roots blower with a cast-aluminum case and rotors. The rotors were 3-lobed, but not twisted like a GMC, and the blowers came in two sizes, the "4" and the "6", which referred to the rotor/case length, in inches. From 1950 to 1958 they were sold in complete kits to mount on VWs, Porsches, and MGs. Reportedly more than 1,000 were made, and several supposedly ended up on VW dune buggies in the 1960s, but they're extremely scarce today.

More recently, and perhaps not surprisingly, Lou Fageol's son, Ray, started his own small supercharger company in San Diego, California, called KF Industries, in the 1980s. His Roots-type blowers resembled the Pepcos in size and design, having straight 3-lobe rotors. The big difference was that he pioneered the practice of making the cases and the rotors from aluminum extrusions, rather than castings, so they could be cut to any length. Using the same cast-aluminum bearing plates and drive snouts, these blowers could easily be made in a variety of sizes. Known as the Max 10, 15, 25, and 30, they varied in length from 4½ to 9½ inches, with the most common, the Max 25, displacing 63.2 ci. Obviously targeted for smaller engines, including motorcycle applications, a Max 10 kit was made for VW flat-4s that were popular on dune buggies, while Max 25s were made for Toyota 20R 4-cylinders and for Chevy 60-degree V-6s in S-10s, Blazers, and Fieros, either in carbureted or factory fuel injected form.

While the KF blowers did not reach a wide market (actual sales numbers are not known), they presaged the use of cut-to-fit extruded aluminum rotors in the highly successful B&M blowers.

Another Roots blower with a similar-sounding name that has been bouncing around the aftermarket (in small numbers) for decades is the Penco. Designed by former GM engineer John Camden sometime in the 1960s, and sold by him (sometimes under his name, Camden) and others through the 1970s and 1980s for a wide variety of applications ranging from flathead Ford V-8s to big-block Chevy and Mopar motorhomes, it is basically a derivative of the 53-series GMC blower (and therefore similar to the first B&M and Weiand blowers). In fact, the standard 140-ci Penco uses GM 4-53 2-lobe rotors and helical-drive gears in its own cast-aluminum case.

The big difference between the Penco and the GM or any other similar blowers is that it uses no rotor bearings or bushings. Instead, the 356-T6 aluminum end plates were reamed and honed to size and fed a constant supply of pressurized engine oil, with a braided oil line connecting the front and rear end plates, and a return line directing oil back to the engine valley through the intake manifold. The top of the case incorporated a 4-barrel carburetor flange. Low-profile cast-aluminum intake manifolds were made for flathead V-8s, small- and big-block Chevys, and big-block ("B" series) Mopars.

There's no telling how many Pencos (or Camdens) are out there. In fact, I recently saw new units being marketed on the Internet for flathead applications. If you're looking to buy a used one, however, the first thing to check is the condition of the end-plate bearing surfaces and, consequently, whether any rotor-to-case contact has occurred. If the blower

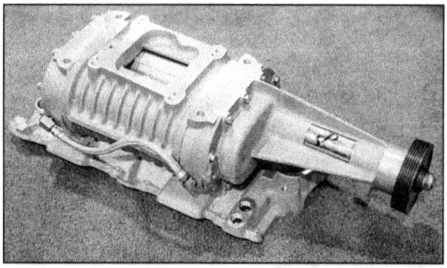

The Penco, sometimes called a Camden, has been floating around for decades. It's basically a cast-aluminum housing incorporating a 4-barrel flange on the top, using GM 4-53 2-lobe rotors for a 140-ci displacement. Note the oil line feeding front and rear gear/bearing plates. This one is on a Chevy manifold; intakes to mount them on flathead V-8s to big-block Mopars were made, as well.

was installed on a hot rod, it has probably seen few miles and been fed a constant supply of clean oil. If it was on something like a motorhome or trailer-towing pickup since the 1970s or 1980s, however, just accumulated cold starts, let alone lack of engine oil changes, could cause even mild wear (at best) that cannot be fixed without boring out the end plates to accept some sort of press-in bearings or bushings.

The Judson and Other Vane Types

We briefly mentioned vane-type superchargers in Chapter 1. They are mechanically quite different than common types of blowers, but though they are fairly simple, and highly efficient, they have never achieved widespread use.

The Bendix Corp. and Holley designed and built working prototypes of vane superchargers in the 1980s, which were shown in some detail in previous editions of this book. However, neither was sold to an auto

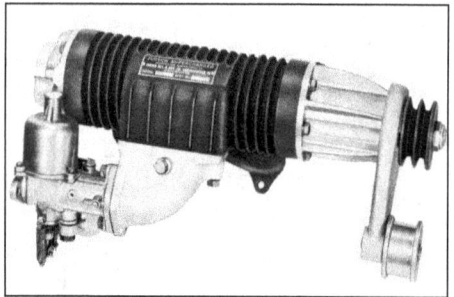

This vane-type Judson, seen in a catalog photo, is typical of the smaller sizes made in the 1950s and 1960s for sports cars like MGs and Triumphs, as well as small cars such as VWs and Corvairs. This model is fitted with a single SU carburetor, so it's probably for a British car application. The oil reservoir, necessary for its proper operation, is not shown.

manufacturer for OEM use, and both projects were shelved. The Holley blower, in fact, was designed in conjunction with the Wankel Co. of Germany, which made a vane-type supercharger that set records on NSU motorcycles many years ago. Further, the Wankel rotary engine that we know in Mazda RX7 cars here in the United States is based on the same principle as a vane supercharger, except that it is of a "fixed vane" design.

The only vane superchargers produced for aftermarket automotive use were the Judson in the United States and the Shorrock in England, both in the 1950s. Obviously they are scarce today, but: 1) they are definitely worth points as rare vintage equipment (especially Judsons, which are more common in the United States), and 2) the vane-type blower should be of interest to anyone studying superchargers (if not, feel free to skip ahead).

The simplest type of vane supercharger—the Judson falls in this category—consists of a simple cylindrical housing, inside of which a smaller cylinder rotates on an off-center axis. Through slits in the surface of the smaller cylinder protrude any number (usually three or four) of thin, flat blades, or vanes. These vanes are linked to, or ride on, a shaft located at the center of the outer cylinder (case), and are able to slip in or out of the inner cylinder, or rotor. Thus as the inner cylinder rotates eccentrically within the housing, the vanes rotate concentrically, maintaining either a slight clearance from, or very light contact with, the wall of the case.

The outer cylinder, or case, has an intake port and an outlet port, which are no more than openings in the case wall. As the inner cylinder and vane assembly rotates within the case, two things happen. The vanes draw air in through the intake port, moving it much like a paddle wheel. However, as a given quantity of air is drawn in and trapped between two vanes as it is carried around the blower wall, the inner cylinder begins moving (on its offset axis) closer to the outer cylinder, thereby compressing the air between the vanes. The vane-type blower is a positive-displacement pump, since it moves the same quantity of air per revolution, but it is also an internal compressor, and therein lies its major attribute.

This is a more efficient way to compress air and pump it into an engine. A Roots blower, for instance, is simply a pump. Compression (boost) doesn't occur until the air is pumped into the manifold below the blower, where it "stacks up." This pressure, however, causes air to backflow into the blower rotor cavities as they open to the manifold, causing pulsing. (Newer Roots designs use higher-helix rotors and higher rotor speeds, as well as modified outlets, to improve this condition.)

Even simple vane-type superchargers will have a higher mechani-

cal efficiency than older Roots types (such as GMCs). But it is in their adiabatic efficiency that they excel. First, very little extraneous motion, or work, is done to compress the air. Second, remembering our basic (PV/T) Gas Law from Chapter 3, we know that increasing air pressure while keeping its volume the same increases its temperature proportionally; but decreasing the volume while increasing the pressure will reduce the amount of temperature increase. If we could reduce the volume the same amount that we increased the pressure, the equation tells us we could actually keep the temperature constant. In real life, however, we are lucky to approach simple adiabatic heat rise in a compressor. The eccentric-vane supercharger comes close.

So why aren't vane superchargers more common? First, like most things mechanical, there are drawbacks.

Made in the early 1950s, this is the first V-8 Ford Judson blower I have ever seen, let alone complete, installed, and working. It is fed by two 97s on a bolt-on plenum, and is mounted on and feeds into the stock manifold, all parts appearing to be original Judson (the matching generator cover was just a lucky find). However, again, the necessary oiling reservoir seems to be missing.

Compared to a two-rotor Roots or screw, or a single-impeller centrifugal, the vane blower has more moving parts, and designing and machining a system to hold the vanes in the eccentric rotor, while keeping them in close contact with (but not touching) the case wall, is complicated.

Second, the off-center rotation of the inner cylinder causes an obvious imbalance in the unit. This could be controlled to some degree by making the rotor of lightweight material or adding a counter-balance shaft to the blower, but either change would add to the cost/complexity of the unit and, ultimately, the offset of the inner rotor limits its effective rotational speed. Plus, auto manufacturers abhor a vibration of any type.

Third, vane-type blowers cannot approach the same air pumping capacity per revolution as Roots or centrifugal blowers. Combined with the fact that they cannot be turned at high RPM, this means that vane-type blowers must be quite large to pump significant quantities of air (though increasing the size increases the eccentric vibration problem).

Thus, with its efficient internal compression but low volume, vane superchargers are best suited to producing high boost levels on smaller engines (such as the record-setting NSU motorcycles).

Since small engines were the norm in England in the 1950s, the Shorrock vane supercharger achieved some success there, especially in hill climbs, rallies, and early drag racing, on motorcycles and small 4-cylinders. Made in two sizes for engines of 850 to 1300 cc and 1300 to 2000 cc, it used four thin-metal vanes held in place by small rings on a shaft at the center of the cylindrical case. The vanes slid through slots in the eccentric inner rotor cylinder, which rotated on trunnion shafts. Thus the vane tips were held in close tolerance to, but did not touch, the case wall. Shorrock blowers were marketed by the Allard Motor Co. from 1957 into the 1970s, but very few, if any, were imported to the United States.

The Judson, invented and marketed by Haddon Judson of Conshohocken, Pennsylvania, beginning in 1952, was an utterly simple device. The initial unit, known as model B-210, was made for the flathead Ford V-8. It mounted directly on the stock intake manifold and had a built-in flange for two Ford 2-barrel carburetors at the intake port. Subsequent models, however, were made in a variety of smaller sizes and sold in complete kits to fit cars such as VWs, MGs, Triumphs, Sprites, Volvos, and Corvairs. Judson claims 50,000 of these were sold by the late 1960s, when he turned his attention to marketing one of the first transistor ignition systems.

Unlike the Ford V-8 version, these later Judsons were smaller in diameter and varied in length. With a finned, cast-aluminum case with inlet and outlet spaced about 120 degrees apart, the unique feature of the Judson was the design, placement, and composition of the four vanes in the eccentric rotor. When I interviewed Mr. Judson years ago, he would not say exactly what the vanes were made of, other than "a synthetic material" (I had been told it was Masonite). But these blades simply slid into slots cut at an angle in the rotor. As Judson described it: "Due to the weight of the blades and the angle of mounting, the centrifugal force is balanced [when the rotor is spinning] so that the pressure against the case is kept to a minimum and yet a zero clearance is assured." With zero clearance between the blades and case, air leakage was minimal and volumetric efficiency was high.

While these blowers seemed to work well, and reliably, in their stated 5- to 7-psi range on small engines, the biggest drawback to both the Judson and Shorrock blowers was that they required some internal lubrication (the Shorrock for moving internal metal parts; the Judson for the vane tip-to-housing contact). If you know about high-compression engines, you know that any introduction of oil into the combustion chambers (past rings or valveguides) promotes detonation. So a supercharger, added to an engine to increase compression—especially one with internal compression itself—that also injects a small amount of oil into the air/fuel mix is not optimum. Further, the Shorrock drew engine oil from a pressure line, meaning that the engine oil level had to be checked and replenished.

The Judson came with its own oil reservoir (usually a glass jar, similar to those for windshield washers on early cars). The blower consumed this lubricating oil at the rate of about one quart every 1,000 miles. Even if the owner filled this jar religiously, the life expectancy of the vanes was about 20,000 miles. If it ran dry, wear would occur on the rotor shaft as well as vanes.

So if you find a used Judson for sale, be aware: 1) that it is supposed to come with an oil reservoir (few I've seen at swaps have it); 2) if you want to install it on an engine, you need to include an oil supply; and 3) it is difficult to judge if, or how much, the vanes are worn; if they need replacing, you'll have to make your own from some suitable material.

Latham

Another rarity among superchargers is the Latham "Axial-Flow." It was originally produced in Florida from 1956 to 1965, and reportedly about 600 units, of various sizes, were made. Designed and produced by Norman Latham, it is actually a turbine fan similar in design and concept to a jet engine. It is the only supercharger known to use this principle for blowing air into an engine.

Basically, the Latham blower consists of a stack of small fans, each made by inserting a row of blades around the circumference of an aluminum ring. These rings are bolted together to make a cylinder covered with small fan blades. This cylinder is then spun at high speed inside a cylindrical housing to blow air from the front to the back. Such a fan arrangement, however, would tend to simply spin the air inside the housing, rather than blow it through. In order to "straighten out" the airflow through the blower, Latham placed rows of blades inside the stationary housing, turned the opposite direction from the rotor blades. Thus he created a multi-stage compressor, each stage consisting of a rotor fan followed by a reverse direction stator

These are two now-rare, working installations of Latham blowers on street rods, both using four side-draft Carter YF carburetors. The one on the small-block Chevy appears to use original Latham components, including the wide, flat drive belt. The big-block Ford unit has been adapted to a 4-barrel intake manifold and has a custom twin-V-belt drive.

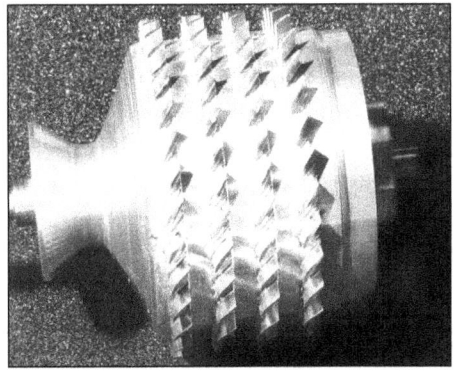

This is a 4-stage version of the rotating Latham impeller. Between each row of its fan blades are opposite-turned rows of blades held stationary in the outer housing rings. Each row of rotor and stator blades propel and compress the air/fuel mixture.

fan, which "catches" the accelerated air, changes its direction, and increases its pressure in a manner similar to the diffuser blades in a centrifugal blower. This compressed air is then accelerated by the next rotor fan, "straightened" and compressed by the next stator fan, and so on until it reaches the back of the housing and is blown into the intake manifold at high volume and pressure. The term "axial flow" refers to the fact that the air travels along the axis of the rotor (that is, from the front of the blower to the back), rather than being spun radially by the rotating fans.

The Latham blower had several advantages. To begin with, it has only one moving part, the rotor assembly, plus two double-row ball bearings. Other than the bearings, no parts touch, so nothing should wear out in one. There are no gears to make noise. Plus there is very little stress on any components. The Latham is also very efficient in terms of engine power required to drive it. Producing as much as 10 pounds of manifold pressure in a large V-8, the Latham reportedly requires as little as 10 hp from the engine.

Latham claimed high volumetric and adiabatic efficiency for the axial-flow design, as well. The fact that the Latham is a draw-through configuration further adds to the cooling and it increases fuel atomization and distribution. Latham even claimed (and apparently could demonstrate) that, in street installations with two Carter YF side-draft carburetors, the blower produced a 12-percent fuel economy increase over stock carburetion.

And Latham blowers worked. Karol Miller used one on a 1956 Ford Y-Block to significantly best all class competitors at both the Daytona Beach and Bonneville speed trials in the mid-1950s, and even drove the car there and back from Texas on both occasions! Les Ritchey installed one on a 312-inch 1957 Ranchero, improving quarter-mile times from 15.2 sec./90 mph to 13.44 sec./103 mph—and drove it from L.A. to the Oklahoma City Nationals and back. GM was very intrigued with the Latham blower in the late 1950s, installing it on a couple of Motorama dream cars. A GM dyno test of a small-block Chevy at that time produced 230 hp at 6,000 rpm with a single 4-barrel, and then netted 334 hp at 5,600 rpm after the Latham was installed.

The major drawback to the Latham was its cost—about $1,000 in the 1950s and 1960s—necessitated by the high cost of necessary machining and assembly processes. And, even at that considerable price, the Latham wasn't profitable to build.

Another problem with the Latham was the drive belt. The blower ran at

You can't really inspect a Latham unless you take it all apart. This 11-stage one, seen at a recent swap meet, has been fitted with a Gilmer-belt pulley and some odd intake elbows, but it turned freely with tight bearings. In any case, it's a rare sighting. There aren't many of these around.

five times crank speed, necessitating high belt velocity. Latham used a flat, non-toothed or ribbed, steel-impregnated belt about 1½ inches wide on a very large aluminum crank pulley and a very small blower drive pulley. It was critical to get the blower and crank pulleys perfectly aligned to keep the belt on the blower. Plus these belts wore out and had to be changed frequently.

Lathams were made in several styles, with complete kits to fit most American cars of the late 1950s and early 1960s. The major difference in blowers was the length, which was determined by the number of rotor and stator rings that were stacked to make it (each being about an inch long). The largest Lathams were 11-stage, and these were most common. The small-block Chevy used a 10-stage, and smaller units were made for smaller engines, including the Corvair. They came with either two or four side-draft Carter YF carburetors. Some kits included a low-profile intake manifold to fit the blower under a stock hood; others bolted onto an existing 4-bbl intake.

Despite its substantial attributes, the technical and cost problems of the Latham doomed it. Using investment-casting technology and improved drive belts, someone tried to revive the Latham in the mid-1980s. Prototypes showed promise, but even then production cost—relative to other types of blowers on the market—made the project unfeasible.

However, if you can find a used Latham, chances are that it will be in good shape, and it would not be difficult to adapt to any engine.

With 3-lobe, straight-cut rotors, small Magna Chargers were initially made for blown fuel motorcycles. Here we see an 80-ci unit being fitted to a Harley-Davidson engine with a right-angle drive, and a similar-size case showing the wide intake port with a directional bar in the center to improve airflow.

With the Latham blower was an even rarer, and in this case partially unmachined, Latham intake manifold for an FE big-block Ford. How many of these do you suppose were ever made?

Magna Charger

Jerry Magnuson started building Roots-type blowers long before his involvement with Eaton superchargers. In fact, in his youth, he was one of the few owners of a Bandimere kit that mounted a 2-71 GMC on a Chevy 6-cylinder. He also raced a 4-71 GMC blown 1955 Chevy Gasser. But when he tooled up to produce Magna Chargers in the early 1970s, his intended market was primarily blown fuel drag racing motorcycles. Consequently, his first 3-lobe Roots blowers were relatively small.

Magnuson was one of the first to really work at improving the design and efficiency of the Roots-type blower. He made his rotors hollow, like GMC's, to keep the inertial weight low, but he made them straight instead of "twisted," and used straight-cut drive gears, to eliminate the problem of "untwist" and separation at high speed. He also added an internal rib to each rotor to eliminate centrifugal growth at high RPM. Thus his small blowers could run (and maintain) much tighter clearances for high volumetric efficiency, and could be spun much faster to create high boost. This design also reduced heat-causing air turbulence in the blower. And the straight 3-lobe rotors also allowed him to increase the size of the blower inlet and outlet to increase VE. According to the tests at Garret AIResearch, the little Magna Chargers attained an overall efficiency of about 65 percent, and they were the standard on Top Fuel bikes all over the world in the motorcycle-crazy 1970s.

For automotive applications, Magnuson made a kit for Buick V-6s that mounted a 110-ci blower on a 4-barrel intake with an adapter. Then he came up with the impressive looking—and performing—MC-220 for small-block Chevys that actually Siamesed two 110 blowers in a single case. This blower is slightly smaller in displacement than a GMC 4-71, though more efficient. Mounted to a 4-barrel intake modified with a welded-on flange, and fitted with a pair of

VINTAGE SUPERCHARGERS

For the automotive market, Magnuson made this 110-inch blower with manifolds and drive kits to fit small-block Chevys, as shown, and Buick V-6s as seen in Chapter 1.

B&M made blowers of many sizes and shapes—tens of thousands of them—to fit a wide variety of applications.

Mikuni, Dellorto, or Weber side-draft carbs, this unit also maintained a very low profile. It could be installed under the hood of most 1980s cars, including Corvettes. Quite a few of the MC-220 blowers were sold and installed on a variety of specialty vehicles including street rods, Corvettes, and Cobra kit cars.

When Magnuson began working with Eaton superchargers in the 1990s, he sold the rights and patterns to the Magna Chargers to B&M, but they were never put into production. Changing hands a couple more times, some small units for racing motorcycles were made, but neither the blowers nor spare parts were available as this was written.

However, finding one of these blowers in the "used parts" market, especially the unusual and impressive MC-220, should not be too hard, and could be a good investment.

B&M Automotive

When I wrote the first edition of this book back in 1984, the small, low-cost B&M 2-lobe Roots-type blower had just appeared on the market. With its cut-to-fit, hollow, Teflon-tipped extruded aluminum rotors and low-profile (for hood clearance) design, I didn't really think it would work all that well. Besides, B&M was an automatic racing transmission company; what did they know about superchargers? So I gave it a brief, tentative mention.

By the time of the second edition of this book, in 1999, B&M not only proved me wrong, but also proved the significant effectiveness of its simple and low-cost blower design and construction. To start, in a head-to-head "Blower Bash" I conducted at *Hot Rod* magazine (August 1983) for the new, smaller blowers then appearing on the market, limited to 6 psi and run on 92-octane pump gas, the then-untested 144-inch new B&M did very well; in fact, better than B&M expected. And in "Blower Bash II" (April 1984), using an only slightly larger (162-ci) High Energy version, it held its own at a 12-psi boost level against several much larger 6-71-sized blowers.

With immediate sales success of its initial small blowers, B&M soon produced larger sizes, including a 250-ci Powercharger using longer rotors and case, and a 6-71-size 420 MegaBlower that proved its drag racing prowess on Boyce Asquith's

The most impressive Magna Charger was the MC 220, which actually housed two 110 blowers in a Siamesed case. Adapted to a 4-barrel intake manifold (so it could fit many engines), it was usually fitted with Mikuni or Dellorto side-draft carbs to give a low overall profile, which would even fit under the hood of a '32 Ford, with air conditioning, as shown. Capable of producing 500 hp on 350 Chevys, many of these blowers were made and shouldn't be hard to find in the field.

CHAPTER 4

How to Check a Used Blower

This could be a classic "good news and bad news" scenario. The good news is that most superchargers, if they are properly maintained and not abused, will never wear out like an engine will. There are no rings rubbing cylinder walls; there is no pounding of bearings; there is no combustion or detonation inside the blower (hopefully!); and it's never subject to red-hot combustion cylinder temperatures. Whether it has one or two rotors/impellers, they should never touch or rub anything in proper operation. Most blowers have bearings of some sort at the front and back of each rotor/impeller shaft, but the only bearing that sees much load is the one nearest the drive-belt pulley, and that's usually minimal for any street blower.

Even the big, old GMC 6-71 blowers were designed and built to serve high-mileage duty on road-hauling diesel big rigs. They were made to go hundreds of thousands of miles before rebuilding. Similarly, the new Eaton Roots-style superchargers, the first to be fitted to any factory production cars in large numbers, had to undergo grueling hours and miles of unfailing testing before any manufacturer would install them as OEM equipment, subject to full warranty. A supercharger is an air pump. It should last longer than your water pump, power steering pump, A/C compressor, or even the oil pump in your engine—and how often do they wear out?

There's more good news, which is even more relevant here. Our topic is street superchargers installed for enhanced performance. That means we're not talking about racing blowers built and used for super-high-RPM, high-stress, and potentially explosive applications. But more pertinently, the types of blowers we're discussing are primarily aftermarket accessories installed on specialty or hobby vehicles that—realistically—don't get driven all that much. These are weekend cars (or boats, or trucks, or whatever). They might get driven hard at times (that's why you put a blower on it, right?), but even that hard use can be measured in seconds, not hours.

So the typical street supercharger is a low-wear device in the first place, and the types of vehicles these blowers are installed on are typically low-mileage vehicles. So, other than GMC units scavenged straight off old trucks or earth-movers (this is not uncommon), most superchargers you find for sale in the used-parts market are not going to be worn out. As just one example, I have

To begin with, this Eaton blower adapted to a flathead V-8 intake was covered with loose dirt at a dusty swap meet— never a good thing with any supercharger. Second, the person who cobbled it together was obviously no machinist. It might work fine, but it's crude. As for the blower itself, it probably came off a used car. You don't know what's inside unless you take it apart and look. Unless the price matches its dirty condition, pass.

seen literally hundreds of S.Co.T. blowers installed on street rods and vintage race cars over the years. These blowers haven't been produced since the early 1950s, and spare parts have never been available. Yet I have never—not once—seen or heard of one of these units being worn out or even damaged. Further, I have seen countless specialty vehicles that have been running the same supercharger, of whatever type, for two or three decades. That dates me, but it makes a point.

A quick visual and manual inspection should confirm if the blower is sound. The first thing to do is turn the drive pulley or shaft by hand. It should turn freely, with no discernable drag. There definitely should be no "rough spots," ratcheting, sticking, or odd noises when you turn it.

Second, move the shaft up and down and in and out. There should be virtually no play either way (which would be a rare sign of worn bearings).

Third, any dual-rotor or centrifugal blower will have a pair of gears inside that should have minimal clearance between them. When you turn the drive pulley/shaft back and forth, you should feel no "slop" or rattle between these gears. A couple of clarifications on this last point: On any centrifugal supercharger, these are "step-up" gears, meaning one large gear driving one smaller gear

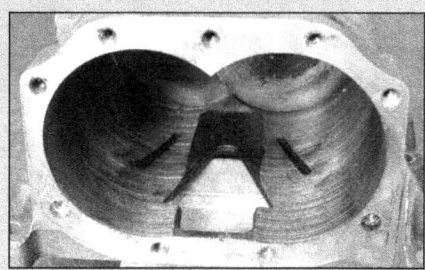

Here's what you might find inside a used Eaton from a production car. Both units came into Magnuson's rebuild shop; the one on the left cleaned up fine, while the one on the right is heavily scored (as you can see in the close-up), probably from dirt going through it. This case is junk, and will be scrapped.

attached to the rotor, to greatly increase its speed. Since the impeller turns at much higher RPM than the drive shaft, this places inertial loads on these gears, especially if the vehicle is accelerating rapidly from a dead stop, or worse, if the driver has a twitchy foot and keeps "winging" the throttle. This is a no-no with a centrifugal blower, and can lead to damaged or even broken gear teeth. You can't see these gears without taking the blower apart, but you should be able to feel if the teeth have been damaged. On the other hand, if you're checking a really old centrifugal, such as a Frenzel, Graham, or original McCulloch, understand that tolerances weren't so tight back then; a little clearance is expected.

As for dual-rotor blowers, at least one, the Eaton, has a sort of "fail-safe" coupler made of synthetic material between the driveshaft and the driven gear/rotor. Especially on factory-installed Eatons that have seen some miles, this pin-driven coupler has been known to wear out, which would cause slop that you could feel, though it should be discernible from loose or broken gear teeth.

Finally, in most superchargers—though not all—these gears (and front bearings) are lubricated either in an oil bath or with pressurized engine oil. If the blower has been allowed to run dry, or the oil to become contaminated, this is one of the few ways to wear one out. Check not only to see if such damage has occurred, but remember to provide proper lubrication once you install this unit on your engine.

Visually inspecting a centrifugal supercharger at point-of-purchase is difficult. But you should be able to see at least some of the rotors and inner case walls on any Roots or screw-type. The rule of thumb is that if you can see any signs of wear, scoring, or even physical contact on the rotors or case, pass. Such visible damage could have been caused by worn bearings or gears, dirt, or mistreatment such as backfires or over-revving.

The two tangs on the lower right of this 4-71 GMC blower case tell you it came straight off a diesel. But that doesn't matter, because this is nothing more than a weathered core case and a pair of rotors. If they're good, are they worth the $200 asking price? Ask your local blower builder what usable cores are going for.

Is this scrap aluminum? The stock diesel 4-71 at upper left looks clean and buildable; the 3-71 next to it is really corroded. The 6-71 rotors on top look good (unscored), but are they large or small diameter? They might or might not fit the cases below them. At best, these are simply stock cores and should be priced accordingly.

This brings us to the bad news. About the only thing easily or inexpensively replaced in any supercharger are the bearings, which can be sourced from any bearing

How to Check a Used Blower CONTINUED

This 14-71 was apparently built by The Blower Shop and, given the carbs, fuel lines, linkage, etc., might be a good deal for the $2,500 asking price—if it's not hurt. You could turn it over to inspect the rotors from the bottom (it seems not to fit the manifold it's on, for some reason). Are they Teflon stripped? Can you turn it by hand? Being a 14-71, was it built for racing? Or maybe for a boat? It's probably bigger than what you want for street, anyway.

The price on this obviously used Autorotor Whipple screw compressor is $750. You can turn it by hand but, again, you can't see inside. Plus there's no manifold and the rear cover/inlet looks odd. What did it fit? How can you make it fit your application? Why did someone take it off what it was on?

If the price were right, this early Paxton might be a find. But be careful; their Achilles heel is the drive balls, which are prone to pitting or wearing. Turn it by hand to feel for any unevenness or ratcheting. But you can't see what's inside. Fortunately, a source for parts and rebuilding these blowers now exists.

house by inside diameter (I.D.), outside diameter (O.D.), and length. But if the bearings are worn out, they usually cause the rotors or impeller to rub or the gears to wear. Remember, nothing is supposed to touch inside the blower, and tight clearances are imperative to efficient blower operation.

There are three problems with this used Vortech: At $1,000 the price is high. Other than the air cleaner, there's no mounting or drive hardware to install it. And the "New Bearings" note makes you ask, "Why did it need them?" and "What got hurt when they went out?" For the money, you'd be better off buying a new blower from Vortech with the proper trim, inlet/outlet, rotation, and all the mounting and hook-up accessories needed to match it to your engine and vehicle.

In previous editions of this book, we showed how to check all the clearances in a GMC blower with feeler gauges, and how to rebuild and set up such a blower, which is a complicated operation often requiring machining. The bottom line today is that a damaged case, rotors, or gears have to be replaced, and they are quite expensive. This also goes for the impeller in a centrifugal blower, which could have bent or broken fins that you wouldn't discover until you take it apart (which would likely also damage the scroll housing). The cost of such replacement parts, coupled with the tools and expertise needed to assemble them to critical tolerances, makes rebuilding a worn or damaged blower at home impractical.

Further, having such a used blower professionally rebuilt by one of the few shops capable of doing it, is usually about as expensive as buying a new unit.

So buying a used supercharger is pretty much a win/lose situation. If you can inspect the unit and it looks, feels, and sounds OK, chances are that it is perfectly good. Conversely, if you can see, feel, or hear anything wrong with it, it's very probably not worth buying at any price. This, of course, assumes you can see, feel, and hear the used supercharger. Buying one advertised on the Internet or other mail-order source is iffy at best. Probably the first question to ask yourself is, "Why is this supercharger for sale?" If it's vintage or rare, that's one thing. But people don't usually take a blower off, or replace it, unless there's something wrong with it. Yes, new superchargers are relatively expensive. But used blowers come with no warranty, and rebuilding one can be just as expensive, or even prohibitive. Buyer, beware.

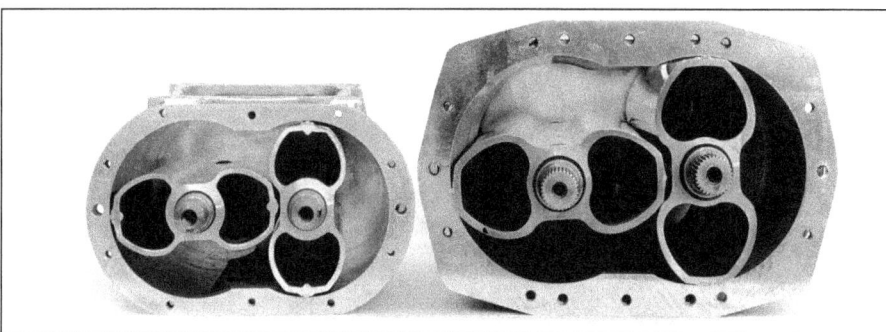

The majority of B&M blowers were made with the same-diameter, 2-lobe, Teflon-tipped, extruded aluminum rotors, as seen on the left, which could be cut to different lengths for longer or shorter cases, most ranging from 144 to 250 cu. in. The big 420-inch MegaBlower, on the right, had obviously larger rotors and case, and pumped at least as much air as a 6-71 GMC.

Running a Gilmer belt drive and a pair of Holleys, this polished B&M MegaBlower has not only the look, but also the performance, of a 6-71 GMC. Several have been used successfully in racing applications.

9-second/156-mph street-driven '32 Ford, among others. By 1998 B&M had sold well over 22,000 blowers, each bench-tested in-house before delivery and none reporting failures on the street or track. Consequently, I admitted my mistake and gave B&M ample coverage in this book's second edition. But, wouldn't you know, within months of its publication, the entire B&M supercharger division (and Weiand's) was acquired by Holley Performance Products, which has decided (as of this writing) to produce four sizes of Weiand superchargers, but none of the B&M line. Consequently, all of the B&M blowers have been relegated to this chapter—though things could change.

The initial B&M 144 was obviously patterned after the GMC 4-53, even to its displacement. The primary differences are the lightweight cast-aluminum case (with integral 4-bbl carb mount), end plates (with an oil bath in front and sealed needle bearings in back) and snout, and the very lightweight rotors cut from long, aluminum extrusions and then machined. The rotors are supported on full-length steel shafts and are of "involute" tip design (rather than "cycloidal," or round-end as in 71-series GMCs), which is in keeping with

Although the big air cleaner hides a lot, this is a typical 144 B&M installation on a small-block Chevy. It's overdriven 90 percent by a Poly-V belt with a spring-loaded tensioner, and produced 450 hp at 7 pounds of boost (130-hp gain) on a 350 Chevy in one test. These blowers work surprisingly well for their size.

53-series design. The single Teflon strip in each rotor tip does not "wipe" the blower case, as in a competition drag blower, but is designed to maintain a .003- to .004-inch clearance so it won't wear out. If, due to over-revving, the rotors should stretch enough to rub the case walls, the Teflon provides a margin of error to prevent scuffing.

The original B&M 144 was designed by the late, soft-spoken George Wallace, to be driven at relatively high overdrive ratios (1.78:1 to 2:1) to produce about 7 pounds of boost on 350- to 400-inch small-blocks. The reason behind the small-blower/high-RPM design (besides cost and hood clearance) was based on calculations derived by Mercedes-Benz in the 1930s, showing that Roots blower volumetric efficiency increases with blower speed, since leakage around the rotors is a function of time (the faster the blower spins, the less time the air has to leak past rotor clearances). Another factor is that air leakage is also a function of the size of the rotors and case (that is, the total area of the leakage path).

There's little question that the small B&M blowers work, and work well. And so do the larger versions. Given the fact that literally tens of thousands of these blowers were sold, most being installed on specialty or hobby-type vehicles that see little actual highway mileage, finding a used B&M blower in good condition at a reasonable price should be fairly easy. They might not be prized as rare or unusual antiques, but as long as one hasn't been abused or worn out, which should be readily apparent from a quick inspection, it could be a good buy in the pre-owned blower market.

CHAPTER 5

THE NEW CENTRIFUGALS

That kind of sounds like the name of an edgy rock band, doesn't it? Well, it's been pretty much the biggest news in power adders for street and drag race cars in the past decade or so. Having started with big GMC blowers in the 1950s and 1960s, we discovered the hidden wonders of nitrous oxide in the 1980s. Then it was big, complicated, and finicky turbochargers that made mind-blowing boost. Now, finally, the type of research and development that has been spent on exhaust-driven turbos has finally been directed to similar, but belt-driven centrifugal superchargers. Given today's refinements, and the fact that centrifugal blowers are not positive-displacement pumps and can increase boost exponentially with driven speed, the bald truth is that if you put a big enough centrifugal blower on your engine, and spin it fast enough, you can feed any size motor all the air—and horsepower—it can physically handle.

That said, we must take a step back and remember that we are addressing street supercharging here. We're looking for a manageable and efficient 6 to 8 pounds of ready boost

Centrifugal blowers were not only used on several low-production, high-end automobiles in the United States before World War II, but they also dominated Indy-type racing, usually on Miller or Duesenberg engines. This one on a 1927 Cooper Indy engine is typical. It uses a straight-blade rotor and a slightly snail-shaped housing, with the inlet in the center and the outlet at the bottom right.

on a moderate street engine. In this regard, centrifugal blowers (like turbos) of the past suffered from proverbial "lag" and less low-end power than positive pumps. But with modern impeller/housing designs, control valving, and intercoolers, today's centrifugal superchargers produce horsepower and torque curves nearly identical to those of the new Roots and screw superchargers in actual street-driving ranges. Some of the real-world differences between these modern street blowers involve packaging, intercooling, and interfacing with factory EFI versus carburetion. But—more than on other types of belt-driven blowers—if you want to turn the wick up on a centrifugal blower with higher-RPM pulleys (or a bigger unit), the sky can be the limit.

Given that fresh preamble, let's go back and look at a basic description of what a centrifugal supercharger is, and how it works, contrasted to positive-displacement blowers—specifically GMC types—as stated in previous editions of this book.

The only similarity between a Roots-type blower and a centrifugal supercharger is the end result they produce, and even in this respect they are significantly different. In the first place, a Roots is literally a pump, whereas the centrifugal is more like a fan, or a literal blower. The Roots traps and moves a given volume of air through it with each revolution of the rotors (not counting for leakage); consequently it is known as a positive-displacement pump. Its pumping output (again, not counting inefficiency) is directly proportional to the speed at which it is being turned.

A centrifugal blower, however, is an inertial compressor. Its one primary moving part is a fixed-blade fan called an impeller, which actually looks like a disc with fan blades protruding on one side. Whereas the Roots blower is similar to a typical engine oil pump, a centrifugal blower is similar to a typical engine water pump.

The impeller is enclosed in a housing shaped more or less like a snail's shell, with an inlet hole above the center of the impeller, and an outlet at the end of the chamber of the "shell." Air enters the blower axially (along the rotating axis of the impeller), being sucked in by the low pressure created by the "fan," which is blowing air out of the housing. As soon as the air enters the blades of the impeller, however, it is rapidly accelerated radially, toward the outer tips of the fan blades, by centrifugal force. Here is how one source describes the action of a centrifugal blower: "The air-moving element is a form of bucket wheel, which hurls air outward from a central inlet against a collector housing called a volute. As the heavy air is hurled outward from the center of the impeller, the partial vacuum thus created at the center pulls more air into the inlet. It's a centrifugal pump."

To get a better idea of the principal on which a centrifugal blower works, think of a merry-go-round of the type found in schoolyards or city parks. One or more children push the merry-go-round, while the others hang on and spin around on it. If you are sitting near the center of the merry-go-round, you won't be spinning very fast. But the farther toward

This Miller blower being restored shows the relationship between the hand-machined straight-bladed impeller and the housing, which in this case has stationary curved fins in the diffuser area before the air is flung into the spiral outlet housing.

These modern Vortech centrifugal blowers clearly show the inlet in the center (with the curved blades of the rotor inside) and the increasing diameter of the scroll-shaped outlet passage.

This cutaway shows the relationship of the inlet, impeller (rotor), and outlet, or scroll housing. Note the narrow, flat opening between the impeller tips and the scroll opening; this is the diffuser area. The increasing diameter of the scroll is evident here. In this case, the impeller turns clockwise as viewed from the inlet (left side of picture).

the outside you move, the faster you go, even though the merry-go-round itself is still turning at the same speed (or RPM). Furthermore, as you may remember from your childhood, the spinning motion of the merry-go-round tends to force your body toward the outside edge (that is, radially) and, if you don't hang on tightly enough as it picks up speed, it will hurl you off the edge with considerable velocity. The children's game of crack the whip operates on the same principle.

The tendency of a rotating body to want to fling objects on it, or contained by it, toward the edges is called centrifugal force. It is a demonstration of the laws of inertia and momentum, which are used in the case of the centrifugal blower as an "energy multiplier."

For instance, let's say you and a friend are playing on a merry-go-round. You are pushing, and your friend is riding. If your friend is sitting on the outside edge, it will be hard for you to get the merry-go-round going (a body at rest tends to remain at rest), because you will have to accelerate his weight at the speed of the outer perimeter of the merry-go-round. However, if he moves toward the middle, it will be much easier to get the thing going because you are pushing rapidly at the outside edge, but his weight is moving slowly in the center. This is the same principle as reduction gearing: using a low gear to get an automobile moving, for instance, and then shifting to higher gears once it's under way. So, since you are an intelligent kid, you have your friend sit in the middle while you get the merry-go-round going. Then, once you have it spinning rapidly, you tell him to move out toward the edge, where he'll have the thrill of spinning around at a higher speed, but you won't have to push any harder or faster to keep him going (a body in motion tends to remain in motion).

In these cutaways of early ball-drive Paxton blowers, the 1950s Variable Ratio unit on the left shows a small impeller with straight blades, the diffuser cavity, an increasing, squarish-shaped scroll, and an abrupt right-angle outlet on the left side. The housing with the springs contains the planetary ball step-up drive.

The reason a body tends to be flung off a rotating object is that momentum (the fact that the body wants to remain in motion) is linear. That is, the body wants to keep moving in a straight line. But the rotating object moves it in a curving line. If the body is firmly attached to the rotating object, its mass will tend to keep the object rotating, but part of its momentum (also called kinetic energy, or the energy "contained" in a moving body) will be lost.

To illustrate this principle, again think of yourself on the merry-go-round. If you are sitting on the outside edge and your friend is pushing at a good speed, the weight of your body will keep the merry-go-round spinning for quite a while after he stops pushing. This is the effect of momentum, or kinetic energy—work continues to be done although no apparent energy is being put into the system. But in this case it is only part of the energy available. If you are sitting on the outside perimeter of the merry-go-round, you're going to have to hang on with lots of your own energy to stay in place—an amount of energy equal, but oppo-

This disassembled modern Vortech shows the diffuser side of the scroll housing (at top), which, inverted, fits over the impeller in its bearing case (at right). It, in turn, fits on the drive case, which houses the step-up gears. The larger gear is driven by the belt pulley, while the smaller one spins the impeller, usually about four times faster (a 4:1 ratio). This model feeds pressurized engine oil into the gear case, and returns it to the oil pan, with external lines.

site, to the amount of kinetic energy, or centrifugal force, that would propel your body in a straight line (tangentially) off the merry-go-round as soon as you let go.

Perhaps we are overdoing the explanation of how a centrifugal blower works—this is just basic, junior-high physics—but it does illustrate why a centrifugal blower is much more efficient than a Roots or other type of positive-displacement pump, which simply pushes the air with direct force. By using the "energy multiplying" effect of centrifugal force (the momentum of the mass of the air molecules) to help move and compress the air, the mechanical efficiency of a centrifugal blower is, consequently, much higher than other types, meaning that it requires less horsepower from the engine to make substantial boost.

The spinning blades of the impeller in a centrifugal blower rapidly accelerate the air molecules, greatly increasing their velocity, which gives them a considerable amount of kinetic energy. How this velocity is transformed into pressure is a bit more difficult to understand. If you look at a cross-section of an impeller and its housing, you will notice that most types decrease in cross-sectional area from the center to the tip of the blades. That is, the cavity enclosed by a pair of blades and the housing is wedge-shaped, tapering toward the outer edge. Therefore, it would appear that air would be compressed in this cavity as it is "squeezed" outward into the smaller area near the impeller tip. But such is not the case, for two reasons.

First, although the cross-section (or height) of the blade decreases toward the tip, the distance between two adjacent blades increases from the center to the edge, thus increasing the enclosed volume. The combined effect might be a constant-area cross-section, but in fact many centrifugal housing designs (as used in turbochargers) actually have parallel walls.

Second, and much more significant, as the air is accelerated along the impeller blade, two things happen. It tends to "stack up" against the

A cutaway of a ProCharger D-1SC clearly shows the 4.1:1 step-up gears and bearing shafts, as well as the scroll housing and impeller (from the backside). Since this unit self-contains oil in the gear case, the thinner cogged wheel aerates and pumps oil onto the gears. From this angle, the drive pulley turns clockwise (same as the engine crankshaft), while the impeller turns the opposite direction due to the gear drive. The scroll outlet is beyond the larger section of the cutaway.

face of the blade, which would compress the air. But at the same time, as the blade accelerates the air molecules radially, they will "stretch out" as their velocity is increased. This latter condition is similar to the effect of a carburetor venturi which, as you know, decreases the density and the pressure of the air by increasing its volume (as the air molecules are stretched farther apart).

All of this may be a little confusing, but don't worry too much about exactly what is going on inside the centrifugal blower housing. The one point we want to make is that it is difficult to compute a volumetric efficiency figure for a centrifugal blower, since it is not a positive-displacement pump. We do not speak of the internal "displacement" of a centrifugal blower, as we do of a Roots, vane, or screw-type blower. In fact, the shape

Early Paxtons used the simple, cast, straight-fin impeller on the right. This type is still adequate for most street centrifugal blowers making 5 to 8 pounds of boost. The modern curved-fin impeller on the left can obviously draw more air into the blower inlet, but must be investment-cast or machined from billet.

of the impeller blades and the housing can have nearly as much effect on the output of a centrifugal blower as does its physical size.

The adiabatic efficiency of the centrifugal supercharger is very significant, however. Remember, the energy imparted to the air by the blower (ultimately by the engine) is minimal in a centrifugal unit because of its good mechanical efficiency. That is, there is comparatively little work done on the air—since we are using the weight of the air molecules to provide much of the energy—and therefore the centrifugal supercharger does not heat the air nearly as much as an old-style Roots blower. The centrifugal blower does not "beat" the air, and the flow of air through the blower is much smoother than in a Roots (especially older-style ones).

Second, the compression process itself is much more efficient in the centrifugal supercharger. After the air molecules are accelerated along the impeller blades, they are flung off the ends at a velocity approximately equal to that of the tips of the blades. As this high-velocity air is hurled into the scroll housing, it literally piles up against the air already packed into the housing and the

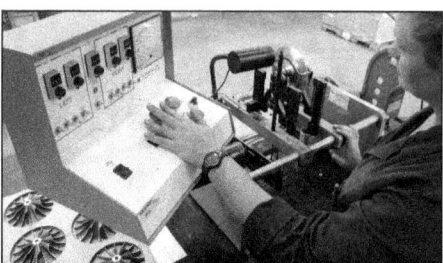

You may have noticed small scallops at the outer edge, or holes near the inner shaft, of the impellers in the prior photo. At the Vortech/Paxton factory, each impeller is spun on this computerized dynamic balancer, and drilled/machined accordingly, much like a crankshaft. Don't forget, with step-up internal gearing plus pulley ratio, the impeller could be turning 10 times crank speed, or more. The larger the impeller, the more critical balancing is.

manifold, which means that the air actually compresses itself by its own momentum. The kinetic energy imparted to the air molecules by the impeller in the form of velocity is immediately and efficiently converted into static energy in the form of pressure. Some heat is certainly generated by this process, since the volume of air is reduced as it "stacks up" (thus increasing the density of the air at the same time that it increases the pressure, which is what we want the supercharger to do), but the heat gain in a good centrifugal blower can be low enough to attain 80-percent, or more, adiabatic efficiency.

A further advantage of the centrifugal supercharger over other types is the mechanical simplicity of the impeller and housing, in which there is only one basic moving part. There is very little stress on the impeller, it is very lightweight, and it does not mesh with, or come in contact with, any other parts. Also, there is no pulsing of the output airflow, nor are there any eccentric moving parts to cause vibration or wear, as in a vane-type, Wankel, or piston pump. And finally, a centrifugal blower can produce significantly strong boost pressures from a relatively small and lightweight unit, which can be mounted in a variety of convenient locations on the engine.

Is this beginning to sound too good to be true? As you might expect, there are a couple of flies in the ointment—otherwise every car would run a centrifugal blower and that would be that.

The major problem is that not only is the centrifugal blower not a positive-displacement pump, but that the kinetic energy imparted to the air molecules by the spinning impeller increases roughly as the square of the tip speed of the blades. This might sound like another asset at first—if you get 10 pounds of boost at a given blower RPM, doubling the blower speed will give you four times as much boost, and tripling blower RPM will give you nine times more boost.

In the first place, your engine can't use that much boost. But think of it in reverse. For a street engine, let's say you want a maximum boost of 10 psi at 6,000 engine rpm, and you select drive pulleys to give that amount. No problem. But at 3,000 engine rpm the blower speed will be cut in half (since the blower is driven in direct proportion to the crank regardless of the overdrive ratio), and the boost level will be reduced by four times, to only 2½ psi. If the centrifugal blower makes 7 pounds of boost at 6,000 rpm, which is typical for a street setup, it will only make 1¾ psi at 3,000 rpm.

Thus the centrifugal blower, by its design, is very "peaky," or speed-sensitive. It will give good, efficient boost at higher RPM, but very little boost or torque at lower engine speeds. As a result, the centrifugal blower is excellent for top-end speed contests, such as Bonneville, or sustained high-RPM racing such as on a long oval track (i.e., Indianapolis). But a centrifugal does not work as well as a positive-displacement type for road racing, for drag racing, or for any type of driving that covers a wide engine-RPM range—and street driving falls into that category.

On the other hand, we are comparing centrifugal blowers to Roots blowers (primarily) here, and this "low-end response" argument against centrifugals usually refers to racing situations. On the street, you don't want gobs of horsepower until you put your foot in the throttle. The centrifugal blower might not pin you to the seat immediately like a Roots will, but it'll come on like gangbusters at the top end. More important, it will be far less of a parasite on your engine when you are not in need of extra power. It is lighter and more compact to carry around under your hood (a big consideration for street driving) and it will be much more efficient when it is making boost. Obviously, these comparisons

A wide variety of sizes and shapes (or "trims") of impellers can be made by dialing them in on the computer.

Early Paxton/McCullochs came in one size, and their ball-drive mechanism was RPM-limited. To get more boost, you could add an extra blower, such as this Shelby-inspired setup recently installed by Paradise Wheel.

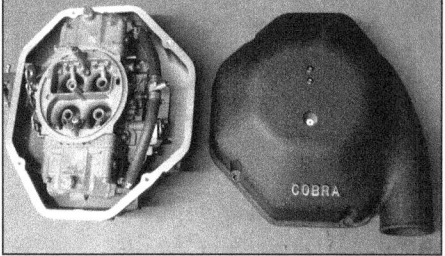

Centrifugal blowers are good at pumping dry air, but not heavy fuel. So, before EFI, the compressed air had to be pumped through the carburetor(s). Paxton's preferred method, then and now, was to house it in an equalizing "pressure box," as shown.

Making molds to investment cast several sizes of impellers would be prohibitive. CNC machining isn't cheap, but it's much more versatile. Therefore ProCharger machines all of its impellers from 6061-T6 billet aluminum blanks, as shown.

are made primarily to large GMC-type Roots blowers.

Another drawback to the way the centrifugal blower makes boost is that the impeller must be driven at extremely high rotational speeds to get effective boost. Impeller speeds in the neighborhood of 50,000 rpm are not uncommon. Consequently, centrifugal blowers, like turbos, require very high-quality shaft bearings and a good oiling system to maintain bearing life at these high shaft speeds. However, the fact that the impeller shaft is not subjected to extreme heat levels, as it is in an exhaust-driven turbo, simplifies the situation.

To attain the high impeller speed obviously requires some sort of wide-ratio step-up gearing between the crankshaft and the impeller shaft, beyond that feasible with belt pulleys. Using simple spur gears inside the blower housing to overdrive the impeller shaft has been the typical procedure in the past (with the notable exception of the ball-drive Paxton), and this works fine over a moderate RPM range. However, if the engine is rapidly revved up or down in RPM, the blower's impeller and shaft would undergo severe rates of acceleration and deceleration. Early centrifugal blowers, which used relatively large and heavy impellers, would strip the teeth off the drive gears under such conditions. Today's automotive centrifugal blowers use small, lightweight impellers, as well as sophisticated drive mechanisms and shaft oiling to eliminate this problem.

However, a given-size centrifugal blower has a maximum RPM limit. The user of a centrifugal supercharger should be careful not to over-rev the engine for two reasons. First, given step-up gearing, the blower RPM can increase to the point that would harm bearings or potentially bend or break fins on the impeller.

Second, winding the engine an extra 1,000 rpm can shoot blower boost to a dangerous level. While most centrifugal blowers in the past lacked any sort of "pop-off" valve or wastegate (as used on turbos for years) to guard against over-boosting, most of today's manufacturers, fortunately, have bypass or blow-off valves and systems to regulate this.

Centrifugal Superchargers vs. Turbochargers

Turbochargers are simply another form of centrifugal supercharger. The compressor section of a turbo is exactly the same. The difference is that the turbo uses another impeller and scroll housing, through which hot exhaust is piped, to drive the unit. Thus the turbo takes no crankshaft horsepower from the engine to run. Instead, it recovers some of the heat energy normally wasted through the exhaust to do the work of compressing the intake charge. Combustion heats the exhaust, causing it to expand, so it is already pressurized. The drive (turbine) side of the turbo works in reverse of the compressor side; it "absorbs" the pressure of the exhaust gas to spin an impeller. The exhaust enters the impeller radially at the blade tips and leaves axially from the center. The impeller driven by the exhaust is connected directly, by a common shaft, to the impeller that compresses the intake.

As mentioned earlier, the transfer of heat from the exhaust turbine to the intake impeller, along the common shaft, is a real problem in the turbo, not only because of the effect on bearing and oil life, but also because of the considerable amount of heat transferred to the intake charge by the heated impeller. A belt-driven centrifugal blower does not have this problem.

Also, although the belt-driven centrifugal blower is more "peaky" in boost delivery than a Roots, it is not as peaky as a turbo. In a crank-driven centrifugal blower, regardless of the percentage of overdrive, the impeller rotation speed is directly proportional to engine speed, even though the amount of boost produced by the blower isn't. In a turbo, however, this

One of the true advantages of centrifugal supercharging today is that, at street-boost levels, you can usually pump the increased airflow directly into the stock EFI system, and the computer will "read" it and adjust fuel flow accordingly. Plus you can mount the supercharger anywhere a belt will reach, and hook it up with a simple duct-tube, as these Vortech examples on a small-block Ford and Chevy demonstrate. At higher boost, an intercooler makes the system much more efficient, but also more complex. For street, this basic modern system is hard to beat.

"peakiness" is compounded, since the rotational speed of the blower impeller depends on the rotational speed produced by the exhaust passing through the turbine portion rather than on a direct link to the engine. So not only is the output of a turbo not proportional to engine speed (as is the case with any centrifugal blower), but neither is the turbine speed that drives it, thus doubling the problem. Consequently the "sizing" of the turbo to the engine, plus the matching of a turbine size and design to the impeller size, is both critical and complicated in any turbocharger installation. Further, any turbo will be greatly affected by camshaft profile, since the cam controls exactly how the exhaust will be released to drive the turbine.

So, while a belt-driven centrifugal blower might not produce as broad a boost curve as a positive-displacement blower, it will outperform most turbos in this respect. The centrifugal

Another big advance in centrifugal supercharger technology is that the blowers are available in a variety of sizes as well as impeller "trims" to match not only large or small engines, but also to feed them in a wide range of boost levels. Further, as these big and small Vortechs show, you can get them with right or left outlets, and in clockwise or reverse rotation (rear drive), to greatly increase mounting location possibilities.

While the centrifugal blower size and trim can be matched to your engine and its intended use range to begin with, like all belt-driven blowers (and unlike a turbo), you can step up the boost level for a little weekend racing by a simple pulley swap. While numerous possible combinations are shown here, usually bolting a slightly smaller pulley on the blower is all it takes. You only have to remove one bolt, and the belt tensioner should take up belt slack.

blower is certainly not as touchy about camshaft profile as a turbo, and it does not restrict exhaust flow in any way. Further, turbos require not only custom-made and convoluted headers and exhaust piping, but the headers or manifolds must both support the weight of the turbo unit(s) and survive extremely high temperatures caused by the turbo backpressure. The required turbo exhaust system and routing not only adds complexity and cost, but it also produces significant under-hood heat that can cause several problems if not dealt with properly.

On the positive side, both turbos and centrifugal blowers lend themselves relatively easily to the incorporation of an air-to-air intercooler in the system. And since the belt-driven centrifugal blower heats the air much less than a turbo to begin with, the intercooler can be that much more effective.

Finally, since the air inlet/outlet ducting in centrifugals and turbos is the same, and both work best in a "blow-through," or "dry air," configuration, they are readily adaptable to today's direct-port EFI systems. The blower can be mounted in a variety of locations in cramped, late-model engine compartments, and then plumbed directly into the mouth of the throttle body. In most moderate-boost applications, no further tuning changes are needed, since the MAF sensor will read the increased air charge and increase fuel flow accordingly. For higher-boost systems, there are reprogrammable computers, bigger aftermarket injectors, and higher-pressure fuel pumps to allow the engine to be retuned to work in harmony with the supercharger.

Vortech and Paxton Superchargers

For four decades the only viable centrifugal supercharger in the aftermarket or in OEM applications was the Paxton. Operated for many years,

Finally, for more serious applications, you can guard against overboosting by adding a pressure-relief valve, such as this, somewhere in the ducting between the blower and the engine intake system. Not only can it be set to "blow off" boost at a set maximum-psi level to guard the engine from damage, but one can also relieve, or bypass, pressure surge in the inlet tract when the throttle is suddenly closed during boost mode, which would create heat and noise and could ultimately damage (bend or break) impeller fins.

going back to the days of the legendary Novi Indy cars, by the Granatelli brothers, Joe and Vince (and sometimes Andy), this venerable company changed ownership in the late 1990s, and then was wisely acquired by Jim Middlebrook, the founder and CEO of the young and successful Vortech supercharger company, in 2001. With the decision to finally discontinue the complicated and expensive-to-produce ball-drive VN and SN models, this left Paxton and Vortech competing with very similar products in factories only a mile apart. Combining the two companies was not only practical, logistically, but created efficiencies that allowed lowered, competitive pricing, especially on Paxton systems. Both companies will retain (as of this writing) their own brand name, product line, and even separate addresses and phone numbers, even though they are now contained under one roof.

In 1995, Paxton introduced a completely new, greatly simplified, but significantly modernized centrifugal blower, called the Novi 2000, which introduced precision-cut helical step-up gears in the blower case for the first time in centrifugal blower history. Rather than an "oil bath" contained in the blower housing, like the older Paxtons, the Novi blower gears are fed a constant stream of pressurized oil from the engine, thus requiring an oil feed and return line as part of the system. Using improved impeller and scroll housing designs, the moderately sized Novi 2000 has a claimed capability of 26 pounds per square inch gauge (psig) of boost, creating up to 970 hp in modern V-8 engines. However, versatility is the strength of belt-driven supercharging, and Paxton touts this with the Novi 2000, stating that it is designed to deliver 8 to 10 pounds of boost for street-driving applications on relatively stock engines.

Greatly furthering the versatility theme, both Paxton and Vortech blowers are available in clockwise or reverse-rotation designs to place the inlet toward the front or the rear of the vehicle, and with straight or angled scroll-housing outlets. This means that these blowers can be mounted in a variety of locations on the engine, which is one of the pluses of the centrifugal blower design.

Speaking of centrifugal blower versatility and large boost/power numbers, however, we must stress here that this book is titled *Street Supercharging*. Just as turbos did a decade or two ago, big belt-driven centrifugal blowers have been getting plenty of press for making gobs of horsepower (1,000-plus) and powering so-called "street-legal" cars into the 7- or even 6-second range in quarter-mile drags. As we said earlier, put a big enough blower of any type (but particularly a centrifugal) on an engine and you can make as much horsepower as it will stand—and then some. Paxton, Vortech, and Procharger all make big superchargers that will blow more than the doors off any car. But we will not cover them here (access their websites for plenty of info). Our focus is on systems you can bolt on your car and truly drive regularly on the street, with plenty of power and performance whenever you mash the

After World War II, the only centrifugal supercharger sold in any great numbers was the ball-drive Paxton/McCulloch. Remaining basically the same in design and configuration, other than its unique Variable Ratio pulley, the early 1950s McCulloch on the left and the late-1990s Paxton SN 2000 on the right span a production run of nearly five decades. As of 2000, however, production had ceased.

This Novi 2000 Paxton is a reverse-rotation, rear-drive model that pumps through an air-to-air intercooler before being directed into the EFI unit on a Shelby Mustang Ford engine.

Although this configuration looks much like it did decades ago, with the blower ducted directly to a pressure box housing a single 4-barrel carb atop a Mopar V-8, the Novi Paxtons are a completely new design, with first-ever bevel-cut step-up gears in a pressure-fed oil-bath housing, and modern curved-blade impellers.

Although Paxton has merged with Vortech, the superchargers and installation systems remain separate. Vortech favors water-to-air intercoolers, as demonstrated by a V2 blower routed directly through a charge cooler and into the injection unit on this LS-1 Chevy V-8.

A profile of the LS installation shows the rear-belt drive for this application, plus the braided-steel oil-feed line from the engine's pump to the blower, and the larger, black return line to the pan.

throttle. Plus you can have even more on selected weekends with a simple pulley change or other more serious—but easily changeable—modifications.

In this vein, Paxton has introduced two new, slightly smaller models called the Novi 1500 and 1200. With a scroll housing 1-inch smaller in diameter and 1-inch thinner, they are designed for better under-hood fit in newer vehicles and street power in the 6- to 8-psig range, yet are claimed to be capable of 825 hp at 26 psig with an appropriate pulley swap. The latest innovation in Paxton blowers as of press time were "SL" models of the various sized units (i.e., Novi 1200SL), which stands for "Self Lubricated." These models, like the original Paxtons, have a self-contained oil reservoir (with a dipstick) to lubricate the bearings with 4 ounces of a unique synthetic lubricant, and therefore require no oil lines to the engine.

Given its heritage with Ford in general, and Mustangs and Shelby vehicles in particular, the Paxton line is definitely skewed toward current Mustangs, plus models going all the way back to its 1964 introduction,

A complete water-to-air charge cooling system includes a radiator that mounts at the front of the vehicle, a small electric pump and heater-size hose to circulate the water, and an air box that contains a smaller "radiator" (or heat exchanger) to cool the pressurized air flowing from the blower to the engine intake. This particular system is for drag racing, with a small, light radiator and a large reservoir tank that can be filled with ice.

with a modernized version of a pressure box for single 4-barrel carbureted systems. Standard systems for direct-port electronically fuel injected models include fuel management/calibration components including high-capacity injectors, a high-flow fuel pump, fuel management unit (FMU), high-flow MAF sensor, and either an ECM chip or module or an ECM re-programmer and timing controller, depending on the specific application. For shops or individuals who have both the equipment and experience to reprogram the electronic fuel management system themselves, or wish to modify the engine beyond the parameters of the standard Paxton components, "Tuner Kits" are available for most applications, which delete the above items and consequently cost less.

CHAPTER 5

In addition, most of the Paxton applications can also be ordered with the addition of a Charge Cooler (also known as an intercooler or aftercooler), which can be an air-to-water system or a simpler air-to-air unit, depending on the vehicle.

Further, these systems are designed to add significant power to basically stock vehicles, to fit under stock hoods, to run on 91-octane pump gas, and are 50-state smog-legal.

Besides a full range of Mustang applications, Paxton also offers different levels of blower kits for Ford, GM, and Dodge trucks, as well as Dodge Viper and Ram V-10s, and even a "classic" Mopar setup with a blow-through pressure box for single 4-barrel carbureted small-blocks.

Vortech, which was founded in 1990, has been growing and refining its line of centrifugal superchargers ever since, using a sophisticated blower dyno and flow benches for development. While all contemporary centrifugal superchargers are similar in basic design and outward appearance these days, the Vortech units are discreet from Paxtons.

For street applications, Vortech offers the same features and componentry listed above for Paxton kits. The major difference is that Vortech offers a much broader line of superchargers, both in sizes of blowers and in vehicle applications. Ignoring the large-to-huge V-4, V-7, and V-20 models designed for racing in the 1,200- to 1,900-hp (maximum) range, street units include the V-1, the newer V-2SQ with quieter helical step-up gears, the V-3 with an internal oil reservoir, and the physically smaller V-5 and V-9 for smaller-displacement engines and/or tight engine compartments.

Another aspect that we mentioned earlier that makes centrifugal blowers even more versatile is that, besides increasing blower speed by changing pulley ratios, or changing to a physically larger unit, the output of a given supercharger can be varied by changing the "trim" of the impeller. This basically means changing the size, shape, or number of blades on the impeller, but it can get quite sophisticated with "back-curves" to blades and such things.

Vortech takes full advantage of this variable, offering at least four different trims for each blower model. For instance, on the V-1 supercharger, the S-Trim is rated at a maximum of 680 hp at 20 psig, while the racing T-Trim is rated at 825 hp at 26 psig. This allows plenty of versatility to match a supercharger to your engine and driving needs. The pitfall, as with most speed parts, is to be too greedy. Installing a centrifugal blower that is too big in size or trim for your engine's needs will be as disappointing as installing a big rumpity cam that doesn't "come on" until 6,000 rpm. By the way, the numbers given above are for *maximum* power levels. The V-1 Vortech with S-Trim is the typical street blower, designed to give "Strong

This Vortech application on an LS7 Corvette uses a large, aluminum air-to-air intercooler mounted just ahead of the radiator. Also note the large, low-restriction air cleaner for the blower's intake, mounted in the fresh-air stream.

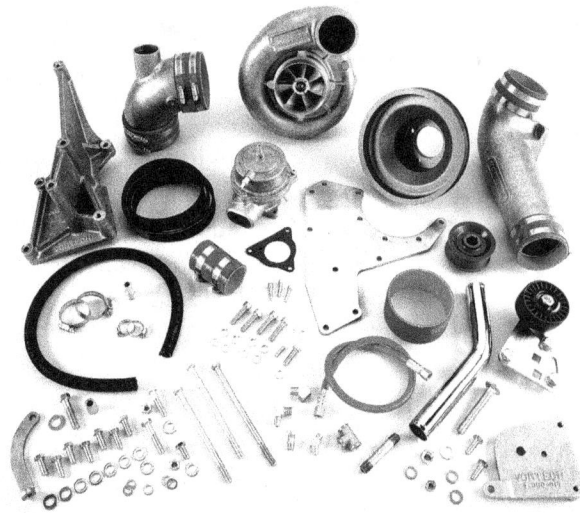

Intercoolers certainly aren't necessary at typical street-boost levels, so don't be daunted by complicated-looking systems. This is a typical non-intercooled Vortech installation kit, including the blower, mounting brackets, pulleys, and every hose, clamp, bolt, and washer needed to install it on the engine.

low-speed boost along with exceptional mid/high-end flow for street and strip," using pulleys that will give 6 to 8 pounds of boost. If you want more boost and high-end power at the strip on the weekend, change pulleys. That's the beauty of belt-driven blowers, of all types.

Several of the Vortech applications duct the supercharger directly to the inlet (throttle body) of the EFI unit on the vehicle, and a few kits for carbureted small-block Chevrolets duct the blower to a pressure box similar to Paxton's. For intercooled applications, however (which Vortech calls Charge Cooling), a water-to-air closed system is used in all cases.

This consists of a pressurized box mounted directly between the blower outlet and the intake inlet, with a water-fed heat exchanger inside. The water, which absorbs heat from the compressed air in the box, is connected by hoses and a small electric pump to a larger heat exchanger (radiator) that mounts behind the grille of the vehicle. Although such a system is more complicated, and heavier, than an air-to-air intercooler (which routes compressed air from the blower, to a heat exchanger at the front of the car, and then through ducting back to the engine's intake inlet), Vortech says it has found through extensive testing that it is more effective because it reduces pressure (and density) loss between the blower and the intake system.

Whereas it was not an issue with the more common Roots-type blowers, which mounted directly to the intake manifold, Paxton engineers and users found long ago that

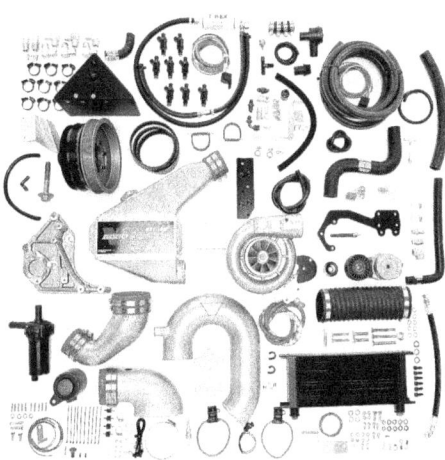

It takes a bit more, however, to squeeze a blower, charge cooling system, and free-flowing intake air ducting under the hood of this LS-1 F-body Pontiac. Not only does everything fit neatly, however, but all the ducting remains free-flowing and the blower intake hooks to the car's fresh-air cleaner.

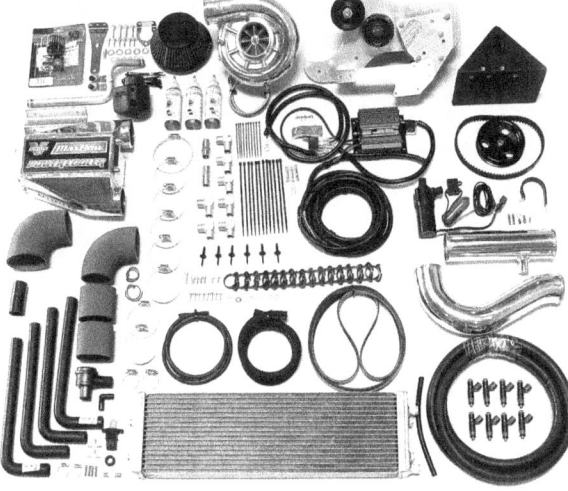

There are a lot of pieces included in Vortech's charge-cooled kit for the 6.1L Mopar Hemi, but the installation is pretty straightforward, from the blower, through the cooler, to the stock EFI system inlet. In the kit photo, note the large, water-cooling heat exchanger that mounts behind the car's grille, and the higher-flow injector nozzles and computer programmer that are included.

This installation on a 4.6L 3-valve Mustang is equally tight but tidy. Again, it uses a rear-drive blower to make things fit, and the inlet to the blower is fed through low-restriction, wide-bend ducting with a high-flow air cleaner located near a fresh-air stream. Vortech systems are available polished, as shown, or as-cast.

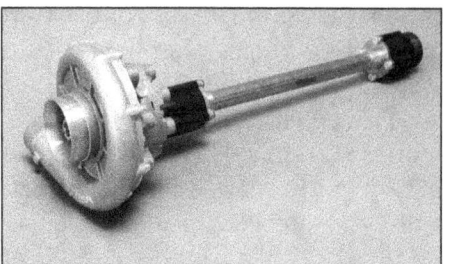

If front or rear drive, plus right or left outlet, doesn't get the blower mounted conveniently, you can always extend the driveshaft. This smaller Vortech V-2SQ is used primarily on front-drive, cross-mount Honda and Nissan 4-cylinders.

flowing air doesn't like to turn corners or go through constricted passages. With the less efficient early Paxtons, they found that one right-angle bend in the tubing between the blower and the carb box could cost 1 pound of boost loss (from a total of 5 or 6 pounds), and that a similar restriction on the inlet side of the blower could be worse. With more efficient and higher-boost blowers the problem might not be as acute, but this is something important to consider when locating a centrifugal blower in the vehicle and routing necessary ducting from it to the engine's intake, and to the blower's intake. Keep the airflow path as short, as straight, and as unrestricted as possible in both cases.

Finally, we have the little-discussed and probably less-understood subject of "surge" in a centrifugal supercharger. Without getting into (another) lengthy technical discussion, surge is basically the condition when a centrifugal blower (or turbo) reaches a point at which it is pumping more air than the engine can ingest, and the airflow backs up into the blower, kind of like a clogged drain in your bathroom. This problem is specific to centrifugal blowers because their boost rate multiplies at a much faster rate than blower (and engine) RPM speed does. In high-boost situations, this surge of "back-up" air into the blower can cause temperature increases (at the least) and possible damage to the impeller, such as bending or breaking fins (at worst). Obviously, this sort of surge can be avoided by sizing the blower properly to the engine, and its operating RPM range, so that it doesn't reach the surge limit.

But there's another problem with belt-driven centrifugal blowers in this regard. It's the throttle in your intake system. If you're running the engine at wide-open throttle (WOT), whether on a drag strip, on a road course, or on the street, you're obviously creating boost with the blower. But at the end of your run (when boost is highest), or when braking for a turn, or you've run out of room for wide-open throttle acceleration, what do you do? You take your foot off the gas pedal, which slams the throttle blade(s) shut. This means that whatever boost your blower was making, be it 6 pounds or 20 pounds, is suddenly stopped by a closed valve and has nowhere to go but back into the blower. As we said, this causes heat, it can cause damage in severe cases, and it can cause a "reversion" effect that makes a lot of ugly and annoying noise.

To control this type of surge in a pretty practical manner, Vortech came up with a variety of types of bypass/blow-off valves. Since the sudden closing of the throttle not only shuts off blower inlet boost on one side, but at the same time creates immediate vacuum in the intake tract on the other, Vortech sells a Standard Bypass Valve that can be plumbed in a 1-inch line "around" the throttle (from the blower outlet tube to the intake manifold), which incorporates a vacuum-actuated valve that opens as soon as it reads vacuum. Simple. Vortech recommends it for street-blower applications in the 6- to 12-psi range to eliminate surge and reduce heat soak in the blower discharge tube. And since the blower is pumping dry air, the excess boost could be vented to the atmosphere.

However, if your intake system includes an MAF sensor, the bypassed air must flow through it for the electronic fuel system to meter properly. If

These are polished examples of Vortech's Maxflow bypass and blow-off valves used on serious systems to limit maximum boost and relieve surge pressure, as explained in the text. Street systems can use a much smaller, simpler valve.

THE NEW CENTRIFUGALS

Again, part of the beauty of centrifugal supercharging for street, especially with factory EFI, is that you can route the blower's dry-air boost directly into the existing fuel injection throttle body (from the intercooler), as seen on this F-body Camaro TPI installation.

On a 2007 Cadillac Escalade, the blower is driven by the same serpentine belt that runs other engine accessories. Vortec on the engine cover refers to the 6.2L GM engine, not to be confused with competitor Vortech superchargers.

there is enough distance between the throttle blade(s) and the MAF sensor (as in certain Ford Mustangs) the bypass tube can be inserted there. Otherwise, the bypassed air should be routed back to the inlet side of the blower (into the tube between the air cleaner and the blower inlet). This will cause some heated air to be introduced into the blower, but it is not significant because the bypass operates only at closed or very low throttle.

For higher boost situations—primarily for racing—Vortech has more complicated, but even more effective bypass/blow-off valves. These similarly install in the outlet (pressure) tube between the blower and the engine intake, and they include a "rolling diaphragm" valve set to open immediately upon reading manifold vacuum. However, they also include a pressure-relief valve that can be adjusted to "blow off" excessive boost at a set level during WOT, as well. This might sound like the adjustable wastegate used to regulate boost on turbocharged systems, but it's not. The wastegate is plumbed into the exhaust manifold feeding the turbine side of the turbo, and is set to bleed of exhaust pressure at a certain limit, thus controlling the drive speed of the compressor. Therefore, it acts as a governor to limit boost to a set maximum (and maintain that boost for continuous power at that level). A blow-off valve on a belt-driven centrifugal blower is more like the spring-loaded "pop-off" valve (or plate) built into the intake manifold on Roots-blown racing engines in the early days. These were used more as an emergency valve in case of a backfire into the manifold/blower (today's Fuelers use a "burst-plate" that literally blows off). Supercharger users learned soon enough that if airflow suddenly backs up in the system, a relief valve can (hopefully) avert serious damage.

Though quite a bit of ducting is involved, an intercooled ProCharger blower kit is relatively simple, such as this one for an LS3 Corvette.

A COMPLETE GUIDE TO STREET SUPERCHARGING

CHAPTER 5

As you might expect, ProCharger has a wide range of shapes and sizes of centrifugal superchargers, though all are now of the same basic design, as seen in the cutaway at the beginning of this chapter, including self-contained gear lubrication. These two units actually represent big and biggest in the ProCharger, being the F-1 and F-3 models, claiming power capabilities of 800 to 1,600 hp, or more, on street-drivable small-block-powered vehicles.

However, these more serious (and expensive) blow-off valves are only needed for systems that can create lots of boost, as in racing. For street systems, a standard bypass valve is simple and smart.

ATI ProCharger

The other major player in the belt-driven centrifugal blower field is Accessible Technologies ProCharger.

Accessible Technologies, Inc. (ATI) of Lenexa, Kansas, began producing the ProCharger centrifugal supercharger in 1993. As we stated, contemporary belt-driven centrifugal superchargers are relatively similar in external appearance, design, and installation, so much of what we described for the Paxton-Vortech blowers, above, also applies to the ProCharger line. (One recent centrifugal blower, the Powerdyne, which was included in the prior edition of this book, was unique in having an internal cogged belt drive

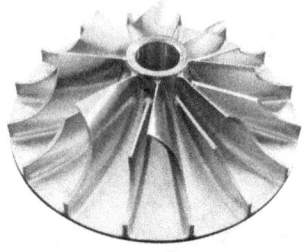

Also as seen at the beginning of this chapter, all ProCharger impellers are CNC machined from billet aluminum, which easily allows for various "trims," or curved-blade shapes, in any given-size housing.

to step up impeller speed, instead of meshing gears. This blower has gone out of production at the time of this writing, though it may return in a revised configuration.) So do not think that we are short-changing the ProCharger by talking about it less. The accompanying photos should give you a good overview of the products available from ATI. If you are contemplating the purchase of a centrifugal supercharger system, we strongly recommend you shop both companies profiled here (and any others that might appear in the future, if they seem to meet the expertise and experience of these).

Here's a reverse-drive ProCharger in a C5 Z06 application, with the blower ducted directly into the unseen intercooler ahead of the car's radiator, and directly back into the factory injection's throttle body.

ProCharger prefers large, aluminum air-to-air intercoolers for most of its installations, especially street packages on factory vehicles that make hefty horsepower, as we shall see in the following examples (though, of course, the front-mounted intercoolers don't show in the photos).

From the beginning, ProCharger has used a variable combination of drive pulley sizes, step-up gear ratios, scroll-housing diameter, and impeller size and design to provide a wide range of boost levels. Its original P600 and P600B blowers, with 9-inch scroll housings and straight-fin cast or machined billet impellers, have been superseded by the P-1SC and D-1SC models, respectively. While ATI calls them "entry level" superchargers—compared to several considerably larger racing versions in the "F" series—they are typical street units. They use machined-billet cases containing an oil bath of proprietary synthetic lubricant, square-cut step-up gears, and an 8- or 12-rib drive-belt system.

This is a typical ProCharger installation; a 6.1L Hemi in a 2007 Dodge Charger, featuring polished blower and drive components.

And if you want more power, such as on the 5.4 Triton and 3V Modular Fords shown here, you have many options with a belt-driven blower, starting with a pulley change, an impeller trim change, or a bigger intercooler, and moving up to a bigger blower, all of which still fits under the stock sheetmetal.

The P-1SC uses a straight-fin machined billet impeller, while the D-1SC has a "helixed" impeller and upgraded shaft bearings, and is "capable of supporting 925 horsepower." One unique (and patented) characteristic of these blowers is an aeration pump for the lube oil, driven by a toothed sprocket off the impeller shaft. Both of these units are available in carbureted blow-through applications for small- or big-block Chevys, using a bonnet-style housing to blow into the top of a Holley 4150 type carburetor, rather than a pressure box to fully enclose the carb, as in Paxton-Vortech systems. The use of a bonnet blow-through system requires a special carburetor designed for this application, or the addition of throttle shaft seals and possibly other modifications to standard carbs. Several systems for blowing directly into factory EFI units are also available.

One area of significant difference between ProCharger and Paxton-Vortech is intercooling. While Vortech strongly prefers air-to-water intercooling for reasons given above, ProCharger feels just as adamant about air-to-air intercoolers. The strongest argument is that this is an inherently simpler system, requiring fewer (and fail-safe) components, which take up less underhood space, weigh less, and simplify installation. Further, ATI claims that air-to-air intercooling is more effective than air-to-water systems in lowering charge air temperature and increasing its density. While they present several arguments for this case, it may be open to further discussion and testing, depending on which parameters are measured.

For applications where an unlimited source of cold water exists (such as marine), or where ice water can be used for short periods of time (as in drag racing), ATI concedes that a water-cooler is better and they make such units. The overall effectiveness of intercooling, however, cannot be denied, especially for street systems. As ATI points out, it not only produces significant horsepower gains under boost, but it allows standard (not retarded) ignition timing, 91-octane pump gasoline on the street, and improved engine life and reliability.

While ProCharger started out with the usual Ford Mustang and small-block Chevrolet installation kits for its superchargers, it has been adding numerous applications and variations to its line, ranging from Corvettes and Camaros, to Challengers and Chargers, to pickups and SUVs of all types, to Hondas, Nissans, Infinitis, Ford Focus, and even Harley-Davidsons.

A 2008 GM pickup truck also uses the Vortec small-block and the ProCharger is run by the engine's single serpentine belt. You can see that the low-restriction air cleaner feeding the blower is drawing heated underhood air, but don't forget that the blower is pumping through a large intercooler mounted at the front of the vehicle before being routed to the engine's EFI intake.

So your late-model Mustang happens to have a small V-6 under the hood? Bolt on a supercharger, preferably with an intercooler, like this, and it'll run like a big-inch V-8.

CHAPTER 6

MODERN ROOTS BLOWERS

GMC Blowers

The 6-71 GMC blower is obsolete. It's a 1938 design and it finally went out of production in the 1980s.

But then so are flatheads, Nailhead Buicks, and old Chrysler Hemis. That doesn't mean today's hot rodders don't want to put them in their cars. Further, the elongated, Teflon-stripped blowers used on today's Top Fuel Dragsters and Funny Cars are still an extension of the old 6-71 design. On top of that, the engines they run are close duplicates of old Chrysler Hemis. At Bonneville you'll find all sorts of serious race cars running GMC-style superchargers, including Al Teague's amazing single-engine (Chrysler Hemi), rear-wheel-driven, 430+ mph streamliner that ran a Mooneyham 12-71 blower. Nostalgia Top Fuel Dragsters are limited to 6-71 blowers, and they're hitting 250+ mph in the quarter mile.

Yes, GMC blowers are nostalgic, but they do still work. They're not nearly as efficient as modern superchargers covered in this book, but they do pump some air—lots of it.

For the street, in fact, a 6-71 GMC blower will give you more power than you can use. So, either, 1) that's not the reason you put it on top of your engine, or, 2) it is. There's an old hot rod adage that says "Sometimes too much is just enough."

Here's how the classic 6-71 GMC blower was designed to be used: hung on the side of an inline, 6-cylinder, 2-stroke diesel engine to blow fresh, dry air into the cylinders, through ports in the walls, at the bottom of each stroke. They were made to run hundreds of thousands of miles doing hard work. They weren't designed to make boost, but they do that pretty well, too.

Despite all the advances in modern supercharging outlined in this book, the bald fact is that a large percentage of hot rodders still want that huge, shiny, noisy, 6-71 or 8-71 mounted right on top of their V-8 engine, with a couple of big 4-barrels on top of that, and probably some sort of big, polished scoop as the crowning glory. It doesn't matter that the driver can barely see around the thing. What's important is that everyone else can see, hear, and appreciate it. Best of all, unlike a lot of other hot-rod eye candy, this thing will work just as good as it looks.

The big difference in the GMC-type street-blower market today, however, is that none of these blower builders use any GMC parts any more, other than the 3-lobe rotors, the supply of which is drying up quickly. Cases, end plates, and (in some cases now, and probably more soon) rotors are all made from new castings today—if not machined from blocks of billet.

In past editions of this book we spent quite a bit of time delineating the different types and sizes of GM blowers, and showing step-by-step procedures for strengthening, machining, and "clearancing" one properly for performance use on the street or strip. Today, building a street-performance blower out of used (and probably abused) GMC parts is not practical. In the following pages we'll present several contemporary GMC-type blower builders who make a variety of supercharger packages made from new integrated pieces. You let the blower builder assemble and set up the unit; then you buy the package and bolt it on your engine, just as you would with the other types of modern superchargers profiled in this book.

However, since the GMC blower was the one that really brought supercharging to the world of hot rodding, let's start with a brief historical outline of the GMC blower lineage, both in terms of types made and how they were designed to work.

Rodders and racers are most familiar with the 71-series of GMC Roots-type blowers. These were designed for GM's first diesel engine, the 6-71, which was a 2-stroke, inline, 6-cylinder engine displacing 71 ci per cylinder for a total displacement of 426 ci. Ultimately the line included 2-71, 3-71, 4-71, and 6-71 engines, each using the same design of blower and rotor diameter, but with rotor and case length shortened to match the engine's capacity. Each of these sizes of GMC blowers, known by the same designation as their matching engines, has been used by hot rodders, though the 4-71 and 6-71 are by far the most prevalent and common today (as well as larger sizes, i.e., 8-71 and 10-71, which were made by the aftermarket, not originally by GM).

Several other types and sizes of GM blowers have been produced over the years. The 53-series, for instance (made for engines with this smaller cylinder size), used straight-cut 2-lobe rotors rather than the helical 3-lobe rotors of the 71s. Their cases, which again differ in length corresponding to engine size (4-53, 6-53, 8-53, etc.) are smaller in diameter and are easily identified by a horizontal rib in the middle of each side. While these 53-series GM blowers were virtually never used by hot rodders, the initial 144-ci B&M and Weiand street blowers were patterned nearly exactly on the 4-53 GMC, though made with more modern materials.

When GM later introduced V-series diesel engines, it introduced slightly different blowers designated 6V-71, 8V-71, and so on. These used 3-lobe helical rotors identical to the 71-series, but of different lengths. The cases are also externally similar, but are readily identified by long attachment bolts that anchor in the middle of double side-ribs and extend down to the manifold at about a 30-degree angle. The only company that has used this design for automotive applications is Dyer's Blowers, which made manifolds and drive kits to mount 6V-71s to a variety of V-8s in the 1980s. These kits are no longer in production.

There were minor changes in GM blower design over the years, primarily to cases and end plates. One significant change in the 71-series line,

The V-series GM 2-stroke diesels are newer, and most add a turbo to the blower in a 2-stage setup as seen on this 568-ci 8V-71. The blower mounts between the cylinder banks, on top of the engine, similar to hot rod applications.

These are the sizes of 71-series blowers made by General Motors for more than five decades, beginning with the 2-71 at the bottom and increasing in length through the 3-, 4-, and 6-71 size cases.

however, occurred in 1978. In a fuel-efficiency move, to reduce horsepower required to drive the blower, GM slightly reduced the diameter of the rotors in all 71-series (and, a bit later, V-71) blowers. The difference is so small (about 1/4-inch diameter) you have to measure them to tell. Plus they used the same cases and endplates (so they look the same externally), but bored them to the smaller diameter. Mixing these components won't work. The older rotors won't fit in the newer cases. But the newer, smaller rotors will fit in an older case; they just won't seal to make the blower work. We mention this just because there are a lot of old GMC blower parts floating around swap meets and the Internet. They don't all mix and match.

To sum up: GM made 71-series rotors in both large and small diameters. GM never made an 8-71 (inline) blower. The GM 6V-71 and 8V-71 blowers (with long, angled mounting bolts) were both made in large- and small-diameter rotor sizes. The 6V-71 rotors are a couple inches shorter than 6-71 rotors, so are not commonly used by performance blower builders. (Two companies, The Blower Shop and Blower Drive Service, recently made "stepped" end plates incorporating angled intakes and/or rear discharge cavities, to allow use of more plentiful large-diameter 6V-71 rotors in a 6-71 case.) The 8-71 blowers made by most builders today use 8V-71 rotors (usually large diameter) in a custom-made housing. They're about 1-inch longer than 6-71 rotors.

Also, these diesel engines were made for versatile applications in everything from trucks, buses, and boats to cranes, army tanks, and stationary water pumps. Therefore they were made in clockwise and reverse rotation, with front or rear drive, and

A close-up of the 3-71 with its end plates removed clearly shows the relationship of the 3-lobe rotors. The right one turns clockwise, the left one counterclockwise, to pump air from the large inlet on top, around the case sides, and out an equally large opening at the bottom. Clearanced properly, the rotors do not touch each other or the case walls.

with the blowers mounted on the right or left side. Consequently, any GMC blower straight off a diesel engine might turn frontward or backward on top of your engine. If the blower turns backward, the rotors can be flopped side-for-side, and the rotor shafts changed end-for-end, to make it work properly. Once the "tang" or "lip" has been machined off one side of the GMC case to mount it flat on an automotive manifold, the case itself has no front or back (the endplates can be bolted to either end).

GMC blowers were never designed to supercharge automotive performance engines. That is a use appropriated, and accommodated, by inventive hot rodders long ago. These blowers were designed to scavenge exhaust and blow fresh intake air into 2-stroke diesel engines (since a 2-stroke doesn't have separate intake and exhaust strokes, it needs help getting the exhaust out and the fresh air in on the same stroke). Specifically, the blower mounts on the side of the inline engine, with its outlet positioned over intake ports (holes) in the cylinder wall near BDC. When the piston travels down the bore to uncover the ports near the bottom, the blower pumps fresh air in at the bottom, while the exhaust valve opens at the top. Thus the fresh air pumped in by the blower pushes out the exhaust as it fills the cylinder. In the diesel, fuel is injected directly into the cylinder when the piston compresses this fresh air at TDC.

Therefore, the GM blower was designed to pump dry air, to turn at relatively slow speeds, and to operate at zero boost levels. This is why GM calls these units "blowers" rather than "superchargers." In the diesel, the function is simply to move air, not to compress it, since the exhaust valve opens as soon as the blower starts pumping air into the cylinder.

But this is where the Roots-type air pump shines—it is excellent for moving very large quantities of air at relatively slow rotor speeds against low back pressure. Since it is a positive-displacement pump, it moves a given quantity of air with

The 53-series GM blowers were slightly smaller in diameter and have an identifying horizontal rib on each side of the case. They use straight-cut 2-lobe rotors, which also vary in length relative to the engine's number of 53-ci cylinders, as these examples demonstrate. Both the 71- and 53-series GMC cast rotors are hollow.

each revolution, which means that it has immediate response. The fact that Jimmies move very large quantities of air, especially at lower RPM, relative to other types of blowers, is what made them so good for supercharging automotive engines, especially those of 300 ci or more. However, when we bolt a GMC atop a 4-stroke V-8 and overdrive it to make boost, we are asking it to do something for which it was not designed.

As is so often the case with automotive engines, especially of the high-performance variety, we end up making lots of minor compromises in order to effect a big overall gain.

In the case of the GMC blower, its volumetric, mechanical, and adiabatic efficiencies are all highest when it is pumping air against no load (making no boost), as it was intended to do. As soon as we begin to use it to compress air, all three of its efficiency ratings go down. Obviously it takes more power from the engine to turn the blower against back pressure, thus lowering the mechanical effi-

Later, GM made V-6 and V-8 71-series 2-stroke diesels, which used these different, center-bolt cases. Using 3-lobe helical rotors of the same diameters, but different lengths, as the inline 71s, these blowers mounted on top of the engine, between the cylinder banks, usually dual-stage fed by a turbo, as well. Note the scored walls inside these used cases.

ciency as the boost goes up. Also, as back pressure increases, it forces more air to leak through the clearances between the rotors and the case, lowering volumetric efficiency. And the more work that has to be put into the blower to turn it, as well as the more backflow leakage, the more heat will be transferred to the air being pumped, thus lowering the adiabatic efficiency.

Furthermore, the Roots design, which is excellent for pumping, is just not a very efficient way to compress air. The Roots is a backflow compressor, which means that it compresses air by cramming it into a container (the manifold) outside of the blower. In fact, when it builds pressure in the manifold, as soon as a rotor tip passes the edge of the blower's outlet opening, manifold pressure will force compressed air to rush backward into the rotor cavity, compressing the air inside—thus the term backflow compressor. As you can imagine, this isn't the smoothest way to compress air, and this continuous back-and-forth motion adds greatly to air turbulence and friction, which in turn heats the air more, thus lowering adiabatic efficiency. As one supercharger expert put it, "The biggest problem with the GM Roots is that it beats the #$%& out of the air."

To the 71-series GMC's credit, however, the rotors are twisted ("helical"). This serves two purposes in the stock blower. It reduces blower noise (since the air backflowing into the cavity produces a shock wave), and more importantly it reduces pulsing in the output airflow. When a GMC is used to compress air on an automotive engine, the rotor twist helps reduce the abruptness of the backflow compression process, making the job of compressing the air smoother and increasing efficiency somewhat. The fact that 71-series

The only company that made kits to mount V-series GM blowers on automotive engines was Dyer's, exemplified by this 6V-71 adapted to a 360 Mopar using a modified aftermarket carburetor manifold. Dyer's no longer offers these kits, though they can supply service parts or blower rebuilding.

GM blowers have three rotors instead of two also greatly reduces airflow pulsing, increases blower smoothness, and helps reduce leakage back through the blower, since more than one rotor tip will be sealing against the case walls at the same time.

The primary reason other blower manufacturers in the past used 2-lobe, straight-cut rotors was because the machining processes needed to make the 3-lobe helical rotors were much too complicated and expensive for most companies smaller than General Motors. Even when race-blower builders started casting their own longer 10-71 and 12-71 cases, they carefully cut, spliced, and pinned sections of GMC rotors together to make longer ones to fit. In these days of computer

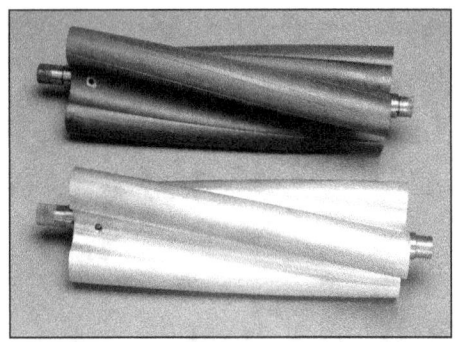
Although they look the same size because of the photo angle, the upper rotor is a longer, original, hard-anodized 8V-71 GM, while the lower one is a new 6-71 "Air Loc" cast and machined by Blower Drive Service.

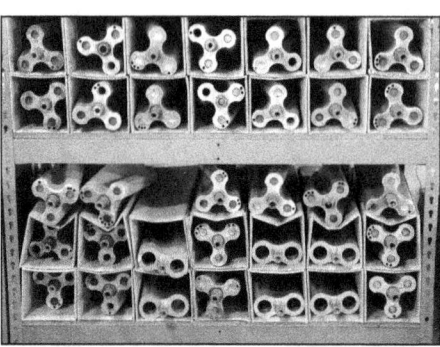
Making new, helical, 3-lobe rotors for GM blowers is quite expensive, whether they're cast and machined or cut from billet. Consequently, most GMC blower builders will rely on usable stock GM rotors as long as supplies last. This stash at Don Hampton's includes 6-71s, 8V-71s, and a few of his own custom-made, straight 2-lobe rotors.

Rotors like these BDS machined-billet Pro-Loc 14-71s are not only very expensive, but they're illegal for NHRA Top Fuel because of their "hi-helix" twist (they can be used in boats, tractor-pullers, etc.). The white Teflon strips fitted in grooves on three sides of each lobe make a "no-gap" air seal, but they also take lots of horsepower to turn, plus they wear out quickly and have to be replaced—often after every run. This is not for street.

design and computer-controlled mills, however, making much-improved Roots-style rotors (and cases) is considerably easier and cost effective.

One final note: In the old days when serious dragsters were running 6-71 blowers set "tight" for racing, a hot rod adage said, fairly correctly, that "When a blower is worn out for racing, it's just right for street." Today's serious racing GMC-type blowers, however, are usually much too large for street use in the first place, but more important, their rotor lobes are grooved and fitted with three Teflon or Nylatron strips each, which actually rub against each other and the case walls, for complete sealing. These blowers are so tight that you probably cannot turn one by hand, and they take gobs of horsepower to drive. When the strips "wear out" (which is usually every run), they are replaced. Such a "stripped" racing blower, even when it is "worn out," is not practical to run on the street. They're for very-high-horsepower engines that run under full boost all the time.

The single nylon strips that were used along the tips of the 2-lobe B&M (and some other) street blowers, on the other hand, are there more for insurance than anything else. The only time they should rub the case is if the engine (and blower) is over-revved, causing the rotors to stretch. If this happens, the strips can be replaced (rather than the blower housing); otherwise, they shouldn't wear out.

Given the above information, if you still want a big Jimmy blower on your street rod, boat, or weekend racer, we think you'll agree that buying one manufactured from new (and very likely improved) components, properly set up, and ready to bolt on with appropriate manifolding and drive to fit your engine and intended use, is the way to go these days.

GMC Blower Builders

There was a time when GMC blower builders made superchargers for race cars, oftentimes in one-stall shops, if not in their backyard garages. Other than Cragar multi-V-belt setups for 4-71s on small-block Chevys, there was virtually nothing else available to bolt a GMC blower on a street-driven engine, incorporating such necessities as a water pump, water outlets, thermostat, fan, alternator, and so on. During the 1980s, that changed significantly and suddenly there were several shops making blower drive systems accommodating street hardware. At first they modified carburetor manifolds with plates to adapt blowers to various V-8 engines, but soon many were casting their own intakes, and other parts. Of course, the focus then was rebuilding GMC blowers to work on performance automotive engines.

Today such "blower shops" are numerous, and nearly all make not only specific drive gear and intake manifolds, but the blower cases and other components, as well. We can't cover all of these shops here; plus, as you might imagine, such businesses tend to come and go. So, in the following section we will highlight some of the pioneering shops that have prospered and grown, some that make unique products or specialize in

MODERN ROOTS BLOWERS

A typical Dyer's blower setup today looks like this dual-carbureted 6-71 mounted on a small-block Chevy.

Like most current GMC blower builders, Dyer's now casts its own 6-71 cases, end plates, and all drive components. And, since they've always been a full-service machine shop, they can do all machining in-house.

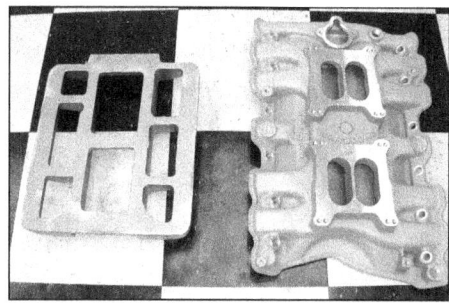

Dyer's pioneered the modification of aftermarket aluminum intake manifolds to mount blowers on a range of V-8 or V-6 engines, retaining street necessities such as the water inlet/thermostat housing. For an Olds 455, the starting point is an Offy dual-quad intake and a cast 6-71 mounting plate.

After a concerted amount of machining on both pieces, aligning and welding, this is the finished product.

certain areas, and one or two that are simply typical of the breed. In the back of the book we will list others, with contact information, and of course we suggest you scan the Internet both for names of new companies as well as new developments at the ones we profile here.

Dyer's Blowers, Inc.

Chicago-area machine shop owner Gary Dyer learned plenty about GMC blowers when he was piloting the well-known, and aptly named *Mr. Norm's* Dodge "Super Charger" Funny Cars in the 1960s. So, in the mid-1970s, under the name Dyer's Machine Service, he pioneered the adaptation of 6-71 GMC blowers to a wide variety of street engines, modifying existing aftermarket carburetor manifolds with bolt-on or weld-on adapter plates, and machining Gilmer belt drives that accommodated street ancillaries. His Street Charger kits for mounting 6-71s on Pontiac, Oldsmobile, Ford, Mopar, and GM V-8s, as well as 4-71s on then-popular V-6s, really opened the doors for the use of GMC blowers on everything from muscle cars to street rods to 4x4 trucks (and even vans...remember?).

Dyer also made a low-profile intake manifold and drive kit to mount then-plentiful 6V-71 GMCs to small-block Chevys, and quite a few of these units were sold. In the early 1980s, he even designed and built his own small-displacement, Roots-type blower called the DMS-1, which pre-dated similar units from B&M and Weiand. This blower, made as a very-low-profile kit for small-block Chevys and Buick V-6s, had a cast-aluminum case incorporating a 4-barrel carburetor flange and custom-made 2-lobe rotors. Unfortunately, the time had not yet arrived for this under-hood system, and few of these blowers were made.

During the 1990s, as several other companies jumped into the street supercharging arena, including those making manifolds and drives for GMCs as well as those making new blowers, such as B&M and Weiand, Dyer concentrated more on his active machine shop business, limiting blower work mainly to rebuilding and servicing units and drive systems.

Today, with the involvement of his son, Bill, they have changed their name to Dyer's Blowers, Inc., and have recharged their supercharger business. Not only do they now manufacture their own blower cases and other components, but they have significantly added to their previously comprehensive line of GMC street blower kits. They've got you covered if you want to mount a big 6-71 or 8-71 Jimmy on: a 409 Chevy; a 389 or 455 Pontiac; a 350 or 455 Olds; a 400 or 455 Buick; a 472 or 500

CHAPTER 6

The process for a 302 Ford starts with a single 4-barrel intake. The use of Offy 360-degree, single-plane manifolds makes machining one open to the blower's dimensions possible. The "adapter plate" is seen here inverted.

This is a completed manifold for a small-block Mopar. The hole visible in the adapter plate is for a pop-off valve.

This aquatic Dyer's application mounts a 6-71 with dual quads on a big-block Mopar. One of the two MSD control boxes is a Boost Timing Master to limit total timing advance in pre-set psi ranges.

You want it blown, big time? BDS has you covered. This company specializes in 6-71 and larger GMC-style blowers, and makes its own cast or billet intake manifolds to fit a wide range of V-8 and V-6 engines. If it doesn't stick out of the hood, don't look for it at BDS. This towering 460 big-block Ford example is an 8-71 blower on a tall cast BDS manifold (to clear the stock distributor), with a water-fed intercooler in between, and a pair of Demon carbs and a BDS Hilborn-style scoop atop all that.

How many people make Jimmy blower kits for 500-inch Cadillacs? BDS does. Note the individual-runner, cast-aluminum intake manifold mounting the BDS 8-71 blower, with a pair of EFI throttle bodies on top of that. Although not installed here, BDS makes the complete Gilmer belt drive, too, of course.

Cadillac; a 290-401 AMC; a 351C, 351W, 400M, 427, 428, 429, or 460 Ford; a small- or big-block Mopar (including 392 or 426 style Hemis); not to mention the usual GM and Ford motors.

Further, Dyer's continues their machine shop services, including rebuilding original or previously modified 4-71, 6-71, and 6V-71 GMC blowers. Plus they are one of the only shops we contacted that will rebuild any sizes of B&M or Weiand blowers (including replacing Teflon rotor strips), as well as reconditioning OEM Eaton blowers.

Blower Drive Service

Another true pioneer in the field of street supercharging is Blower Drive Service of Whittier, California, otherwise known as BDS. As its name implies, this company started out making drive systems for GMC blowers that were compatible with necessary street accessories. Soon they were making custom manifolds to mount 4-71 and 6-71 Jimmy blowers on a wide range of V-8 and V-6 engines. BDS has continued in doing so, though most of their products these days are made from proprietary castings or even from billet. Today the BDS line of street blower kits, based primarily on 6-71 and 8-71 GMC-style superchargers, is probably the most comprehensive of anyone's.

Early on, BDS also specialized in an equally comprehensive line of supercharger accessories and support components. A BDS carburetion setup is readily recognized by its precision-made linkage and its neatly-bent

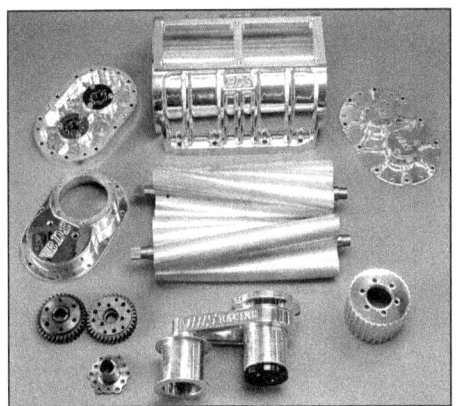

We've mentioned that today's GMC-style blower builders now make most of their own components. Everything in this photo, from the polished 6-71 case, to the end plates, to the drive parts, and even the rotors, are cast and machined by BDS. This is a brand-new 6-71 blower, made to produce horsepower on a hot rod, not pump air into a diesel.

Since new rotors are still much more expensive to make than good, used GMC cores, BDS came up with this creative combination for a more affordable street blower. It uses inset and flow-contoured end plates to fit slightly shorter, previously unused, and therefore relatively plentiful, 6V-71 rotors inside a new BDS 6-71 case.

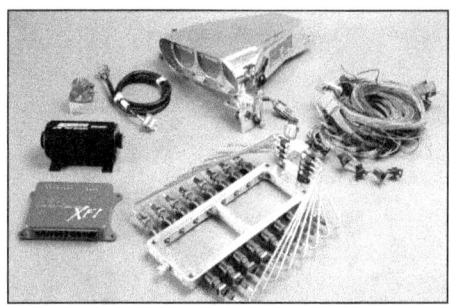

BDS was also an innovator in converting various types of top-of-blower fuel injection to fully streetable EFI. This complete, stand-alone BDS system includes a bug-catcher-style hat, a neatly plumbed injector plate with 16 nozzles, an Aeromotive high-pressure fuel pump, and a F.A.S.T. electronic programmer. BDS has been doing this for a couple decades, and offers several injector styles, with or without the blower.

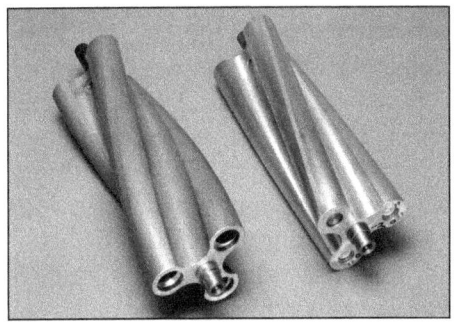

Not only does BDS cast and machine its own standard-helix 6-71 and 8-71 rotors (right), but it also machines more-twisted "hi-helix" rotors from billet aluminum (left). While the cast rotors have hollow lobes, the billet ones are rifle-drilled through each end to lighten them.

One of the things that earned BDS a good reputation early on was its finely crafted stainless steel fuel hard-lines for dual quad setups. This is still a specialty.

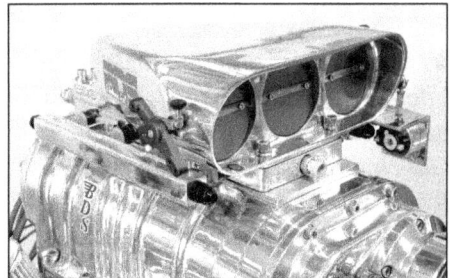

This BDS-made bug catcher is fitted with eight injectors fed by fuel rails. Note the Throttle Position Sensor on the far side. For street, one or two of the injector "holes" are blocked off, behind the butterflies, to give more sensitive throttle control at street speeds.

stainless steel fuel lines with red and blue anodized A-N fittings. The BDS Hilborn-style polished aluminum air scoop, with air cleaners inside, has also become a staple of dual-carbureted GMC-blown street machines. They also sell "blue-printed" Holley carburetors of various sizes, and will also rebuild your new or good used carburetors to work properly with one of their blower systems.

Further, BDS stocks components such as blower pistons, either flat-tappet or roller cams and kits in blower-compatible grinds, and other blower-specific accessories such as distributors, ignitions, fuel pumps, and gauges.

Another area that BDS pioneered, and continues to lead relatively unchallenged in the street blower field, is the adaptation of electronic fuel injection to blown (and even unblown) street engines. Specifically, since the 1980s BDS's Craig Railsback has been converting race-style fuel injection units, such as 4-port Hilborns or, more often, a Bug Catcher or other style of "hat" injector, to custom-plumbed electronic injectors, run by an ECU custom-programmed to operate the system in street-driving modes.

Finally, BDS has been actively involved in all types of motorsports,

CHAPTER 6

As new engines emerge, BDS keeps adding to its repertoire. For the new cathedral-port aluminum LS-series GM small-blocks, BDS has created this fabricated and machined-billet intake that is a work of art in itself. The engine maintains its serpentine belt system, and this 8-71 is topped by another BDS variation on an EFI 3-hole hat injector.

With its 6-71 and injector finished in Darth Vader black anodizing, one of BDS's latest combos is this manifold and drive for the third-generation Mopar Hemis. The tall cast and polished intake leaves room to mount the eight plug coils underneath, for a very clean look. The billet belt guard is another popular BDS item.

This highly polished package on a 302 Ford small-block is a low-profile 174 Weiand (formerly B&M) that has a single 4-barrel pad cast in the top.

from Pro-level supercharged drag racing to stadium monster trucks, so they can handle just about any type of GMC-style supercharger installation from street machine, to boat, to off-road, to racing.

Holley-Weiand

The previous revision of this book, published in 1999, included ample sections on B&M and Weiand superchargers, both of which were rapidly expanding lines at the time. B&M, which had pioneered the small, low-profile, relatively inexpensive Roots blower made with 2-lobe extruded rotors and cast cases incorporating a 4-barrel carburetor flange (in 144- and 174-ci sizes), had added a longer 250-ci model using the same diameter rotors, as well as a much larger 420 Megablower, which still used extruded 2-lobe rotors, but of larger diameter and length. Intake manifold manufacturer Weiand, meanwhile, introduced a very similar line of 2-lobe, low-profile Pro-Street blowers in 142-, 177-, and 256-ci sizes using cast and CNC-machined rotors very similar to the GM 53-series (without Teflon tip strips, as used in the B&M blowers). Further, since Weiand had made 4-71 and 6-71 blower manifolds for years for Chevy V-8s and older engines such as Chrysler 392 Hemis, as well as distinctive ribbed drive snouts and rear covers for GMC blowers, it added a new line of 6-71 through 14-71 blowers to fit Chevys, 392/426 Chryslers, and other engines, drive systems, and components.

However, shortly after that book's publication, Holley Performance bought both the complete B&M supercharger line (leaving B&M to concentrate on automatic transmissions), as well as the whole Weiand company. Under the Weiand brand name, Holley has been marketing a line of intake manifolds, aluminum water pumps, and superchargers for "Auto & Marine" applications.

At first glance, the Holley/Weiand supercharger line appears to be a selection of former Weiand blower models (144, 177, and 256 low-profile and 6-71 and 8-71 GM styles), with the elimination of B&M blowers altogether. But this is not the case. As of late 2008, the Weiand blower line included a slightly confusing mix of 142, 144, 174, 177, 250, and 256 2-lobe low profile blowers, as well as a 6-71 and an 8-71. All of these blowers incorporate the Weiand logo and are called Pro-Street, although they appear to be made from a combination of previous Weiand and B&M components. A couple variations are called Low Profile, though this seems to indicate the manifold height, not the blower's.

And some have Teflon rotor-tip strips, while some don't.

As of this writing, Holley/Weiand offers 142s through 8-71s (six models) for: small-block Chevrolets (non-LS style); 174s through 8-71s (six models) for big-block Chevys; a 174 for the 289-302 small-block Ford; and a 6-71 for the 392 Chrysler Hemi. The smaller-diameter blowers come in very-low-profile models (a la B&Ms), as well as ones that mount to a taller manifold with external bolts, looking more like GMC cases. Of the GMC-style blowers, both of which use new cases with the Weiand logo cast in the sides, the 6-71 is fitted with new, straight-cut 2-lobe rotors, while the 8-71 uses reconditioned 8V-71 GM 3-lobe helical rotors.

Besides automotive applications outlined here, the Weiand catalog lists several marine units designed for Mercruiser, OMC, Volvo-Penta, and Chevrolet powerplants.

Further, since Holley is foremost a performance carburetor company, it's logical that they should offer an ample line of Supercharger Carburetors. The latest catalog listed six different models, ranging from 600 to 950 cfm in both street and race versions, featuring "boost-referenced" power valves and calibrated jetting for draw-through blower use. Also listed are several varieties of Weiand Supercharger Cams in hydraulic flat-tappet and roller grinds.

However, given our past experience, not to mention market conditions, we must say check current availability on all these products at the time you read this.

In an unpolished version, a similar 174 mounts to a very low-profile manifold on the big-block Chevy. Since Holley is primarily a carburetor company, it stands to reason that all of its current blower applications are designed to accept single or dual 4-barrel carburetion.

This similar-sized unit, dubbed the 256, is the former Weiand middle-size 2-lobe blower, which bolts to a taller big-block Chevy intake with external bolts, GMC-style. A top plate accepts dual quads, and this kit includes a Poly-V belt drive with a coil-spring-loaded idler pulley.

The next step up in size for Weiand blowers is the 250 series, seen here with a 2-inch Gilmer belt drive and dual Holleys on a small-block Chevy. This is the former B&M blower.

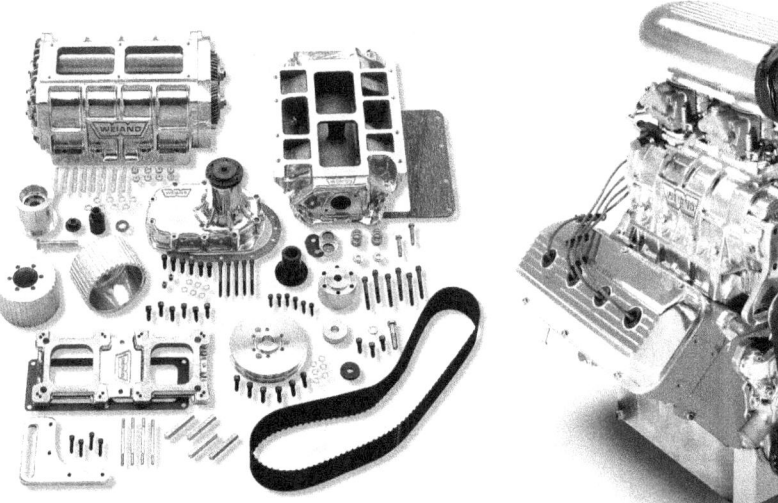

Weiand 6-71 blowers, shown in kit form and installed on an early Chrysler Hemi, use the familiar Weiand ribbed drive snout and rear cover plate, and even a 1/2-inch-pitch Gilmer belt, for a nostalgic setup. However, the blower is fitted with 2-lobe, straight-cut rotors.

Weiand also makes this 8-71 blower, which uses GM 8V-71 3-lobe helical rotors. It is offered with manifold, 8-mm Gilmer belt drive, and dual carb top plate for small- and big-block Chevys.

We don't know who whittled the injector, but the polished billet 8-71 from The Blower Shop is the focal point of this jewel-like all-billet assembly on a big-block Chevy in an impressive early Corvette.

A line-up of cases available from The Blower Shop includes a polished GMC 6-71, the distinctive 6-rib former Bowers 8-71, and a freshly machined (as yet unpolished) TBS billet 8-71. Note that these new cases are hard-anodized on the inside.

The Blower Shop

One of the more recent entrants in the Roots blower arena is The Blower Shop (TBS), noted for its unique cases CNC milled from 6061-T6 aluminum billet. Actually, this company is an outgrowth of the old Bowers Blowers, well-known among Top Fuel and other racers during the 1960s and 1970s. In 1984, under the name Odyssey Superchargers, the current company acquired the Bowers blower line, including its distinctive 6-rib 6-71/8-71 case patterns, and even Larry's 351 Ford-powered blower test stand (as seen in previous editions of this book). For the next 15 years TBS continued an emphasis on competition blowers for the Top Fuel and Alcohol dragster and boat markets.

In the 2000s, however, Ron Hayes has redirected The Blower Shop's priorities to street and marine applications, with an emphasis on, as he aptly puts it, "blowers that are as beautiful and well made as they are devastatingly powerful." While TBS still offers original GMC 6-71 cases, as well as the cast 6-rib Bowers style, the vast majority of 71-series blowers they make today use not only CNC machined and polished cases, but also end plates, drive snouts, and other components. These range from a 6V-71 (327 ci, using 6V-71 GM rotors in a 6-71–length case, with inset and relieved end plates) up to 14-71. The 6V through 8-71 blowers use reconditioned GM 3-lobe rotors, with the 8-71s being available in either large- or small-diameter (360-ci) rotor sizes.

This is a typical TBS installation of a polished 6-71 GMC on a small-block Chevy with an 8-mm Gilmer drive. TBS offers a full line of Demon and Holley blower carbs, pre-bent fuel lines, linkage, air cleaners, and so on.

The 10-71 and 14-71 blowers use machined billet 3-lobe helical rotors, and can be made in either front or rear outlet styles (with the case extended toward the front or the rear).

Also unique are the smaller TBS Low Profile 192- and 250-cid blowers. Like previous B&M blowers, these use 2-lobe rotors made from extruded aluminum, then machined and fitted with Teflon strips on the leading edge. However the rest of the blower,

The installation of a fully-polished billet TBS blower is similar, except this one is fitted with 6V-71 GMC rotors.

MODERN ROOTS BLOWERS

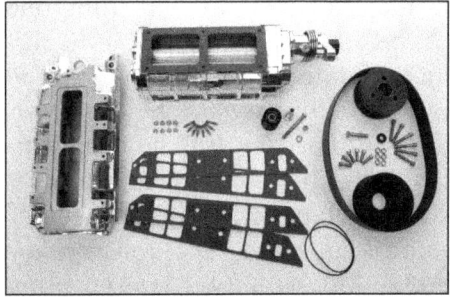

This is a TBS 250 billet blower shown in kit form and installed on a big-block Chevy. All parts, including the cast manifold and the single carb adapter plate, are polished. A spring-loaded tensioner is needed with any Poly-V belt drive to allow for expansion of aluminum parts.

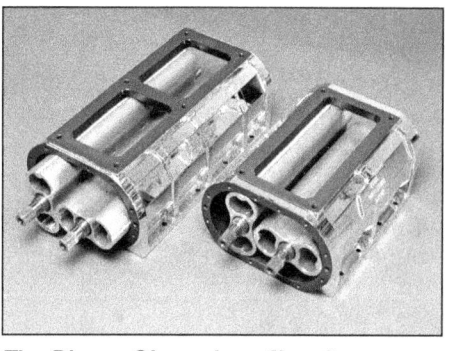

The Blower Shop also offers its own unique line of Low Profile all-billet-case blowers in 192- and 250-ci sizes to fit large- and small-block Chevys. The Teflon-tipped, 2-lobe rotors are cut from extrusions made to order for TBS.

Earlier, we showed a photo of TBS's billet water-fed intercooler. This is a look at the assembled unit with its brass core, and how it fits between a polished Bowers-case TBS 8-71 and a

big-block Chevy. This unit, like the flame-arrester TBS air cleaner, is intended primarily for marine applications (where plenty of cold water, to pump through the intercooler, is readily available).

including the case, ends plates, and drive components, is made from CNC-machined billet aluminum. As this is written, even the two-piece small-block Chevy manifolds for these blowers were machined from billet, though a cast version was in the works.

At present, all of The Blower Shop's manifolds and complete installation kits are designed for small- and big-block Chevy applications, including tall-deck, large-port, and high-profile manifold variations. Primarily for marine applications, TBS also offers a billet aluminum intercooler using a water-fed heat exchanger, which bolts between the blower and manifold for 6-71 through 14-71 blowers. Plus, TBS carries a line of 650- through 1195-cfm Demon carburetors with boost-referenced power valves and fuel curves calibrated for supercharger needs.

Further, TBS offers a full rebuilding service, not only for any GM-style blowers, but also for B&M and Weiand blowers, including the large 420 B&Ms, with certain machined-billet upgrade components available. And, since TBS had just taken delivery of its own brand-new CNC milling machine the day we were there taking pictures, an expanded product line will undoubtedly be forthcoming by the time you read this.

Don Hampton

Don Hampton started building GMC blowers in the early 1960s, when he was very successfully campaigning a Competition Coupe made from a dragster frame, a Fiat Topolino body, and two Chevy V-8 engines with a Hilborn-injected 6-71 on each. He learned quickly. So Hampton's is our example of a typical, perhaps old school, blower builder that specializes in GMC-style superchargers, built or rebuilt for racing or for street. Similar blower shops would include Mooneyham, Littlefield, Kuhl, Dyer's, and other familiar names, some of which are now gone, while others may be joining the field.

And Hampton is a perfect example in that he has probably the most extensive line of manifolds and drive assemblies to mount 4-71, 6-71, and 8-71 (or larger) blowers on a huge variety of V-8 or V-6 engines, new or old. Some of these applications use cast, one-piece intake manifolds, but many others are custom-made at Hampton's by machining out an applicable 2 x 4 or 3 x 2 carburetor intake and welding a specially cast and machined plate on top to accept the blower.

His line of street blower kits covers everything from Nailhead Buicks (and 455s), to early Oldses (and 455s), to AMC's, to Dodge/De Soto/Chrysler Hemis of any size and shape. He also makes a variety of carburetor mounting plates, and if you would like electronic fuel injection he would direct you to someone like Hilborn for a bolt-on, race-looking, but street-drivable, unit. If Don doesn't have a blower setup for the engine you've got, he has a shop full of mills, lathes, and skilled operators that can very likely make one for you. As Don put it, in his usual blunt style, "I do anything the customer asks." For example, he had just made custom 8-71 setups for a Viper V-10 and a Jaguar V-12.

But to say that Hampton is old school is not wholly accurate. He was one of the innovators of 2-lobe rotors for large GMC blowers at least three decades ago. His thinking was simple: if a racer (such as Top Fuel) is restricted to a certain length and diameter of blower, eliminating one of the lobes of the typical GMC will increase the pumping capacity (the open space between lobes) approximately 30 percent. The problem with his early, hand-machined, straight-cut prototypes was that these "flat" rotors tended to flex under heavy boost. Just recently, however, using new CNC technology, Hampton has redesigned his 2-lobe blowers with a 60-degree helical twist, making them both rigid and legal. In fact, a Top Fuel Hydro boat set an E.T. and MPH

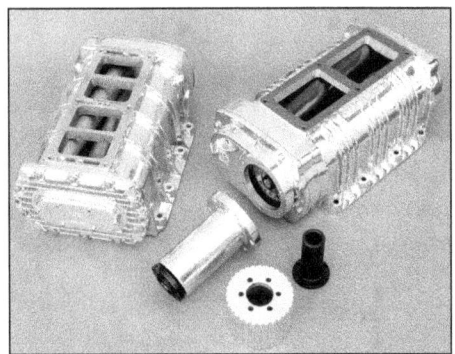

Don Hampton was one of the first to make his own blower cases, and his distinctive 9-rib style, seen in a polished 8-71 size to fit 8V-71 GM rotors, is still one of the best-looking. But he'll make whatever the customer wants. The 6-71 on the left uses a GM case and rotors, with Hampton bearing and drive plates.

These two, to fit a 351-Cleveland and 351-Windsor Ford, are built with a higher blower plate to make room for the front-mounted distributor.

Whether your Buick V-8 is an old Nailhead (left) or a slightly newer 455 (right), Hampton has a manifold to put a 6-71 blower on it.

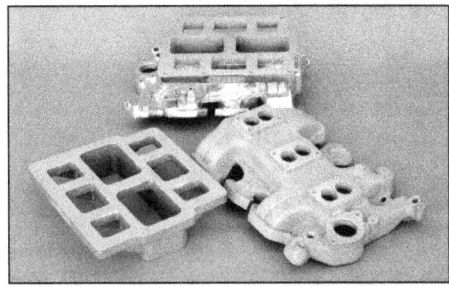

Besides building blowers, Hampton was also a pioneer in fabricating his own intake manifolds to fit a plethora of V-8 and V-6 engines. Although his well-equipped machine shop can do it several ways, the most common is to start with a 2- or 3-carb single-plane manifold, and cut it out to fit one of several sizes of cast Hampton blower plates, align and heli-arc them together, then polish the finished product, as seen here. This one fits an early Olds V-8.

If someone makes a good one-piece blower manifold for non-mainstream engines, Hampton knows where to get them, such as the high-rise one (left) for 460 big-block Fords and the more-obscure one (right) for 427/428 FE Fords. Then he polishes them for good measure.

Everybody has small-block Chevy stuff, but not necessarily a one-piece Cragar-style 4-71 intake. The fabricated manifold at rear mounts a 6-71 on a 409 Chevy, which some might think is sacrilege, but Hampton thinks is cool.

New Old Roots

H&H Flatheads/S.Co.T.

H&H is a third-generation enterprise founded in 1972 by Max Herman, Jr., and Sr., in La Crescenta, California, initially to rebuild Model T and A 4-bangers, and later including Ford V-8 flatheads as well. Much more recently, with sons Mike and Max III joining the business, H&H (which had a longstanding relationship with Barney Navarro in nearby Glendale, California) was able to acquire the entire line of Navarro flathead V-8 Ford speed parts, including original patterns, upon Barney's retirement a couple of years before his passing in 2007.

Navarro, as mentioned earlier, was a pioneer in the use of GMC blowers for automotive racing, and among products acquired by H&H were Barney's patterns for his original 4-71 intake manifold for flathead Ford V-8s. Not only is H&H producing this manifold, but they also offer a multi-ribbed snout and Gilmer-belt-drive pulley combination to mount a 4-71 GMC (or 3-71 with an adapter plate) on Ford flatheads. This manifold requires a "pruned" GMC case, meaning that the lower mounting flange is milled away and the case is drilled and tapped around the outlet opening for bolts installed upward through the manifold flange. In their complete, fully polished kits, H&H includes a 4-71 blower that has been

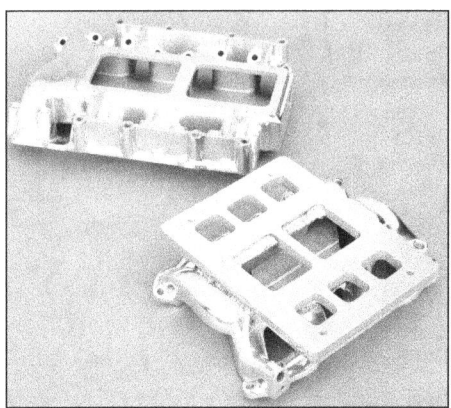

One-piece 6-71 manifolds for early Chrysler Hemis are still easy to find (rear), but how about that cute 4-71 piece Don made to fit the little Dodge Red Ram?

record with one of these new Hampton blowers the first time they tried it.

So Hampton, a very lively 72 years old when we took the accompanying photos, is certainly not relegated to old school. In fact, he was driving one of his other customer's 250+ mph nostalgia Top Fuel dragsters, and teaching his 24-year-old son Wes the business, so we'd say that Hampton Blowers—like GMC-style superchargers for street and racing—are going to be around a good while yet.

Excuse the messy background; that's the way things are at H&H. But the installed 4-71 is not only good-looking, but strong performing on any flathead. The water-pump pulleys and tensioners are part of the package, and the whole thing comes polished.

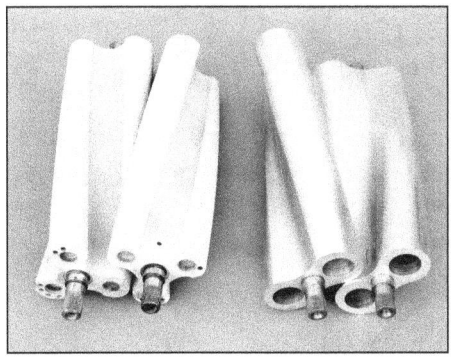

Hampton's latest trick, shown next to a pair of crusty 8V-71 GMC rotors, are what he calls "Super Too" 2-lobe rotors CNC-machined from billet with a 60-degree helical twist. You don't need these for street, but they pump enough air for Top Fuel, and they don't need Teflon strips.

Besides the Navarro flathead blower intake manifold and 3-carb adapter, H&H can supply a rebuilt and pruned 4-71 GMC blower and ribbed drive snout. The only difference from the original Navarro setup is the Gilmer belt drive, which Barney would have used if it were available back then.

Not only has H&H reproduced the entire S.Co.T. blower for the flathead, but the original manifold and drive, as well.

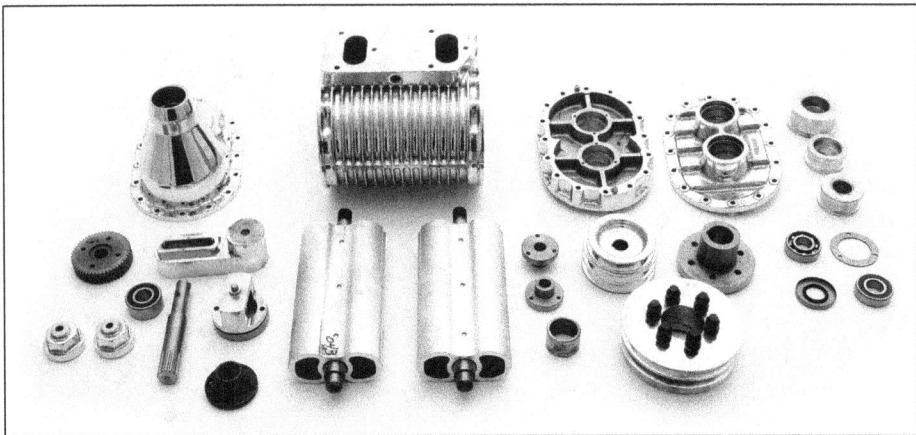

The major differences between the H&H blower and the S.Co.T. are the extruded and machined 53-series GMC-style rotors, with straight-splined shafts and helical gears in place of tapered keyway shafts and straight-cut gears—all significant improvements.

Another upgrade is sealed bearings, so the zerk fittings are just for looks. The front cover has S.Co.T. lettering, while the rear has none.

The new S.Co.T. is driven by two V-belts, as original, and it only comes one way—fully and beautifully polished.

thus machined, as well as fully prepped and clearanced by one of the above performance GMC rebuilders.

Bigger news is that, using the same foundry that made Navarro products for decades, H&H has exactly repatterned and is reproducing the 144-ci Ford V-8 version of the S.Co.T. Roots blower for the first time since the early 1950s. Externally this blower is identical to the original, including S.Co.T. insignia (not Italmeccanica), S.A.E. bolts and threads, and an integral 2-carb inlet. Internally, however, the blower is significantly upgraded with GMC 53-series style rotors made from machined extrusions, with straight-cut splined driveshafts (rather than the tapered keyway shaft of the original). Further, the new version has helical-cut drive gears and sealed rear bearings (zerk fittings are retained for looks only). The original intake manifold has been exactly reproduced, including pop-off valve, except that the idler pulley mount has been slightly improved. These blowers are available separately, or as a complete, fully polished, twin-V-belt driven system, as original.

The New Roots

Earlier in this book we discussed several types of superchargers that were installed on factory-built vehicles, both in the United States and Europe. But these were high-end, limited-production cars such as a Bentley, Bugatti, and Mercedes overseas or a Duesenberg, Cord, and Studebaker Avanti here. Even the Paxton blowers fitted to mid-1950s Fords were strictly for homologation so they could use them for racing. The total number of these early factory-supercharged vehicles could probably be counted in the hundreds.

The only true production blower made and installed on assembly-line vehicles in large quantities over a long period of time that we have discussed so far is the venerable 71-series GMC. Over its 60-some-year lifespan, literally millions of these blowers (and other models, such as 53-series) were produced and used on daily working trucks, buses, boats, trains, and who knows what else? Today, the vast majority of them have gone to scrap.

Eaton Superchargers

Only one supercharger comes close to the GMC's production numbers, and that's the relatively new, and still evolving, Eaton. If you know anything about cars or Detroit, you know the Eaton name. Founded in 1911 as a "Gear and Axle Co.," today it has 80,000-plus employees making a huge variety of products worldwide. You probably know them best for transmissions and rear ends, but they have been supplying all the Detroit manufacturers with driveline, powertrain, and electrical components for decades. They are an original equipment manufacturer. They don't make

MODERN ROOTS BLOWERS

In this colorful cutaway of an early Eaton blower, we are looking at what we would consider the bottom, or outlet side. The large elbow on the left is the inlet duct, feeding into the inlet port located in the "top" of the back plate. The drive pulley is at the right, or front.

aftermarket, or "specialty," parts. And since 1984 they have been making superchargers for OEM applications—millions of them.

The first production Eaton blower appeared on the 1989 Ford Thunderbird V-6 Super Coupe. Its M90 (90-ci) model was used as factory original equipment on these T-Birds through 1995. In 1992 Buick switched from an intercooled turbocharger on its vaunted Turbo Regal V-6, to the same M90 Eaton blower. And in 1995 Mercedes-Benz added them to C-class and other models. As of 1998, more than 550,000 Eaton superchargers had been installed on new cars. As of 2006, that number reached a staggering 3,500,000 units installed on production vehicles ranging from little Ford Festivas, VW Golfs, and BMW Mini Coopers to Saturn Ions, Chevy Cobalts, Mercedes coupes, Pontiac Grand Prix's, Jaguar V-8s, Cadillac STSs, certain Ford Mustangs, and even the SVT pickup truck, to name some. Since 2006, Eaton's production plant in Athens, Georgia, has been pumping out 500,000 units per year, while another in Tczew, Poland, has been supplying Europe (and Japan, Korea, China, and South America) with another 200,000 annually. You get the picture.

What is very interesting is that, after researching all the different ways to supercharge an automotive engine, Eaton chose the century-old, belt-driven, Roots design. That says a

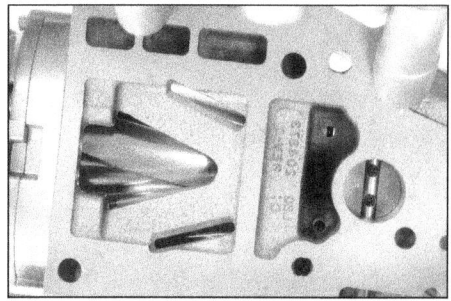

This look at the underside of a mid-Gen Eaton gives you a better idea of the location and shape of the outlet, as well as the location of the integral bypass valve butterfly.

whole lot about its effectiveness, simplicity, and reliability. But what is really exciting is that not only has Eaton built millions of these blowers, but that it has devoted its huge research, engineering, and testing capabilities to modernizing and idealizing this simple but ancient design for the first time since GM did it back in the 1930s. You might think that high-powered drag racers such as John Force, Kenny Bernstein, or Don Prudhomme have optimized the GM-style blower with their mega teams and sizable facilities, but they are hampered by restrictive rules in the first place, and their operations don't hold a candle to a world corporation like Eaton.

Much more significantly, this is the first time the Roots blower design has been rethought and reconfigured specifically to pump more air into an automotive engine to increase its performance. Remember, the old GMC 71, even though it was optimized with helical 3-lobe rotors, was designed specifically to pump non-pressurized air into a 2-stroke diesel engine that ran at low RPM doing heavy-hauling grunt work. It was never intended to force-feed high-performance, high-revving automotive gasoline engines. The Eaton supercharger is.

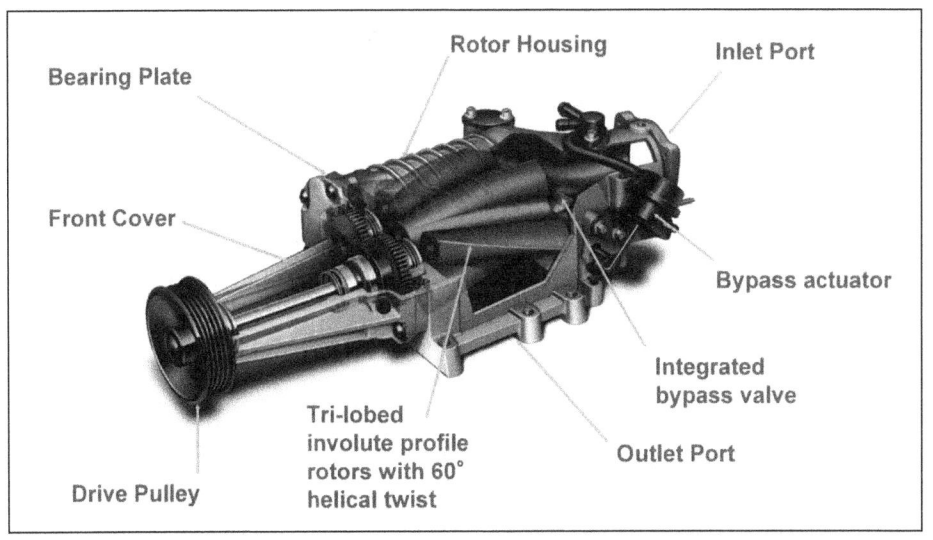

In this cutaway of a more recent generation of the 3-lobe blower, viewed from the top, we get a better view of the inlet duct entering the rotor case at the upper rear. You can't see the bypass valve in this view, but you can see where it's located.

A COMPLETE GUIDE TO STREET SUPERCHARGING

A cutaway of the drive snout shows the location of bearings, seals, and a preload spring. The black piece between the shaft and the drive gear is called the Isolator/Coupling. Made of some sort of plastic or composite, it acts partly as a vibration damper, and is the one part prone to wearing out.

Unlike GMC blowers, whose helical gears can be shimmed in or out to adjust "timing" clearance between the rotors, the Eaton uses straight-cut gears, which are pressed on the keyed rotor shafts, and require no further adjustment. As long as the bearings, seals, and gear teeth aren't worn, don't touch this assembly.

Interestingly, after much research and testing, Eaton selected a 3-lobe design with a 60-degree helical twist, the same as the GMC 71. The big difference is the shape of the rotor lobes, which are more oval, with pointy tips, called "involute" by Eaton. The other major difference is the inlet and outlet of the new blower, which draws air in at the rear of the case, propels it forward between the twisted rotor lobes (like the GM does), then pumps it out a triangular exit port located on the forward bottom side.

These Eaton blowers have been made in four sizes (lengths), consequently designated M45, M62, M90, and M112 according to their cubic-inch displacement per revolution. As of this writing, these blowers have also evolved through five generations, the most noticeable changes being to the inlet/outlet ports. The first generation (1989–1993) is easily recognizable by an oval inlet port. The second generation has a rectangular, slightly lowered inlet port and a revised outlet shape, and is 4-percent more efficient. Later generations included improved powder coating on the rotors as well as further enlargement or relocation of the inlet/outlet, especially on the larger models.

While the Eaton engineers have developed the most efficient and powerful Roots blower, by far, much of this has ironically been abetted by strictures imposed by the automotive manufacturers. First, it had to be relatively low in cost overall, uncomplicated to install, and not prone to warranty failures, which were met by the Roots blower's simple and reliable attributes. Second, it had to fit under modern low-profile hoods and in crowded engine compartments. This meant the blower had to be small in overall size, yet still pump a lot of air efficiently; this was a primary factor in the low, rear location of the inlet port. The fact that this inlet design increased the blower's volumetric efficiency was a double plus.

Another major concern of all vehicle manufacturers today is not only meeting ever-stricter emissions requirements, but also meeting government-imposed fuel efficiency (CAFE) standards. Eaton chose the Roots blower as the best combination of bottom-end power (over a centrifugal) and low parasitic drag (over a screw-type, which takes a small amount of power to compress air internally). To further minimize any "pumping loss" or heating of the air passing through the blower during part-throttle driving, Eaton added a vacuum-operated bypass valve and passage to all its blowers. We tend to forget that in normal driving the engine is very seldom in wide-open-throttle, full-power mode. But WOT is the only time the blower is actually being used. The rest of the time, at part-throttle, cruise, idle, or deceleration, even a supercharged engine has vacuum in the intake manifold. With the Eaton, this vacuum activates a valve to open a passage between the throttle plenum and the intake manifold, bypassing the supercharger completely. Tests show that a second gen M90, with this valve, produces only a 1/3-hp parasitic loss while cruising at 60 mph. Later generations are even more efficient.

Finally, a huge amount of design time and energy at Eaton has been spent to meet a nebulous requirement commonly known in Detroit as NVH. This stands for Noise, Vibration, and Harshness, and it's something those in suits at the Big Three want none of. They seem to have no clue that most of us want to put a supercharger on a car to make it shake, rattle, and roll. What is the logic of tuning the rumble of the free-flow dual exhaust on a V-8 Mustang, and then demanding that the supercharger make no noise? Anyway, several of the smaller design peculiarities of the Eaton blowers, such as the small slots alongside the triangular outlet port, are done simply to lower the NVH of the unit.

The big news from Eaton, just as this book was going to press, was the introduction of an all-new generation of Eaton supercharger designated the

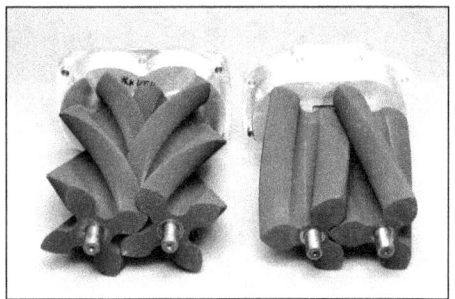

The big Eaton news as of 2008 was the introduction of the all-new, 4-lobe, high-helix TVS model. As you can see, the "involute" rotor shape stays the same, but the amount of "twist" over the rotor length increases from 60 to 160 degrees. This not only greatly increases the pumping capacity of these new models, but also significantly increases their efficiency.

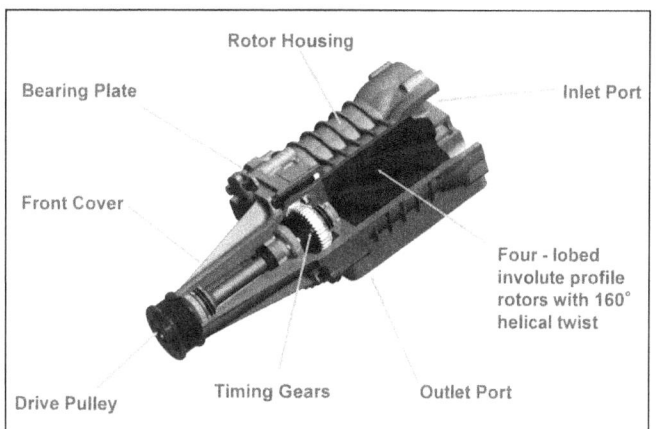

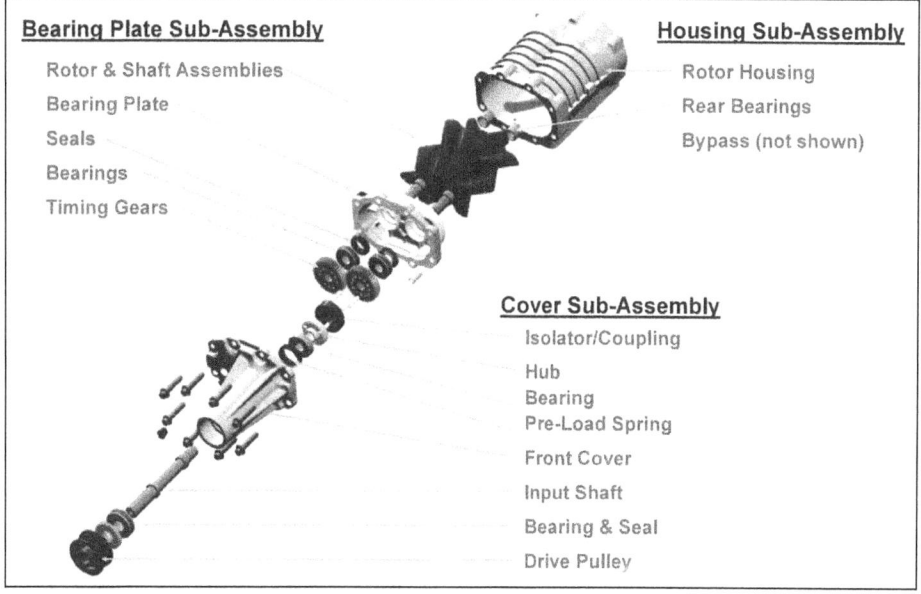

These cutaway and exploded views of the new TVS Eaton clearly show its inner workings and hidden mechanisms, which aren't many. It's still a Roots blower, which is a very simple—yet effective, and now efficient— mechanical device.

TVS (for Twin Vortices Series). While it maintains the same involute rotor-lobe shape, the major difference in this new blower is that it has four lobes instead of three, and they are twisted 160 degrees over the length of the rotor, as opposed to 60 degrees for the previous style (the new rotors, in GMC-type racing blower parlance, would be called "high-helix"). Since adding an extra lobe to the rotor reduces air-pumping cavity space in the blower, these new units are slightly larger in diameter than the M-series to make up for it. The inlet and outlet ports have also been significantly enlarged and streamlined, varying somewhat from model to model, and obviously continuing to change with future application needs.

Further, by refining the efficiencies of this supercharger to the point they have (the fifth-generation M112, in rigorous Eaton testing, showed an isentropic efficiency maximum of 62 percent; the new TVS R1900 recorded 75-percent efficiency in the same testing), the Eaton engineers have found that spinning this blower faster simply results in more air pumped and more power made in the engine. For example, in the first factory OEM installation of an Eaton TVS R2300 on the 2008 ZR1 Corvette, the blower is driven 2.3 times crank speed (that's 130-percent overdrive!) to make 10.5 psi of intercooled boost. This produces an SAE-certified 638 hp at 6,500 rpm and 605 ft-lbs of torque at 3,800 rpm, making the LS9 6.2L small-block the most-powerful true production engine ever offered by Detroit.

As this was written, the new TVS line included R2300, R1900, and R1320 size blowers (size denoted in cubic centimeters; the R2300 has a 2.3L pumping volume), but several other sizes were planned, mostly for smaller engines.

But the example of the brawny new Corvette probably explains why, even with millions of Eaton blowers now in duty on factory-built, daily-driven vehicles, virtually no aftermarket cottage industries have sprung up to make parts to modify or "hop up" any of the myriad factory-installed Eatons. A few have come and gone, and there may be more. If you look, you'll probably find sources for things such as overdrive blower pulleys to increase boost and power, but they haven't been plentiful. The simple fact seems to be that the Eaton superchargers are so refined and effective that they really

CHAPTER 6
Adapting an Eaton to Your Engine

When hot rodders first discovered the powers of supercharging, shortly after World War II, the first trick was to find a usable blower. The second was to figure out how to adapt it to a hot rod engine and make it work. The first problem was lessened considerably when GMC started bolting blowers on its diesel truck fleet. But these blowers took some rebuilding to make them work on hot rod engines, and the builder still had to adapt it. Soon, certain entrepreneurial hot rod types identified a market and filled it with GMC blower rebuilding services and installation and drive kits to mount and run them on popular performance engines. And, as you've just read, that market continues to thrive, even after that huge source of factory blowers has gone.

But now we have a new source of excellent OEM superchargers designed specifically for increased performance on automotive engines of all sizes, and only one enterprising hot rod blower builder has seized upon this ready resource to build systems to bolt them onto popular hot rod engines (Jerry Magnuson of Magna Charger, as we shall see next), and individual adaptations of these blowers is uncommon. Maybe the vast majority of automotive tinkerers and enthusiasts today would strongly prefer a pre-engineered, ready-to-work, bolt-on system, rather than try to cobble something together themselves. Nothing wrong with that.

But the fact remains that Eaton has been building these excellent superchargers since the 1980s, and OEM manufacturers have installed them on several million vehicles currently in the field. If you happen to be one of the apparently now-rare types of do-it-yourself hot rodders, and you'd like to adapt a supercharger to your engine, these Eaton blowers are out there. They don't need to be reworked for automotive performance use, they come in all sorts of shapes and sizes, and given the huge supply and relatively low demand, prices are amazingly affordable.

Larry Metz, a retired fireman and member of the Street Rods Forever car club from Arcadia, California, is just such a hot rodder. In the modest garage/shop behind his house he has a mill, a lathe, and a heli-arc welder, among other handy tools, and he and his sons have built all sorts of fun cars, for their own enjoyment. For his past few projects, Larry has discovered the ready accessibility, easy adaptability, and surprising performance-plus-

Larry's very orange, completely home-built '32, seen here visiting the Bonneville Salt Flats on one trip, features a unique fiberglass body from New Zealand patterned after a 3-window coupe, but with a chopped, lift-off fiberglass top. The 1949–1953 Ford flathead is a modest 276 ci, with a 600-cfm Edelbrock 4-barrel adapted to the M90 Eaton blower. The trans is a Ford T-5 5-speed with overdrive.

reliability of used OEM Eaton superchargers. When we visited, Larry was inspecting the blower system he adapted to the 276-inch 8BA flathead engine in his '32 Ford roadster, which had traveled 4,300 miles on Americruise in 2000, competed very successfully in the 2003 Rod & Custom Ego-Rama, and had driven 30,000+ trouble-free miles to plenty of other places.

Larry decided the first-series M90 Eaton from the 1989 to 1994 T-Bird V-6 Super Coupe would adapt well to his flathead. He found one on eBay for $150 and another at a swap meet for $100, both in excellent condition. This is the blower that had been on the car 30,000 miles. The reason he took it off was because his home-made aluminum drive pulley had started to gall on the blower shaft/bearing. Rather than try to replace the bearing or shaft, he found it much simpler and cheaper to install the front-drive assembly from another good, used blower. That's why the body is polished but the snout isn't yet. A hardened, flatground washer between the remachined pulley and the bearing solved the problem.

This blower was used when he got it, and had just gone 30,000+ miles in a hot rod, including drag racing and other such use, and the rotors still look like this. As we said in the prior section, rotor clearance is set at the factory, and as long as there is no visible wear or damage, leave the rotor/gear set alone. This one looks as good as new.

The first part that might wear is this isolator/coupler that connects the driveshaft to the drive gear by pins. You can't get individual parts like this from Eaton, but check the Internet for sources, or a blower rebuilder such as Dyer's.

Larry is a pretty crafty guy. He built this manifold to fit the blower to his flathead from aluminum flat stock and tubing. He cut and machined the pieces, tack-welded them together with his TIG, then took it to "Someone who can weld lots better than me" to have the final welding done. These early Eatons have an external bypass valve that's part of the manifold on a Ford, so Larry got a bolt-on bypass-valve assembly, with actuator, from Magnuson, and added it at the rear of the intake. He also added a homemade pop-off valve at the front to guard against any back-fire damage.

Adapting an Eaton to Your Engine CONTINUED

The fabricated plate (left) mounts to the front of the intake manifold and helps mount the A/C compressor and alternator, as well as the idler/tensioner pulleys for the Poly-V belt. Larry went with a 6-rib belt, rather than an 8-rib as on the T-Bird, because many more lengths were available, plus he runs 5 to 6 psi on the small flathead, whereas the T-Bird cranks 10 to 12 psi. He has also found that a spring-loaded tensioner is not needed for this small-size system.

Here's a close-up look at the carburetor mounting unit Larry whittled from a chunk of billet aluminum. Not bad for an amateur. A bolt-on plate mounts the AFB-style carb, and the chrome tube connects to the bypass valve. The airflow path could be more streamlined, but this is simple, fits the available underhood space, and has worked fine under all driving conditions.

This rear view with nearly everything hooked up shows the relationship of the carb housing to the blower and the bypass valve. The black diaphragm opens the valve whenever there is vacuum in the manifold (idle, decel, cruise), routing the air/fuel mix from the carb directly into the manifold, bypassing the blower. This saves a little horsepower (fuel) and engine heat. As soon as you hit the throttle, vacuum drops, the valve closes, and everything is pumped through the blower. Such a system isn't needed on a hot rod, and you could eliminate it. But if you really drive your car, as Larry obviously does, why not include it?

Larry's next project, seen here in mock-up stages, mounts the same model Eaton on a similar flathead slated for a 1940 Ford. In this case, Larry shaved the top off a 2-carb aluminum intake manifold with his mill, carved out a matching top plate to accept the blower, and will weld the two pieces together. But we mainly wanted to show how he fabricated and routed the Poly-V belt system to drive not only the blower, but the A/C compressor as well. A large flathead V-belt drives the two stock water pumps and the alternator.

In between the two flatheads, Larry whipped up this combination of an M112 Eaton blower from a 2003 Ford Lightning pickup adapted to a 270-inch Dodge Red Ram Hemi in his "barn find" 1932 Plymouth coupe. This particular Eaton has a wide bolt-pattern base on the bottom and an unusual top inlet at the rear of the case. Making this manifold was a bit more complicated and required a bit more professional help—though it's still relatively simple and incorporates the bypass valve. The 3-carb housing Larry made (with outlet at the bottom rear) was trick and old-timey, but didn't allow room for air cleaners, which are very important for street blowers. So he made a new one for a lower single 4-barrel, and drove this car extensively, as well as drag raced it several times, with no problems and tons of fun.

CHAPTER 6

We've shown several Magna Charger blowers and accessories throughout the book, so this is a continuation. This display motor demonstrates a typical, polished, Gen 5 MP 112 3-lobe blower in a typical installation on an LS-style GM small-block. Since most OEM Eaton installations mount the blower with the belt drive at the front and the inlet facing the rear, to get a more direct, unrestricted inlet flowpath, Magnuson turns the blower around, using an intermediary shaft and belt to drive the blower from the rear, allowing a large, direct inlet at the front. The housing, drive, inlet, and manifold (including intercooler) are all made by Magna Charger. Only the rotors are Eaton.

While Magna Charger stresses the latest technology, and most systems are designed to directly interface with existing EFI and serpentine belts on late-model vehicles, Magnuson has a soft spot for traditional hot rods, as exemplified by the MP 112 carbureted kit seen on a display motor and completely assembled on Jerry's own 1929 roadster pickup. This very complete setup includes everything from a 2-piece intake manifold and blower with integral 4-barrel carb mount, to extended water pumps, front distributor drive, and necessary pulleys, tensioner, etc, for a Poly-V belt drive. Depending on other modifications, this blower can add 50 to 100 hp, yet incorporates the bypass valve for efficient cruising.

don't need any further tweaking in the opinion of the vast majority of happy drivers who have purchased vehicles equipped with them.

Magna Charger

Jerry Magnuson has been designing and building superchargers—specifically 3-lobe Roots-type blowers—for decades. We discuss his original Magna Charger line, built in the 1970s originally for Top Fuel motorcycles, and later for automotive V-8s, in Chapter 4, Vintage Superchargers. When Jerry became aware of Eaton's development of an all-new Roots blower design, he knew a good thing when he saw it. He sold his existing Magna Charger line to B&M in 1987, and decided to concentrate his efforts on the new, emerging Eaton line of OEM superchargers. Not only did Jerry work with Eaton engineers as a consultant on this new project during its ongoing development, but he became (as Magnuson Products, Inc.) the sole factory-authorized rebuilder of OEM-installed Eaton blowers for North America, as well as the sole distributor of Eaton superchargers and replacement parts.

However, Jerry has always been a typical hot rodder who, when he sees a good thing, wants to make it better. So he was soon tweaking the Eaton design, primarily in the areas of inlet/outlet size and configuration to improve volumetric efficiency. Remember, the Eaton Corporation had to design a product that would satisfy a wide range of corporate executives from different companies, meet regional legal requirements, and hit the bogey on nebulous—but important—strictures such as NVH. Jerry didn't throw these design criteria out the window. In fact, his current Magna Charger installation packages for late-model American cars and trucks are not only 50-state emissions legal (each having its own CARB EO number in most cases), but also maintain factory warranty. Still, he was able to make design changes to improve the blower's performance.

Having started in the early 1990s with retrofit kits, using his own reworked blower housing, for GM pickup trucks and SUVs, Jerry's Magna Charger line today (as of 2009) covers the full GM truck/SUV line (including Escalades, Chevy SSR, and Hummers), Pontiac GTO and G-8, Cadillac CTS-V, Corvette (including Callaway), and 4.6L 3V Ford Mustangs.

These supercharger systems include not only the fully revised and optimized Magna Charger blower, but also: all related components including an equal-flow intake manifold; high-volume fuel injectors, fuel rails, and pump; drive system with

Over the years, Magnuson Products has built and branded blower kits for several subcontractors, Toyota Racing Division (TRD) being one of the largest. Most of these tend to look more like factory installations, such as this Cosworth kit that mounts an MP-62 blower on a Mazda MX-5. Yes, there's a blower in there. You'd know it if you were in the driver's seat.

On the other hand, if you want to bolt a blower on top of your 1955–up small-block Chevy, and add a carburetor on top, Magna Charger has that, too. This rodder made his own adapter to mount three chromed 2-barrels on the 4-barrel flange. Note that the vacuum actuator/internal bypass valve is included.

This Magna Charger MP 112 installation on a 2005–2006 4.6L 3V Mustang engine is typical in that it includes the blower, manifold, high-flow fuel injectors and fuel rails, a computer reprogrammer module, and a complete water-to-air intercooler system (you can see the two water-hose connectors at the rear of the manifold). But it accepts the stock Ford throttle body and other EFI components, uses the stock serpentine-belt system, fits under the stock hood, and maintains smog certification, while adding about 50-percent more street horsepower.

belts, pulleys, and idler; and a computer module that reprograms the factory ECU for proper calibration of the system (including automatic transmission shift points, line pressure, and converter lockup, if applicable). All of the above examples also include a water-to-air intercooler system consisting of a heat exchanger built into the manifold below the blower, a second (larger) heat exchanger that mounts at the front of the vehicle, and related hoses and electric pump. Each of these systems also uses the stock vehicle throttle body and MAF sensor (which mounts to the custom Magna Charger intake port or elbow) to maintain emissions legality, and they all fit under the stock vehicle hood.

To give some idea of the effectiveness of one of these systems, the Radix Max Magna Charger for 2007–2009 GM Vortec trucks and SUVs, using the new MP1900 TVS supercharger, delivers an increase of 124 hp at the rear wheels—which is substantial—yet carries its own emissions-legal CARB E.O. number. In another example, using the Gen 5 3-lobe blower, an LS-2-powered 2005 Pontiac GTO, factory rated at 400 hp at the flywheel, produced 470 hp at the rear wheels and ran 11.28 at 126 in the quarter mile. More importantly—and reflected in

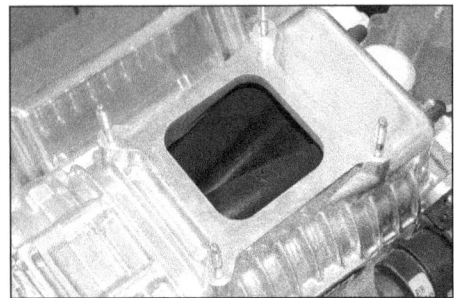
This view shows the integral 4-barrel mount on the top of the MP 122H, which is a fifth-generation, 3-lobe blower displacing 122 ci per revolution.

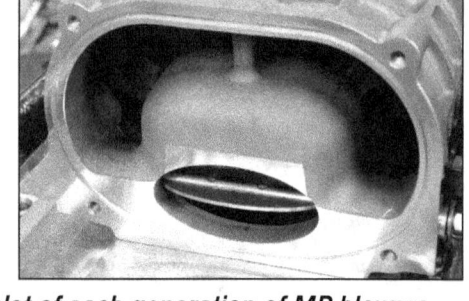
As you can see in the prior photo, the inlet of each generation of MP blowers has increased, with Gen 4-up incorporating the bypass valve and passages in the blower case. Previous models use a round butterfly valve, like a carburetor, but the newer TVS models not only have a cavernous inlet, but also a larger oval bypass valve, seen here in opened and closed positions.

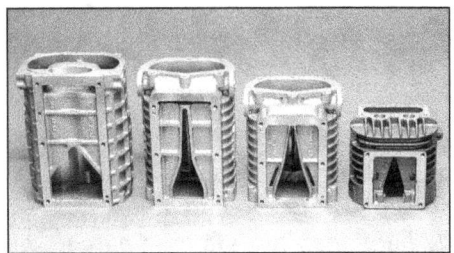
To demonstrate the evolution of Magna Charger housings for Eaton blowers, this lineup starts with (right to left) a 62-ci third-generation, a 90-ci fourth gen, a 112-ci fifth gen, and ends with the MP 2300 sixth-generation, which uses the 4-lobe, high-helix TVS rotor package and displaces 140 cubic inches.

The 4-lobe TVS Magna Chargers are not only slightly larger in diameter, but have a characteristic waffle-pattern case. This one is finished in optional black powder coat, with a carbon-fiber intermediate shaft, and is the slightly smaller MP 1900 (116-ci) setup for installation on a 2008 Pontiac G8, including the Pontiac throttle body already installed. Note the water outlets under the belt drive for the intercooler contained in the manifold.

the quarter-mile E.T.—the horsepower increase afforded by the Roots blower is substantial from 1,200 through 6,000 rpm, meaning that it adds much more low-end torque and considerably more aggregate horsepower "under the curve" than either a naturally aspirated engine or most other types of superchargers.

Besides these complete installation packages for late-model cars and trucks (with more undoubtedly added by the time you read this), Magnuson also offers generic or "hot rod" systems for the various generations of Chevrolet/GM small-block V-8s, including LS versions, and even for the venerable Ford flathead V-8. Most of these are available either in single 4-barrel carbureted or electronically fuel injected designs.

We should also point out here that, while Jerry began by making modifications to Eaton superchargers for his initial aftermarket kits, today his Magna Chargers use either the Gen 5 3-lobe or the TVS 4-lobe Eaton rotor package, but all other components—case, gears, end plate/drive snout, bypass valve, manifolds, and so on—are designed and manufactured by Magnuson.

Plus, over the past decade, Magnuson Products has produced and "labeled" Eaton-based supercharger kits for numerous factory-adjunct and aftermarket entities, beginning with Ford SVO/Ford Performance Parts, GM Performance Parts, and Toyota's TRD line, and including

MODERN ROOTS BLOWERS

This is the larger MP 2300 TVS blower, in as-cast finish, installed on a 2008 C-6 Corvette.

Known as the Radix Max for installation on 2007–up GM Vortec Max engines in pickups and SUVs, this MP 1900 blower does away with the intermediate shaft, having an extended rotor drive shaft that runs through the huge inlet housing, thus putting drive and the inlet at the front of the blower. Even with the high-flow fuel injectors that come with it, this system interfaces with the GM Active Fuel Management, and is 50-state legal with its own CARB E.O. number.

Finally, every Magna Charger, large or small, is run-tested and gauge-checked before it is shipped out. Even though the TVS blower in the background requires a huge electric motor to drive it against static boost on this test stand, it takes less than one horsepower to drive it on an engine.

And, as we showed earlier, Magnuson does constant research and testing on a fully equipped SuperFlow engine dyno (shown here during a magazine test of a carbureted MP 122), as well as a chassis dyno cell.

numerous others in the United States and abroad such as Lotus, Cosworth, Moss Motors, Roush Racing, Jackson Racing, Neuspeed, Downey Racing, Weslake, Alpine, and Marine Power, to name some.

And Magnuson remains a remanufacturing source for all factory-installed Eaton superchargers, as well as any of the aftermarket units mentioned above. While Magnuson doesn't sell individual rebuild parts (such as bearings, seals, etc.), they do sell replacement or upgrade components such as nose covers, drive assemblies, drive pulleys, inlet housings, throttle bodies, and ancillary parts like fuel injectors, pumps, and intercooler/heat exchanger components.

Finally, while the aftermarket may be slow to offer "hop-up" goodies for the millions of vehicles out there running Eaton superchargers now, one way to increase the performance of such cars would be to swap the factory blower for a Magna Charger. The current Magna Charger line includes the MP 45, 62, 90, and 112 in fourth or fifth generation; the fifth-generation MP 122 in either rear-inlet EFI style or top-inlet 4-barrel carb body; and the sixth-generation (TVS 4-rotor style) MP 1900 and 2300. With the exception of the Buick/Olds V-6, which requires an available adapter plate, each of these Magna Chargers will bolt on in place of a similar-size factory Eaton blower. Plus Magna Chargers are available as-cast, polished, black powder coated, or in a new Chrome Coat.

CHAPTER 7

SCREW-TYPE SUPERCHARGERS

The third type of supercharger in common use today is known as the screw-type, the twin-screw, or by its parent name, the Lysholm screw compressor. These units look much like the Eaton-style Roots blower, and appear to operate similarly. Both have similar cases, with nearly identical inlet and outlet ports. They both house a pair of multi-lobe, helical-twisted, meshing rotors. And the belt-drive and rotor timing gear arrangement appear the same. Both are also positive-displacement pumps, meaning they take in and pump out the same amount of air with each full revolution of the rotors.

But similarities can be deceiving. In operation, the screw compressor acts opposite a Roots blower. That is, in a Roots the two rotors turn "away" from each other, carrying air in their cavities around the case walls, to dump it out the opening at the bottom. The meshing of the rotors in the middle of the case forms a seal so the air can't escape back up through the blower; instead it is pumped into the intake manifold, where it is compressed. As we learned in the opening of the Roots blower section, this is not the

Other than the fact that this Whipple Supercharger is painted white, which is unusual, it looks very much like the Eaton Roots-type blowers in Chapter 6. The ribbed case is similar; it has two parallel rotors inside, turned by a belt from the front, with a pair of gears inside the front cover to turn both rotors. The inlet, fed by a large duct from the engine's EFI throttle body, is at the blower's rear, while it exits out the bottom, directly into the engine's intake manifold. But looks are deceptive.

smoothest or the most streamlined way to compress air, but the Roots blower does an excellent job of moving a lot of air simply and quickly.

In a screw compressor the rotors turn the opposite direction, "toward" or "into" each other. These rotors are also dissimilar, one having female (concave) cavities and the other having male (convex) lobes that closely fit—but do not touch—the female cavities. To make it work properly, it usually has more female cavities than male lobes. But let's not get bogged down in technicalities at this point.

The easiest way to see the operational difference between a Roots and a screw blower is to think of a simple Roots with straight-cut rotors, an inlet on the top, and an outlet on the bottom. When the rotors turn, they simply pump (or paddle might be a better term) air straight from the top hole, around the case walls, and out the bottom hole. The screw compressor, as its name implies, must have twisted, or helical, blades on the rotors (like threads on a screw) to pump air axially, or longitudinally, from one end of the blower case to the other (i.e., back-to-front) rather than top-to-bottom. The ancient Greek inventor Archimedes devised this type of pump around 200 BC. It had a single "rotor" that looked like a giant piece of spiral pasta, inside a barely-larger-diameter pipe. By turning the spiral rotor with a handle, this device would raise water from one

SCREW-TYPE SUPERCHARGERS

While the previous example looked more like a factory installation, here's one all shined up on a show car, in this case a late Ford Modular Motor in an early Mustang. The blower is a Kenne Bell, which has a squarer, flatter case, but it mounts to the engine, and is driven by a belt, in exactly the same manner.

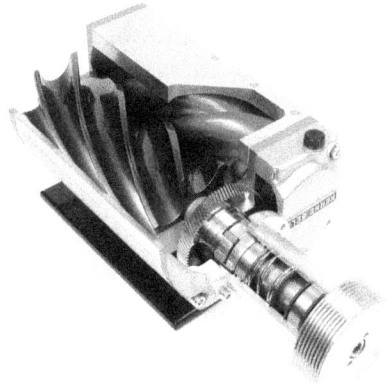 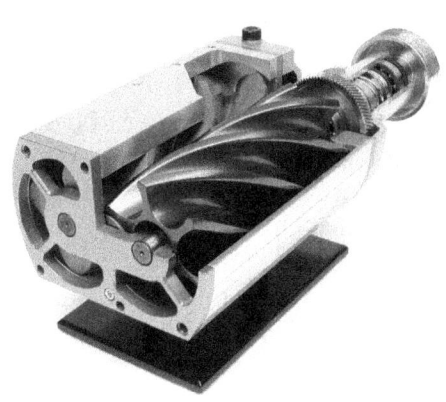

But what's inside the screw compressor is quite different, as these cutaways of a Kenne Bell show. To begin with, the rotors turn the opposite direction from a Roots blower. The two rotors are also completely different-shaped, one having protruding lobes, the other having "cavities." Plus the path of air is different; while a basic Roots draws air in through a hole in the top and pumps it out a similar hole in the bottom, the screw compressor draws air in at the rear of the case/rotors, and propels it forward (like a screw or propeller, as its name implies), expelling it from an outlet near the front of the case. If the rotor gears weren't in the way, it could go right out the front; in this example, the triangular outlet opening is toward the top.

level to another, through the pipe. Similar devices are still used today in rock quarries and gravel plants to elevate this heavy stuff. For much lighter air, you can see why two meshing spiral rotors would work better to pump it through the case.

But wait, as they say, there's more. Not only do these spiral rotors pump air from one end of the case to the other, but their very carefully designed, machined, and timed male/female rotors also "squish" the air between them as they move it. That is, the screw compressor is not only a positive-displacement pump, but it also has internal compression (like a vane supercharger), so it is also a true compressor. To keep it in simple terms, the compression inside the screw blower is done in a linear, streamlined fashion, which adds little extra work or agitation to the air, as opposed to the abrupt backflow compression of a Roots, which occurs mostly in the manifold. For these reasons, both the volumetric and (especially) the adiabatic efficiencies of the screw-type compressor are quite high, especially at higher-boost levels.

The Lysholm screw compressor for pumping air was designed and patented by Svenska Rotor Maskiner AB (SRM) in Sweden in the 1930s, whose chief engineer was a Alf Lysholm. For years, because of the exceptionally high cost of machining the two mismatching, convoluted rotors, these compressors were used primarily on large stationary engines, or in applications requiring a highly reliable source of oil-free air, such as airplane or submarine cabin pressurizing. Over the years, SRM made or licensed hundreds of designs and sizes of screw compressors for industrial, aeronautic, refrigeration, and other uses around the world.

In the United States, between 1986 and 1988, Norm Drazy painstakingly developed a large screw-type supercharger, using a 4-lobe male rotor and a 6-lobe female rotor (turning 30-percent slower), called the PSI, hoping to introduce it to Top Fuel drag racing. In dyno testing, the 385-ci prototype PSI made the same horsepower (1,260 on alcohol) at 28 pounds of boost as a 14-71 (552 ci) at 36 psi. Plus the outlet temperature of the PSI was 85 degrees compared to 150 for the 14-71. Unfortunately the PSI was banned from Top Fuel by the NHRA, but the PSI and a special large Whipple screw compressor have become the standards in Top Alcohol drag classes and boat racing, not only because of their high efficiency, but also because they don't need to be "re-stripped" with Teflon after every round.

In the first edition of this book (1984) I stated that we would probably never see small versions of screw superchargers for automotive use because the cost of making them was prohibitive compared to other superchargers already available. I was obviously proved wrong, partly because of the capabilities of today's computer machining. SRM's parent company in Sweden, Opcon AB, formed a new company called Autorotor to develop screw compressors for the automotive market. It made several sizes of screw compressors for street and race applications, in at least a couple of design generations. In the early 1990s, Whipple Industries of Fresno, California, approached Opcon-Autorotor in Sweden, suggesting a few changes to its screw compressor design, which Autorotor made. Whipple then secured the rights to be the sole distributor for these blowers in the United States. Subsequently, Whipple made an agreement with Kenne Bell, whereby Whipple would concentrate on GM and racing applications and Kenne Bell would design and market kits for non-GM vehicles.

These initial Autorotor screw compressors had an extruded billet aluminum case, which could be cut to different lengths to vary blower displacement, the first being 1.3L and 1.5L. Later Autorotor redesigned its rotors—being the first redesign of a screw compressor specifically for automotive internal combustion engine use—and increased the output of these blowers to 1.8L and 2.2L using the same length cases. In about 1995, however, Opcon reorganized and SRM decided to release a new automotive screw compressor under its original name, Lysholm. This blower used rotors similar to the first-design Autorotor, but housed in a cast-aluminum case with distinctive fins in two sizes displacing 1.6L and 2.1L.

Since that time, both Whipple and Kenne Bell have begun making their own screw compressors, while Vortech Engineering recently announced that they had made an agreement with Lysholm Technologies of Sweden to import new Lysholm screw compressors in two sizes to fit applications for Ford Mustangs and LS-type GM V-8s. (There is more on this in following sections.)

In general, however, the beauty of the screw-type compressor is that it combines the advantages of the Roots blower with those of the vane compressor, without incurring the disadvantages of either. That is, it is a positive-displacement pump, so it provides good low-end boost; it has no contacting parts or friction drag other than the rotor gears; it therefore needs no internal lubrication; and it is perfectly balanced, like a Roots blower. Still it affords internal compression, like a vane supercharger, which greatly increases its adiabatic and volumetric efficiency over early-style Roots, especially in boost levels above 15 to 20 psi. In fact, screw compressors tend to see adiabatic efficiencies in the 80- to 85-percent range compared to about 50 percent for a well-clearanced GM-type Roots blower. It's definitely a good design, doesn't wear out, and is efficient under boost (in a vehicle) or in constant-pressure industrial applications.

The only drawback to a screw compressor in a vehicle—and it's relatively minor unless you're an OEM manufacturer trying to meet CAFE standards—is that the act of compressing air in the blower (even at 100-percent efficiency) takes a given amount of work, which creates a small amount of parasitic drag during the majority of street-driving time when the blower is not in boost mode. This has been addressed with blower-drive clutches as well as (now more common) vacuum-operated blower bypass valves.

Whipple

Art Whipple of Fresno, California, learned plenty about supercharging as owner and/or crew chief on a number of Top Fuel and Funny Car operations, including Ed "The Ace" McCulloch's *Revellution* Funny Car and the *Mr. Ed* fuel floppers. In 1986 he formed Whipple Industries and began looking into the prospects of screw-type compressors for drag race competition as well as for street use. Unfortunately the huge 9.8L Whipple Charger he designed for Top Fuel was banned by the NHRA, but it

 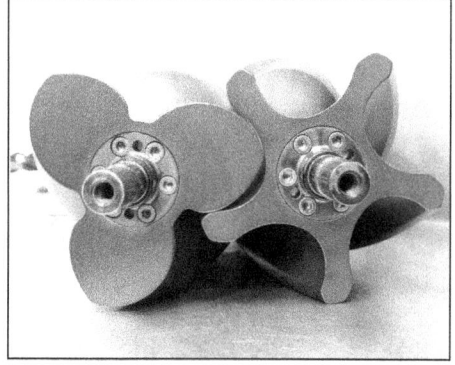

This look at a pair of Whipple rotors shows more clearly how they work. In these views, the male rotor on the left turns clockwise, the female one counter-clockwise. We are looking at the back of the blower, where they draw air in, and propel it forward. But as they pump the air forward, they also "squish" it between them, in the middle, therefore compressing it, before expelling it out the outlet at the other end, which would be at the bottom front in this view. Also note that the number of lobes on the rotors is different; consequently they must turn at different speeds, so the drive gears at the front are different sizes to make them mesh properly.

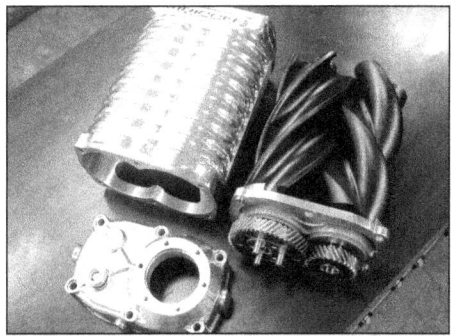

Earlier Whipples used Opcon and then Lysholm compressors from Sweden, but now Whipple makes its own rotors and rounded, finned cases in the United States. They can be ordered in polished or black powder-coat finish. Note the difference in rotor drive gear size evident here; the 3-lobe male rotor obviously turns faster than the larger female 5-lobe one. Current Whipples are made in 2.3L and 3.3L sizes.

This is a fully polished 3.3L Whipple and manifold (with water-to-air intercooler) for EFI installations on pre-LS small-block Chevys (a slightly different version is made for LS applications). The inlet at the back is covered in black tape, so it's hard to see (it accepts an elbow duct to mount a GM throttle body and MAF sensor). But note the vacuum diaphragm that actuates a bypass valve just inside the blower's inlet, which operates much the same as those on Eaton blowers.

These Whipple installations on late-model Mod-motored Ford Mustangs look "factory" and use Ford components such as the EFI throttle body. In fact, Whipple worked with Ford Racing to develop a Whipple/FRPP powertrain control module (PCM) to adjust fuel, spark, knock detection, transmission control, and other parameters to match blower output on 2005–2008 4.6L SC Mustangs. However, Whipple offers a wide range of "adjustable" options on all such blower applications, including intercooled or non-intercooled systems, and boost levels from 6 to 20 psi.

continues to be used in Top Alcohol and other boat racing classes.

At the other end of the scale, the 1.2L Sprintex screw compressor he initially imported from Australia proved too small for U.S. V-8 automotive applications, but in 1990 Whipple secured rights to import proper-sized screw compressors from Opcon Autorotor in Sweden. So the initial 1.3L/1.5L and then 1.8L/2.2L Whipple Charger systems for big- and small-block GM applications were based on these distinctive, squarish-cased blowers.

Then, after the 1995 change at Opcon, Whipple adopted the new Lysholm as the new Whipple Chargers, offering them not only as bolt-on kits for certain GM applications with electronic fuel injection, but also as stand-alone carbureted systems, with a Holley Dominator-size 4-barrel base opening cast in the top of the blower case. Further, Whipple even offered manifolds to mount two of these 2.1L blowers side-by-side, called the Quad Rotor. This system is still available from Whipple by special order.

In the 2000s, we're not sure exactly what was occurring with the Autorotor/Opcon/Lysholm companies in Sweden, but Lysholm cut a deal to supply its screw compressors directly to Ford for OEM use on the 2005–2006 Ford GT Supercar (and announced, in 2008, an agreement to supply units to Vortech, as you will see below).

A Whipple added to a recent Ford Lightning pickup looks clean, yet brawny. Note the large, low-restriction air cleaner isolated for cool-air intake.

CHAPTER 7

Speaking of brawny, this is the large, fully polished Whipple in what they call the Small-Block EFI Universal SC Kit. The manifold can be fitted with a "cupronickel" water-fed intercooler (especially for marine applications), and the wide-mouth inlet and high-flow injectors can be mated to your choice of F.A.S.T., Accell DFI, Holley, Autotronic, or other stand-alone EFI controlling system.

If you prefer carburetion to electronics, especially for your street rod, Whipple offers this blower that incorporates a single 4-barrel mount/inlet cast in the body. As you can see, its billet 10-rib Poly-V belt drive can be integrated with similar billet serpentine accessory drives.

Don't forget this company was founded by a Top Fuel/Funny Car racer. So if you want to go racing with a Whipple Charger, you can bolt a fuel injector hat on top, too.

Consequently, Whipple decided to bring all manufacturing, design, and testing in-house. Its current twin-screw Whipple Chargers are completely U.S.-made in 2.3L and 3.3L sizes, using a distinctive double-rounded, finned aluminum case that can be ordered in a polished or black powdercoat finish. The twin-screw rotors have three lobes on the male rotor and five cavities on the female counterpart. Cases for factory EFI applications feature a large rear-of-case inlet and a triangular outlet at the bottom front. These units can be adapted to single 4-barrel carburetor use with an intake elbow adapter, but cases with a large rectangular top opening are also available for performance applications with dual 4-barrels or a "hat"-type fuel injector bolted directly on top.

While they continue to refine and develop new products on a well-equipped dyno test cell, Whipple's current focus is primarily on street automotive and marine systems.

To give one example, for 2005–2008 Ford 4.6L Mustangs Whipple offers two bolt-on options.

The SC system includes the W140ax supercharger (similar to that used on the Ford GT), intake manifold, 34 lb/hr fuel injectors, 95-mm MAF sensor, and cold air/low restriction intake/filter system. This setup also includes an oversize intake-air bypass system for non-boost driving conditions, and a Whipple/Ford Racing computer reprogrammer to optimize fuel and spark functions to torque output. According to Whipple testing, at 6-psi of boost on 91-octane gasoline, this blower produces 415

Now if you want to build some real hot rod horsepower, Whipple makes this open-top case that accepts two big 4-barrels. This is not exactly how a screw compressor is supposed to work, but Whipple will tell you (and show you dyno sheets to confirm) that it works.

And if that's not enough to turn your crank, there's still the Whipple Quad Rotor, seen here proving its mettle on the Whipple dyno. It's rated at 850 to 1,500 hp. How much do you want?

hp—a 75-percent increase across a broad RPM range.

If that's not enough, Whipple's HO system for this application adds a large air-to-water intercooler and a different PCM re-flashing module to bump power levels to 500+ hp and 475 ft-lbs of torque on 91-octane gas with an otherwise stock engine.

And if you want to rebuild your motor to take it, do some custom tuning, and up your fuel octane, Whipple claims it can produce up to 20 psi and 700 rear-wheel horsepower with one blower, and as much as 1,500 hp with a Quad Rotor.

For much more information, photos, and diagrams on current Whipple offerings, as well as on screw-compressor operation and technology in general, we recommend visiting their website, where there's plenty of information.

Kenne Bell

Kenne Bell Performance of Rancho Cucamonga, California, was founded by Jim Bell in 1968, specializing in Buick engines and performance products. Through the 1970s and 1980s, much of the company's emphasis was obviously skewed

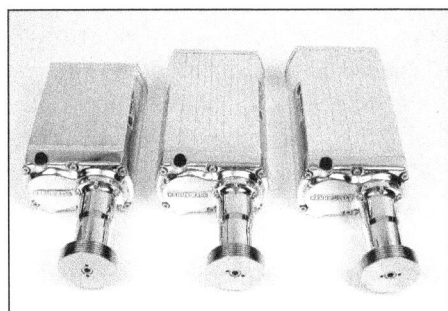

Although current Kenne Bell screw compressors look similar to the Autorotor units used previously, they are about 10-percent larger in diameter and are rated at 2.1L, 2.6L, and 2.8L. All come polished, as shown, with black anodizing as an option.

 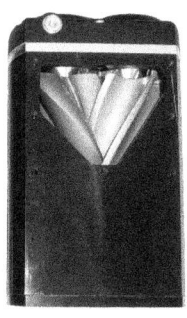

You saw a cutaway of the Kenne Bell supercharger at the beginning of this chapter. It uses a 4-lobe male and 6-lobe female rotor combination, unlike the 3/5 Whipple. These are two variations of the triangular outlet port, in black anodized cases.

toward Buick's V-6 engine, especially the vaunted Turbo Regal models. But not long after Buick decided supercharging was the better way to go in 1988, Bell came to the same conclusion. By the early 1990s Kenne Bell (K-B) became strictly a supercharging company, using the Autorotor twin-screw blower made in Sweden by Opcon AB and imported by Whipple. The first K-B supercharger packages were made for 1986–up EFI 5.0L Mustangs and other Fords, emphasizing complete, factory-looking bolt-on kits with the blower mounted on top of the engine, but still under the stock hood, with minimum moving of factory components.

K-B also made kits for 351- and 460-powered Ford trucks, 4.6L "modular" and 5.4L SOHC Mustangs, 360-hp V-8 Dodge trucks, and even the small PT Cruiser.

In 2004, however, when Opcon reorganized as a "green energy" company and shifted the focus of Autorotor blowers "exclusively on the development of air supply systems for [hydrogen] fuel cell applications" (according to the company's website), Bell was able to contract with the former Autorotor design engineers to retool a similar, but approximately

How do you make the convoluted rotors for these screw compressors? Obviously, very carefully on a big multi-axis mill like this, with specially-shaped cutting tools. Since they've been making these kinds of compressors in Sweden for decades, Jim Bell went there to find machinists with the equipment and experience to make these components to his specifications.

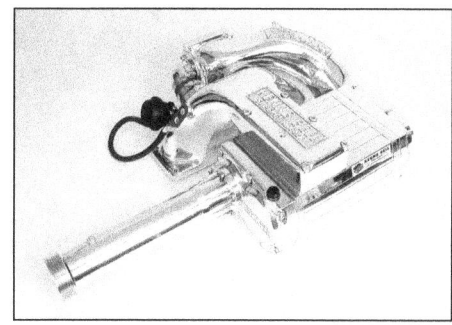

Besides the rotors, gears, and case, the rest of the Kenne Bell components are made in the United States. This blower is fitted with inlet and outlet ducting to bolt it on the lower half of an early small-block Ford EFI manifold, and accept the stock Ford throttle body. Note the bypass diaphragm and tube connecting the inlet/outlet housings.

10-percent-larger (rotor and case diameter) supercharger. These were now made exclusively for Kenne Bell in Sweden. This blower features 4-lobe male and 6-lobe female rotors

This larger supercharger comes with its own specific manifold, complete with injectors and fuel rails, to fit LS Chevrolet applications. The large black tube is the non-boost-mode blower bypass. The brass fittings in the manifold feed cooled water to the heat exchanger inside.

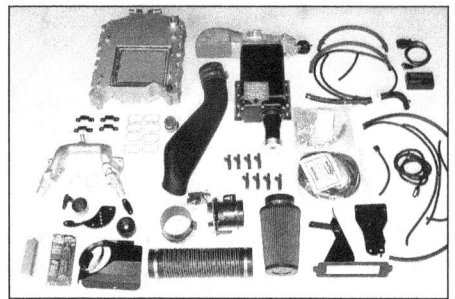

A typical Kenne Bell kit (this one for a 3V Ford) includes a manifold that will accept an intercooler core, and a blower inlet housing to take the factory throttle body. This one also includes high-flow fuel injectors and a computer reprogrammer module.

Bell likes to keep his systems under the stock hood and as factory-looking as possible, though a little polishing doesn't hurt in the looks department, as seen on this Dodge Challenger Hemi installation.

Unlike most other blower builders, Kenne Bell makes its own Mammoth throttle bodies, featuring dual 75-mm throats/butterflies for high-boost applications. The black anodized blowers, like this one, are polished first for a sleek finish.

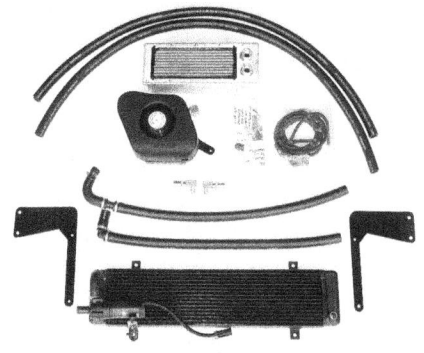

This water-to-air intercooler system includes: the front-of-vehicle radiator, with integral electric pump, at the bottom; the smaller aluminum heat exchanger that fits inside the manifold, at top; a fill tank with cap, in the middle; and the necessary hoses, brackets, and wiring to hook it all up. It's really pretty simple.

This sanitary installation fits under the hood of a Z06 Corvette.

machined from billet, and an extruded billet case, both of which can be made in different lengths to vary supercharger displacement.

Current K-B blower sizes include 2.1L, 2.6L, and 2.8L. The rotors and inside of the case are hard anodized, while the outside of all blowers are polished, but can also be black anodized, over the polished finish. While the blowers are machined and assembled in Sweden, all other components are made in the United States.

Kenne Bell now focuses primarily on various size and performance-level late-model Mustang supercharger systems, as well as C5, Z06, and LS Corvettes or similar GM engines, and a Dodge Hemi system that was in prototype as this was written. Most of these kits include air-to-water intercoolers and are rated in 5- to 18-psi-boost ranges. From the beginning, Kenne Bell designed kits that were intended to be installed on factory stock engines, using factory EFI components without reprogramming the computer.

However, Bell says that many of his customers are using his H-series Big Bore superchargers, which produce 15+ psi, on the street. In fact, the 2008 limited-production Shelby Super Snake GT 500 uses the Kenne Bell 2.8H supercharger to produce 725 hp to make it "the world's most powerful production muscle car." This system also includes K-B's Mammoth dual 75-mm throttle body.

In fact, K-B's 2008 website catalog lists three stages of supercharger kits for 2005–up Mustang GT 3V, with Stage 1 producing 501 to 675 rear-wheel horsepower (rwhp), Stage 2 producing 539 to 675 rwhp, and the Mammoth 2.8H claiming 775 rwhp, all with "100-percent stock factory

SCREW-TYPE SUPERCHARGERS

If you note the small-diameter pulley on the blower and the Mammoth intake tract, you have a hint that this otherwise-tame-looking system is ready to pump out some big horsepower for this Mustang.

engines." The Mammoth kit for the Ford Shelby GT 500 Mustang claims 801 rwhp, as tested on K-B's in-house dyno. As in-the-field examples, the site shows two street-legal 4.6L Mustangs, running only the Kenne Bell 2.8H supercharger kit (no nitrous or other enhancer), both rated at over 800 rwhp, and running quarter mile times of 9.28/150 and 9.50/142.

As we will show in Chapter 8, we would not recommend running these horsepower levels, at 15+ psi of boost, or running these kinds of speeds on a regular basis with a completely stock factory engine. But Jim Bell is very willing to back up these claims, and it shows the sort of potential supercharging offers when you simply turn up the boost, especially with a supercharger that is efficient at higher-boost levels. Check the latest Kenne Bell website, contact the company if you wish, and make your decisions based on information you've learned from reading this book.

Vortech-Lysholm

At the 2008 SEMA Show in Las Vegas, along with its full line of Vortech/Paxton centrifugal superchargers as seen in Chapter 5, Vortech introduced two new supercharger packages for Ford and GM engines using the Lysholm VL-series twin-screw supercharger. As mentioned earlier, Lysholm and Autorotor apparently merged with parent company Opcon in 2000. Then the company was reorganized in 2004, with Lysholm becoming the twin-screw supercharger division focused on gasoline automotive and marine engines. However (according to Opcon's website), the agreement to use the Lysholm blower on the Ford GT "supercar" was made with Eaton Corporation. Yes, it's a bit confusing.

But the new agreement with Vortech, announced in late 2008, was to use 2.3L and 3.3L versions of the Lysholm compressor, which is the design with a finned, cast-aluminum case and a 3-lobe-male/5-lobe-female rotor package (as used on the Ford GT and previously used by Whipple).

Initial Vortech applications include 2007–2009 Shelby GT500 and Shelby GT500KR Mustangs plus the 2003–2004 Mustang Cobra (as a direct replacement for the O.E. Eaton Roots blower) in the 2.3L and 3.3L screw-compressor sizes, reported to produce up to 700 hp with the larger blower in boost levels up to 20+ psi. These are direct-replacement bolt-on kits including an integrated bypass valve and an adapter/high-flow plenum to mate to the existing air-to-water charge cooler. A DiabloSport Predator hand-held programmer is used to recalibrate ignition timing and fuel enrichment. Initial GM applications, using the same two blower sizes, include pickups and SUVs using LS-type V-8 engines, plus Tuner Kits (which must be reprogrammed by the installer) for other LS-based applications, such as street rods.

An initial installation of the Vortech-Lysholm screw compressor for LS-style GM engines is seen on this 2009 Chevy pickup.

Vortech stated that other applications will likely follow, using these or other available Lysholm supercharger sizes and styles. Check the company's website for the latest developments.

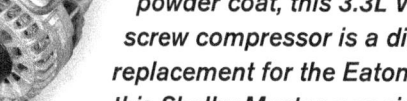

Finished in a black wrinkle powder coat, this 3.3L Vortech VL screw compressor is a direct replacement for the Eaton that was on this Shelby Mustang engine.

CHAPTER 8

BUILDING THE STREET-SUPERCHARGED ENGINE

If you've read car magazines for any length of time, you've read your fill of engine-building articles. You've seen—dozens of times—how to check the bearing and piston clearances, how to gap the rings, how to install the pistons/rods and the camshaft, how to pre-lube the right parts, how to torque the mains and rods, how to dial-in the cam (maybe), how to prime the oil pump, and all that. All internal combustion engines screw together much the same way, and that goes for supercharged engines. So we don't need to go

The new MP 2300 Magna Charger wasn't installed before the engine was dropped back in the car (actually lifted back into the Corvette), but this gives you an uncluttered look at how it fits on the engine. The stock throttle body has already been installed on the blower intake, but the belt drive can't be completed until engine accessories are added.

through all that, again, here. In the first place, the majority of engines being fitted with superchargers for street use and possibly some weekend racing don't need to be torn down and rebuilt. Most of the blower types and kits covered in this book are designed to be installed on stock, late-model engines as-is. To optimize the package, in some cases you might consider a camshaft change, or possibly some cylinder head work or a swap to out-of-the-box aftermarket heads. If you want to make some big horsepower, turn some high RPM, or otherwise stress or abuse your motor, you should definitely consider some stronger rods, pistons, and other critical parts, which means rebuilding the engine. We'll cover these areas in the following pages.

Rule number one: if your engine is old, tired, or perhaps already hurting from previous speed excursions, bolting a blower on it—any kind of blower—will only exacerbate those weaknesses. If the compression is weak or uneven, if the head gaskets are iffy, if the bearings are a little loose, if any of the valves are burned or leaking, if the valvesprings are old and tired, you need to rebuild the engine before you add a supercharger to it. If not, you'll probably be rebuilding it, or replacing it, with a new block, crank, rods, and so on, after you really hurt—or scatter—the ones you had.

Rule number two: since the smog-control days of the 1970s, hardly any factory engines have been built with compression ratios over 10:1. Today's highly efficient engines hover around that number, but most are fitted with much stronger pistons that can withstand the added cylinder pressure of a blower making 6- to 8+ psi for street performance. If, for any reason, your engine has old-fashioned high-compression pistons in it—like 12:1 or 14:1; anything

After cleaning all parts, the first stop was the Sunnen honing machine. Duttweiler stresses that straight cylinder bores are essential on these newer aluminum blocks with iron cylinder liners, and has tried several honing techniques. Here he's using thick torque plates and a couple of different stone grits, very carefully, hoping the bores would "clean up" at a .005-inch overbore. Fortunately they did. This engine obviously hadn't been abused or hurt.

above 10:1, really—especially if these happen to be cheap sand-cast pistons, do not put a blower on it. Change the pistons to a lower compression and a stronger type. Period.

A lot of people don't understand fuel octane rating and compression ratio. Octane is simply a number that denotes the point at which the given fuel will ping, "knock," or detonate in your engine, given its effective compression ratio. The volume of the combustion chamber (including the height and shape of the piston top) sets the static compression ratio of your engine. Pumping extra air into this chamber with a supercharger increases the "effective" compression ratio of the engine. In either case, if your engine audibly pings or knocks (in the cylinders) when you accelerate—you should know this sound—then either 1) the octane of the fuel you're using is too low, or 2) the effective compression in your engine is too high. (This is oversimplifying, because factors such as ignition timing, engine temperature, even cam timing come into play.)

Pinging and especially detonation are serious problems. First, when the engine begins to ping or knock, it won't make any more power, so you're defeating your purpose. Second, if pinging is allowed to continue, or if detonation occurs, it can quickly damage engine parts including burned valves, cracked rings, and broken pistons. Adding a supercharger, depending on its size and type, may make hearing such knocking more difficult and will likely hasten its results.

The first (easier) solution is obviously to use higher-octane fuel; however, this might not be practical, or even possible, for street driving. Another simple fix is to lower the blower boost by changing to a larger top pulley, but you probably don't want to do that (and it might not fix the problem, anyway). The surer, more permanent solution is to set the static compression at a level that is equally compatible with the octane of gasoline you plan to run and with the amount of boost the blower will make. This usually means changing the pistons in the engine (or possibly the heads). But all of the above are very important considerations for any street supercharged engine. That's why we're telling you now.

Now, as far as building your street supercharged engine goes, as we said, all engines go together pretty much the same way. Specific engines can have small idiosyncrasies that should be addressed when rebuilding them for higher performance, and in virtually all cases these same procedures or modifications apply to supercharged versions, as well. We will neither give you a step-by-step engine-building lesson here, nor try to cover a swath of different performance engine proclivities. If you need to know about the basics of engine building in general (performance or otherwise) there are excellent books on that subject.

The main difference between building blown and unblown performance engines is that the traditional modifications for increasing horsepower without a blower—increasing cam timing, increasing compression ratio, porting heads, tunnel ram intakes, and so on—all shift the engine's optimum performance level to a higher RPM (because horsepower is a direct function of RPM), and significantly hurt performance, fuel economy, and smoothness of running at lower RPM ranges, where you're normally driving on the street or cruising on the highway. The beauty of street supercharging, as we said in the beginning of this book, is that it takes the place of these other performance modifications, so you don't have to do most of them, plus it greatly increases power and performance in the lower, street-driving ranges of 2,500 to 4,500 rpm (especially with a positive-displacement blower). So not only do you need to "unthink" many of the traditional power modifications when adding a street supercharger, but if your engine has already been modified in such a manner, you might even have to *undo* some of them, especially in terms of cam specs or compression ratio. But we'll get to that.

Let's start by assuming that you are bolting a street blower kit onto a stock, late-model (or fresh) engine, since this is the common case these days. If you have any doubts about the compatibility of a 6- to 8-pound street blower on your healthy, relatively low-compression engine, my advice is to go ahead and install the blower on the car, being sure to add a boost gauge so that you know exactly how much the unit is putting out. If you experience knocking in the motor when the blower is under boost, and you are already using the best gasoline available, start by richening the fuel system and making sure the ignition isn't overly advanced. Second, if the blower system doesn't include an intercooler of some sort, and one will fit, adding one will help. If boost is kept in the 6- to 8-psi range, you shouldn't have any problems.

If, for whatever reason, you do blow a head gasket, burn a valve, or even break a piston land or ring, *then* pull the engine out and go through it. On the other hand, if you're the type of person who doesn't like surprises, and would rather be safe than sorry, it certainly doesn't hurt to blueprint any engine that will be driven in any sort of high-performance mode. But with mild blower boost (below 8 psi), and low static compression (below 10:1), the instances in which production parts will fail will be the exception, by far, rather than a common occurrence.

However, if you plan to bolt a 6-71 with a pair of 4-barrels on your smallblock Chevy, and you fully intend to get your foot in the throttle now and then, you better think about upgrading some of the components below that blower. The same holds true if you're planning to bolt any sort of supercharger on your new Mustang, Corvette, or Mopar Hemi, and then pump 15 to 20 psi of boost into it and run 9-second quarter miles on Sundays. Again, many of the same conditions apply that we mentioned above—if you keep your big blown motor out of detonation, you're not going to have to worry a whole lot about parts damage. Likewise, if you're *not* going to abuse the engine, over-rev it, or race it every week, you don't need parts like a forged crank, 4-bolt mains, O-ringed heads, and so on. Many customers have bolted 4-71 to 6-71 size blowers onto relatively stock low-compression engines without any problems at all. But once you start making 10 to 15 pounds of boost, or buzz the motor over 6,000 rpm, you are in marginal territory with factory components, especially in terms of pistons, rings, and head gaskets.

Here's the bottom line: if you are adding a supercharger to your engine for high performance, and you plan to drive it in a high-performance fashion, then you better build the engine to high-performance specifications. Any high-performance engine, supercharged or not, should be blueprinted. This includes checking and fitting all clearances, matching ports, dialing in cam timing, balancing the rotating and reciprocating assemblies, and so on. The procedures for blueprinting a street supercharged engine are basically the same as those for any high-performance engine. In the following sections we will discuss peculiarities in parts selection or assembly procedures unique to a blown engine, but there aren't many, actually.

The only real problem to watch out for in a supercharged street engine (besides a heavy right foot) is that the blower will inevitably cause some increase in intake air temperature, which will cause both the cylinder temperature and the exhaust temperature to be higher than they would in naturally aspirated engines at similar power levels. In truth, however, today this only really applies to higher-boost situations (above 10 psi) and/or to older-style blowers (i.e., GMCs). Modern, more efficient blowers, especially when coupled with a good intercooler, virtually eliminate this problem.

Further, remember that even a high-performance street blown motor sees the full stress of maximum boost very rarely, as opposed to a race car, which is built to operate under constant boost. The vast majority of the time, a street blown motor will be running on a much lower effective compression ratio, with more-optimum cam timing, than a comparable unblown high-performance engine. Also keep in mind that, when a blown motor is under boost, the denser air charge forced into the cylinder "cushions" the piston/rod/crank assembly during the cycle. Peak cylinder pressures are much higher in a naturally aspirated, high-compression engine. This causes greater stress on parts, as well as potential detonation, than is seen in a comparable blown engine.

Block, Crank, Rods

There's not much to say here that we haven't just stated above. If you are going to be using a moderate-boost street blower, you probably do not need to tear into the short block. If, on the other hand, you plan to make more than, say, 10 pounds of boost and you figure the engine might see some high RPM, then you should plan on a typical performance blueprinting of the entire block and lower engine assembly. Magnaflux the crank and rods, straighten and polish the crank, chamfer the oil holes, shot peen and polish the beams on the rods, resize all the holes and align all surfaces, and so on. There's nothing special a

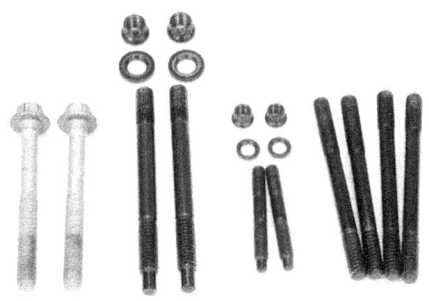

Probably the most essential element of a performance rebuild of one of these engines, especially if a blower is to be added, is a good set of screw-in studs (these are from ARP) for the main caps and the heads. In both areas, the factory engine uses "torque-to-yield" bolts (left) which must be replaced after each use, anyway.

blown motor needs that any high-performance engine doesn't need in this department.

A 4-bolt main cap block and a forged-steel crankshaft are certainly not requisites for a supercharged street engine, unless you are planning to make around 15 pounds of boost and intend to punish the motor with it. On the other hand, 4-bolt mains and a good crank are excellent insurance, and such blocks for Chevys are relatively easy to come by. Billet 4-bolt main caps are available from specialty houses for many types of engines, but these are usually quite expensive, require custom machining of the block, and really aren't necessary for anything but an all-out racing engine.

If you are using a cast crankshaft (and rebuilding the engine), it would be wise to give it a surface-hardening treatment such as Tufftriding. Choose a crank with rolled journal fillets if you have a choice. But since you cannot perform crankshaft preparation in your garage, all you really need to do is give your crank to a good engine shop and ask them to prepare it for the use you expect your engine to see. They should know what to do.

If your engine has some miles on it, you'll want to send the crank out for polishing and balancing, at the least. But this one was in fine shape, and Ken has no problem with the cast LS crank. He installed new CL 77 main bearings and reinstalled the crank.

Nevertheless, it seems that lots of people who build blown street engines like to spend money. A typical case in point is high-dollar connecting rods. In visiting countless engine shops over the years, I have seen far more sets of the "super trick" forged or billet steel connecting rods being installed in street engines than I have in actual race motors. I'm not saying that certain racers don't use—and need—the good rods, but I am saying that street engines surely don't. How often have you seen a supercharged street engine throw a rod? Or break a crank? Personally I've never heard of such a thing. Broken pistons or rings, yes; or blown gaskets, or even valve problems, but not bottom-end failures.

Your main insurance on a street engine is to check (Magnaflux, Zyglo, etc.) the stock components for cracks or fatigue as part of the blueprint. As far as connecting rods are concerned, the weakest link is usually the bolts. Always replace used rod bolts when rebuilding a performance engine. And it is wise, and relatively inexpensive, to use stronger SPS-type (i.e., ARP) bolts as a replacement.

Bottom-end clearances in a supercharged engine should not differ from those in any high-performance application. All engine builders that were interviewed for information in this section of the book strongly recommended Clevite-77 (CL-77) main and rod bearings for a supercharged engine. These readily available bearings feature a tri-metal surface with a lead-tin Babbitt overlay, which is softer than that of standard bi-metal bearings, yet still has a high-load capacity.

To feed these bearings, you want a good oil system. Performance building books on various engines spell out all sorts of specific oil system modifications, including enlarging certain passages and restricting others. Most of this is for high-RPM racing duty. For a street blown motor, make sure all oil galleys are clean and deburred. Other than that, your best and simplest insurance is a good high-volume oil pump.

Finally, several builders strongly recommend surfacing both the block decks and the heads to make sure they are perfectly flat for gasket sealing with a blower. With today's improved head gaskets, O-ringing of the block or heads is really not needed for anything but a serious-boost race motor (we'll discuss this more in the Cylinder Heads section). However, experienced big-block blown-boat-engine-builder Mike Kuhl was a firm believer in O-ringing supercharged engines, and stated, flatly, "I wouldn't run a 454 without O-rings at any boost." What we would add is that most Kuhl River Rat engines ran 8-71 blowers (at least) and, more significantly, boats don't coast or cruise like a car does. A boat engine is under constant load, which means near-constant boost if it is supercharged.

Since we're discussing the short-block assembly, we should address the subject of crate engines here, versus a custom engine build. Crate motors in a wide range of sizes and performance levels—primarily Chevrolet or Ford V-8s—are available from many sources these days. Often the price of one of these engines, given the new components included, can be less than the cost of having a similar one built. The problem is that, as far as we have seen, all of these engines—and the horsepower ratings quoted for them—are for naturally aspirated configurations. Many come with high-flow aftermarket aluminum cylinder heads, big-duration cams, and often a high-performance intake for carburetion or electronic fuel injection, and the price for such engines not only reflects the cost of these parts, but goes up proportionally with rated horsepower.

But remember, 1) the supercharger alone can probably produce as much, if not more, horsepower without these aftermarket parts, and 2) you'd probably have to change the pistons and cam to more blower-compatible specs, and you won't use the intake system in most cases. On the other hand, buying one of the "low-po" stock-replacement-type crate motors to bolt a blower onto is not a good idea, either, because these are not precision-built, performance-oriented engines.

So, if you're not adding a supercharger to a relatively new car with a healthy stock engine, it appears your best alternative is to build (or have professionally built) your own engine, using high-quality parts and engine-building procedures, but tailoring it to its intended supercharged use.

This brings up one final consideration for this section. Given the labor-saving, cost-cutting attributes of modern CNC machining, coupled with the considerably lower cost of doing it "offshore," certain aftermarket companies are offering very affordable high-performance "crank kits" that include H-beam or I-beam billet rods and possibly even a billet steel crank for prices that rival those of new,stock components. Many such kits also include pistons, which

The main caps on these engines have four bolts plus side bolts, which is plenty. Proper torquing is an acquired skill. Duttweiler cautions against undertorquing any bolts. Don't forget the special hardened washers under the nuts for any aluminum surface.

might or might not be available in the proper compression ratio for a blown motor. But such a bottom-end package is worth looking into for a stout, street-supercharged engine.

Pistons and Rings

This is the primary area in which the construction of a supercharged engine differs from that of other high-performance engines. One of the ways to high performance without a blower is high static compression, commonly achieved with high-dome pistons. The limit to compression increase in any engine is the point at which it begins to ping or detonate on the fuel being used. In a supercharged engine, the extra air pumped in by the blower effectively increases the compression ratio, as it adds greater air charge. So you make your compression with the blower, not with the piston configuration.

Rule number one: you cannot run high-compression pistons with a blower. In the old school (and previous editions of this book), we said a blown motor must run a compression ratio below 9:1. That was based mainly on low-efficiency GMC

This one photo says a lot about proper engine building. Just as important as "blueprinting," besides checking all torques and clearances, is complete cleanliness (of parts and work area), organization, and proper sealants and lubricants.

The stock LS powdered-metal, "broken cap," I-beam connecting rods and lightweight hypereutectic pistons are excellent pieces, and none turned out to be damaged, so they probably could have been reused.

superchargers. One reason high static compression leads to knock is because it creates heat. If you are running one of today's much more efficient superchargers, at street-boost levels (6 to 8 psi, or so), you won't be making nearly as much heat in the cylinder. If you're adding an intercooler to the system, the situation is even better. So we are seeing either factory-stock or purpose-built engines with static compression in the 10:1 range running modern superchargers with no problem.

If you are running a big GMC blower, or if you want to make big boost on the street (or strip on weekends), then you should adjust the static compression ratio accordingly, down to 9:1 or even 8:1 (or lower). This might mean changing pistons in an already assembled engine. But the rule of thumb is the point of knocking. If the engine pings or detonates with the blower, and other elements in the system are optimized (such as cooling system, ignition timing, etc.), you have two basic choices: lower blower boost by changing drive pulleys, or change your pistons.

Rule number two: You can't tell what the compression in the engine is unless you measure it. Factory engines can vary a point or more above or below the specified compression (in

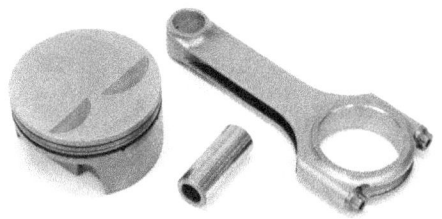

As a bit of overkill insurance, Ken and Jerry decided to use a set of .005-over Mahle forged and coated pistons (LS 131 4005), with floating pins and snap rings, plus a set of Scat H-beam forged rods. One of the main reasons for the new pistons was to allow the clean-up hone in the cylinders. And the Scat rods are very affordable.

fact, they can often vary considerably in CR from cylinder to cylinder—that's just one reason why blueprinting is necessary). Even aftermarket pistons that are rated at a certain compression ratio must be matched with the specific components in your engine. Minor differences in connecting rod lengths, piston pin heights, dome heights, valve head heights, valve seat depth, and combustion chamber core shift can all add up to alter the actual compression in each cylinder considerably. Furthermore,

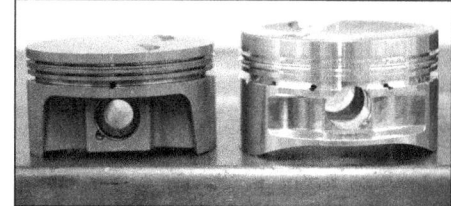

Another reason for using Mahle pistons, besides their strength, is that the top ring groove is .200-inch down from the top, which is an important consideration in any blown engine. For serious boost (like 30 psi) in his blown race engines, Kenny uses a forged piston like the one on the right with the first ring more like .400 to .500 down. Note that this puts the oil ring groove down into the pin hole.

"listed" compression ratios for aftermarket pistons are stated for a specific-volume combustion chamber and a certain thickness of head gasket. Combustion chamber sizes have varied over the years on most types of engines. And if you are using older heads, how many times have they been surfaced in the past and by how much?

Figuring the exact static compression ratio in an engine involves a lot of measuring and a lot of arithmetic (although it is simple arithmetic), but it is the only way to be sure how much compression the engine really has. Obviously, we are talking about a serious engine buildup—a high-performance engine that will see some healthy boost and will therefore require a tear down, parts upgrading, and blueprinting. If you are going to bolt a mild-boost blower onto a relatively stock engine—that is, if you aren't planning to change the pistons anyway—there's little point in pulling the heads off to check the compression. This would only be necessary if your engine encounters detonation that cannot be eliminated by other means.

The above statement is important to today's street supercharging, so let's phrase it another way. If you are starting with a late-model, relatively low-compression engine (9.5 to 10:1 or lower) in good running condition, and you want to add a bolt-on, moderate-boost (5- to 8-psi range) blower kit to improve performance, there is no need to pull the engine apart either to change the pistons or to check the actual compression ratio. Add the blower, dial in the system (adjust the fuel mixture, set the timing, add an intercooler perhaps), and figure that everything is going to work fine. If the engine does experience knock or detonation under boost, even though you have

Clevite-77 main and rod bearings are the standard for performance engines these days. And the Mahle pistons come with their own ring set, using a "moly" top ring and a cast second ring.

taken all the "external" steps to eliminate it, then consider pulling the heads, measuring the actual compression ratio, and possibly changing to pistons of a lower ratio and probably higher quality material. Yes, we are repeating ourselves, but sometimes it's necessary to make a point.

Speaking of adding a blower to an existing, running engine, let's restate another fact, because it's important. If the engine is old, it could be tired and worn; if it's been raced, it could have parts that have been scuffed, stretched, or cracked; and even if it's new—whether in a car or in a crate—you don't know if it was assembled properly without taking it apart and blueprinting it.

We're not saying every street supercharged engine should be blueprinted. You can safely assume a factory-built engine has been assembled correctly (especially if it's running correctly, with no knocks, rattles, smoke, or blowby). But, if the engine is tired, hurt, or improperly assembled, adding a blower will only aggravate these problems. If the engine has tired rings, a cracked piston, worn guides, a burning valve, or marginal head gasket seal, adding a blower is certainly going to worsen the problem. Don't add a blower to a worn engine. Furthermore, adding a blower to a relatively fresh factory engine, or a standard rebuild (or low-po crate engine), might—hopefully in isolated cases—immediately point out the flaws that sometimes creep past assembly line employees. If so, assuming the failure is not catastrophic, a tear down and blueprinted rebuild is in order.

Now, if you are going to be adding a healthy boost blower to the engine, and you intend to make some big power with it; or if you're worried your combination might encounter some detonation or cooling problems; or if you just prefer to be on the safe side in any case (and don't mind spending money for it), then you should consider a set of custom forged pistons and good rings in the engine.

Such pistons are available from all the name-brand race-piston manufacturers such as Venolia, JE, Ross, KB, Arias, and so on. Besides being the strongest pistons you can get, the plus side is that they can be custom-ordered to fit most any type of engine,

Checking ring end gap clearance on every ring in its respective bore, and filing the ends to fit if necessary, is critical to any performance engine blueprinting, but even more on a blown engine. If the gap is too tight, the rings will butt with heat expansion, and seize in the cylinder. If they're too loose, they'll let cylinder pressure leak through. Since the blower increases cylinder temp and pressure, you can see why it's very important. Many builders increase gaps .002-inch on blown engines, but Ken kept these pretty tight at .020 (top) and .022 (second) in this 4.005-inch bore.

in any specified compression ratio, and made for whatever type (width) of rings you want, located at your specified distance from the piston top.

The down side is that they are naturally the most expensive; you must custom-order them and wait for them to be made (the time can vary by manufacturer, whether it's racing season, and how many sponsored racers have their orders ahead of yours); and forged-aluminum pistons expand much more than other types, so they must be installed with wider piston-to-wall clearance (.008 to .009 for forged, .002 to .003 for cast or "semi-forged"). Consequently, forged pistons will audibly rattle in the cylinders when the engine is cold, and you must allow the pistons to warm and expand before you drive down the road (or track). This can obviously be an annoyance in a street engine. But it's the price you have to pay for the strongest pistons available, and the only type truly custom made to the exact specifications you need.

The other alternative, and the one that is, in most cases, more practical for a street blown engine, is to use a replacement-type "forged" piston from an aftermarket supplier. These were known as Power Forged under the TRW brand, denoted by an "F" after the part number. As of this writing, TRW has been consumed by Federal-Mogul/Speed Pro, but the familiar TRW part numbers still apply. For instance, a Speed Pro L2256F is a Power Forged Chevy piston that gives 9:1 compression with a 68-cc combustion chamber.

Other brands offer similar pistons, possibly called "hypereutectic." The advantages are that such pistons are readily available across the country, they are less expensive than custom forgings, they come in various compression ratios compatible with blower needs, and they expand at a rate similar to cast pistons. Therefore they can be installed at "normal" clearances (.0025 to .003 in most cases), don't rattle on cold-start, and don't require extra warm-up time. The drawback is that such pistons, especially in lower-compression ratings suitable for blower applications, are made only for the more common engines.

One side-note here: Piston availability in custom sizes and compression ratios is better today than ever. In the past, however, it was common to chuck higher-compression pistons in a mill or lathe and trim the tops down to get the lower compression needed for a blower application. This should not be done, for two reasons. First, milling the dome makes the top of the piston thinner and blower pistons need a thicker top, if anything, to withstand the increased cylinder pressure and heat produced by the blower. In most cases, milling the dome of a high-compression piston enough for blower use would severely weaken it.

Second, milling the top of the piston lower, particularly on low-dome or flat-top designs, will reduce the distance between the piston top and the first ring groove. The shoulder of the piston above the first ring land is an area of critical stress in the piston. If the thickness of the piston top above this groove is made thinner, the edges of the top can crack, burn, or even break off when cylinder pressures and temperatures are increased. On a blower piston, the first ring groove should be about .250-inch down from the top, at minimum.

As far as piston rings are concerned, the rule of thumb for supercharged engines is: use the best. Actually there are three major considerations for the choice of rings in a blown motor: they must seal the cylinder against higher pressure; they must withstand and dissipate greater heat; and they must have a high tensile strength so that they will not break under heavy load or detonation.

A tapered ring compressor is a luxury for installing pistons. But this photo and the previous one show the crosshatch Ken wants in the cylinder bores. Don't forget to check each piston deck height once they're all installed.

There was no need to surface the decks on this aluminum block, but Ken adamantly chooses ARP studs to secure the heads. They install in the block with an Allen wrench and a spot of Loctite.

CHAPTER 8

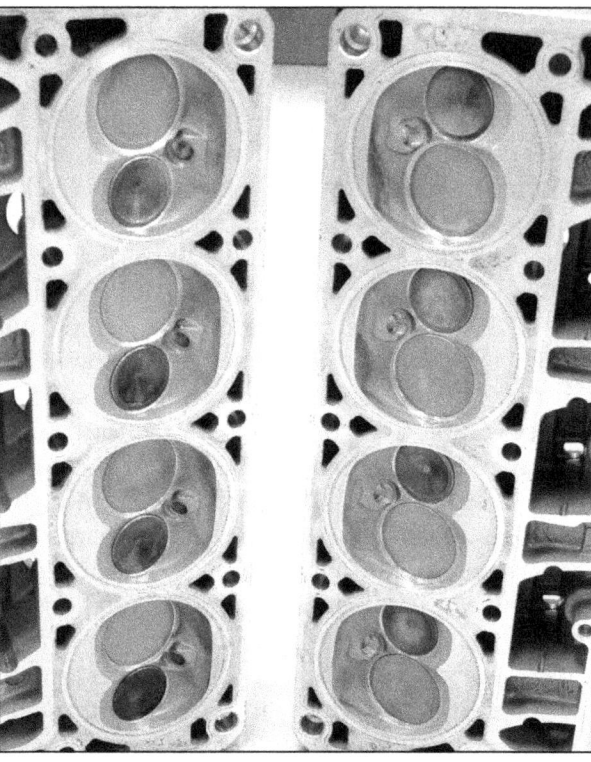

Ken found nothing wrong with the heads or the stock valves, so he gave the valves and seats a 3-angle clean-up, and left everything else as-is.

Standard production rings are made of cast iron. Their major attribute is that they seat quickly and provide fine sealing in standard engines. However, cast iron is brittle rather than ductile, and it has a melting point of 2,000 degrees F. Chrome-plated iron rings have a melting point of 3,212 degrees F, but they are still brittle and they are much more difficult to seat in the cylinders. A popular choice for performance engines today are "moly" rings, which are nodular iron rings sprayed with a molybdenum filling on the face. Molybdenum has a melting point of 4,750 degrees F, the nodular body is ductile rather than brittle, and they seat easily, like cast-iron rings. "Double moly" ring sets include moly-filled top and second compression rings, usually with a chrome oil ring. These readily available rings would be a good choice for most street-supercharged engines.

Finally, given higher temperatures in high-boost blower applications, most builders recommend increasing ring end-gap clearance about .005 inch in blown motors, to allow for greater heat expansion of the rings. In any case, with any rings, it is critical to check and fit the end gaps of each compression ring in each cylinder during engine assembly. Most high-performance rings are made slightly longer than necessary so that you can file them to exact fit. Failing to do so will allow the ends of the rings to butt when they heat and expand, causing them to seize in the cylinder or to break.

Cylinder Heads

Unlike pistons and rings, the cylinder heads on a supercharged street engine really need little attention. The purpose of the blower is to get the fresh air and fuel in and the exhaust out, and that's what nine tenths of performance head work is all about. As far as port size, port shape, and valve size are concerned, as long as they aren't so small that they will restrict the blower's boost, leave them the way they are.

There are some special considerations for cylinder heads on a supercharged engine, however. First of all, you want to make sure that the heads seal in the extra pressure pumped by the blower. We would highly recommend that you have the heads surfaced to make sure they are flat. For the majority of street blower applications, you will not have to O-ring the heads (or block); this should only be necessary on very-high-boost installations, or possibly on engines with poor head sealing to begin with (usually because of too few head bolts surrounding each cylinder). If you feel that O-ringing might be necessary—or you become convinced after one or two head gasket failures—you will have to find gaskets to fit your engine that are compatible with O-rings. A steel-faced sandwich gasket is best (steel on each side with "composition"—whatever they replaced asbestos with—in the middle). A steel shim gasket will work if you can carefully match the O-ring to the rib on the gasket, which can be touchy. Solid copper gaskets are best left to race cars since they are prone to water leaks. Of course cutting the O-ring grooves should be done by an experienced machine shop.

However, few street blown cars will need to be O-ringed. An excellent compromise these days are high-performance head gaskets that have a built-in stainless steel "O-ring" seal around each cylinder. These gaskets are expensive, but they are much easier to install than true O-rings. Obviously, with these or any other gaskets on a supercharged engine, a careful and sequential torquing and subsequent retorquing of the heads is mandatory.

Another obvious area of concern on any supercharged engine is head-gasket sealing with increased cylinder pressure. We're not sure exactly what these new, multi-layer head gaskets from Fel-Pro are made of, but Kenny says he has used them, successfully, on engines like this boosted to 1,200+ hp at 40 pounds of boost! Who needs O-rings? These are 4-layer and carry part number MLS 1161.

The second consideration for cylinder heads on a supercharged engine is to guard against heat and detonation. While the intake and exhaust ports probably won't require enlarging or polishing, it would be helpful to clean up the combustion chambers to remove any burrs, flash, or sharp edges, which could become hot spots and lead to pre-ignition. On a high-boost motor, you might as well polish the entire chamber, which will not only help reduce detonation, but will also help lower the compression ratio. Just don't grind so much out of the heads that you weaken the chamber walls; remember that blower boost can break through combustion chamber walls just like it can break through piston tops if the surface gets too thin.

For valves and valvetrains there are only two considerations for a supercharged engine that would differ from other performance-engine buildups. First, since the operating temperature of the valve is controlled by its contact with the water-cooled head, and since the valve seat is the area of contact through which heat can be transferred from the valve to the head, it is recommended to not narrow valve seats (particularly on the exhaust valve) as much on a blown engine. A 3-angle valve job is effective for increasing airflow past the valve on naturally aspirated engines. But cutting the valve and seat at three angles greatly reduces the width of the actual valve seat contact area. Some engine builders seem to disagree or disregard this point today (especially if they cut seats with a pre-formed 3-angle tool), but the rule used to be to keep valve seat width to at least .080 inch (and perhaps wider, especially on exhausts, say, .100 inch). Remember, the blower will do most of the job of getting air past the valves. On the other hand, with today's more efficient blowers (plus intercoolers), cylinder heat isn't nearly as much a problem as it once was, especially at street boost levels.

Second, any performance engine will usually require stiffer valve springs to guard against valve float at higher RPM and to keep the lifters on the cam with more radical profiles. But a supercharged engine will also need greater valvespring pressure on the intake valves to keep them on their seats, since blower pressure will be acting on the backsides of all the intake valves. Admittedly, even 15 or 20 psi isn't enough air pressure to blow an intake valve open, even with stock springs. But the addition of blower pressure to the momentum of the valvetrain components at high engine speed compounds the spring tension requirement on the intake valves. This can be critical in a supercharged engine.

If an intake valve does not fully close (or "hangs up"), combustion in that cylinder will backfire into the intake manifold, which is filled with

No tricks here. Torque the heads carefully to spec for the studs, in the proper sequence, and don't forget the hardened washers.

pressurized, atomized air-fuel mix—a highly volatile substance. If you have watched Top Fuel drag racing you know the result, and the reason why restraint straps are required on T/F blowers. You certainly don't want to "light off" the blower on your street machine. By the way, a broken valvespring will have the same result, so be sure to invest in a good grade of fresh springs from a reputable manufacturer.

Of course, a broken or stuck valve would be even more destructive. Most street blown motors won't require special valves, but if you are planning to make some RPM with a stout blown streeter, a good set of stronger stainless steel valves are relatively inexpensive insurance. Valve stem seals are a matter of opinion with engine builders. Many use PC-type positive seals on all performance engines. You certainly don't want any oil running down the valve stems into the combustion chambers on a blown engine, because this promotes detonation. Other builders, however, say a bit of oil to lubricate the stems keeps them from sticking. Further, some builders recommend slightly looser stem-to-guide clearance on a blown engine, especially on the exhausts, to guard against sticking from heat-growth. Possibly a combination of tighter seals with looser clearance is the best compromise. Ask your engine builder.

Otherwise, head prep for a street blown motor is basically the same as for any performance engine, but without all the time-consuming, touchy, and expensive port and polish work.

Camshaft and Valvetrain

Just as it is a definite no-no to run high-compression pistons in a supercharged engine, it is equally and emphatically against the rules to use a typical high-performance, long-duration, big-overlap camshaft in a blown motor. These are by far the two most common mistakes in building street blown engines, and of the two, overcamming is the more flagrant.

Typical high-performance camshaft technology has been developed to get unpressurized air into and out of the cylinders. This technology does not apply to supercharged engines. Actually, camming a blown engine is quite a bit easier than trying to match cam timing and profile to the various components of a naturally aspirated, high-performance engine (especially manifold type, size, and runner length). As we have said before, in a blown motor the supercharger will do the work of getting the mixture into the cylinder.

As one experienced cam grinder (Isky) put it: "A blower kind of covers up the holes in a motor." In other words, the blown engine isn't as touchy about several aspects of engine tuning, including cam timing and profile. In many cases, a moderate street blower will work fine with the stock cam in the engine (preferably with heavier valvesprings). A stock cam would certainly work better than a typical high-performance cam.

Most cam companies now list specific blower grinds in their catalogs, often for varying levels of boost, or else they specify which grinds would be good for certain supercharged applications. Further, many of the supercharger companies offer camshafts and related hardware tailored to work with their blowers. In other cases, the supercharger manufacturer should be able to recommend a cam profile that would be good for your given application. For a very general rule of thumb, you want something in the 260- to 300-degree (advertised duration) range, or not more than 240 degrees as measured at .050-inch lifter rise, with net valve lift in the neighborhood of .450 to .500 inch. These are strictly ballpark figures, but most moderate street blowers would be happy with a cam in the 260- to 280-degree advertised duration range; bigger engines with bigger blowers could use a bit more.

One of the first street blower manufacturers to do a lot of experimenting with camshaft profiles for blown engines was Jerry Magnuson. Through this testing, he developed a cam for a 220-ci blower on a small-block Chevy that measured 224-degrees intake, 226-degrees exhaust (at .050 inch), and .480-inch net lift, on 114-degree lobe centers (lobe separation angle). Used in a 350 Chevy engine for a dyno test of five different street blowers limited to 6 pounds of boost, it produced excellent low-end power, an exceptionally flat torque curve, and good power through 6,000 rpm.

The Magnuson cam was manufactured by Schneider Cams of San Diego, California, a respected cam grinder (especially in circle track racing), and they explained the basic theory behind this, or any, good street blower cam. First, the cam should have minimal overlap, which means the lobe centers should be spread as far apart as possible—in the neighborhood of 112 to 115 degrees. Overlap is the period during the cam timing cycle when the intake valve has already opened and the exhaust valve is not yet closed. In a naturally aspirated engine such a situation is tolerable—in fact, preferable—because it takes a certain amount of time to get the air moving. But in a blown engine the air is under pressure. As soon as the intake valve opens, the air/fuel mix bursts into the cylinder, filling it rapidly. If the exhaust valve remains open, part of the air/fuel mix will be pumped out the exhaust by the blower. This is obviously a waste of fuel and power.

Overlap can be decreased by decreasing the duration of both the intake and exhaust valve cycles. That's why you don't want a long-duration cam in a blown engine. However, even though the blown motor doesn't need as much timing as an unblown motor, you still want to keep as much duration as practical to fill the cylinder as much as possible and to get the exhaust out. Widening (increasing the cam timing between) lobe centers reduces overlap without changing the length of time each valve remains open. However, doing so advances the exhaust valve timing and retards the intake; or, seen the other way, it retards the intake timing relative to the exhaust timing.

Consequently, to get the intake valve timing back where it should be, Schneider recommends advancing the entire cam for a supercharged

BUILDING THE STREET-SUPERCHARGED ENGINE

When your stock factory engine comes with a steel billet roller cam and is rated at 400 hp, unblown, the last thing you want to do is put a "bigger" cam in it. We discuss blower cam timing in some detail elsewhere, but the simple case here is that stock is excellent.

engine by 2 to 4 degrees. The net effect is to get both the intake and the exhaust valves open early to get the pressurized air/fuel mix in quickly, and get the consequently pressurized exhaust also out as soon as possible, and at the same time to close each valve as soon as possible so that a minimum of cylinder pressure leaks back out. If the intake stayed open too long, the beginning compression stroke of the piston would want to push the "supercharge" back out the intake valve. This is similar to reversion in a naturally aspirated engine, except that it would have the effect of "backpressure" on the blower, which would ultimately reduce its mechanical, volumetric, and adiabatic efficiencies. If the exhaust valve stays open too long, as we said, part of the new incoming air/fuel charge will blow out the exhaust port.

Finally, Schneider usually cuts street blower cams on a dual-pattern profile, giving the exhaust more duration than the intake (as much as 10 to 12 degrees). Widening the lobe centers and advancing the cam timing also helps to make this possible without negative effects. The reason for giving the exhaust more timing on a supercharged engine should be obvious—the blower pumps a whole lot more air and fuel into the engine on the intake stroke, but the exhaust has to get out on its own.

Many people (myself included, come to think of it) have stated that the supercharger will actually help to "blow" the exhaust out of the cylinder, but this isn't really accurate. The blower will increase overall cylinder pressure, since it will pack a greater mass of air and fuel into it. After combustion, this "super charge" of air and fuel expands, filling the cylinder with a greater pressure and mass of hot exhaust gas than would be present in a naturally aspirated engine's cylinder (that's why you put the supercharger on the engine, remember?). Consequently, when the exhaust valve opens, the significantly increased pressure of the heated gases in the cylinder forces them out the exhaust port at a greater velocity. However, there is more mass of exhaust in the cylinder, so it will still take more time to get it all out. Make sense?

Now, just to throw another contradiction at you, if you remember back in Chapter 3, we were talking about mean effective pressure and the thermal efficiency of a supercharged engine versus a naturally aspirated one. Although we ultimately get much more power out of a supercharged engine (because its mean effective pressure is higher), its thermal efficiency is, nevertheless, lower than that of an unblown engine. The reason is that all of the extra energy pumped into the engine in the form of fuel by the supercharger simply cannot be converted to heat, then to pressure, and then to work within the cylinder, before the exhaust valve opens. The very fact that the exhaust rushes out of the blown engine under greater pressure, and at a higher temperature, than in other engines, tells us that a greater portion of the potential power is being wasted.

Of course all internal combustion engines have terrible thermal efficiency, supercharged or not, so this is not a major point. But, to a certain extent, the thermal efficiency, and therefore a fraction of the power, of the blown motor is determined by the opening time of the exhaust valve. The sooner the exhaust valve opens (the more advanced the exhaust timing), the lower the thermal efficiency, and the more the potential work (power) goes out the exhaust pipe. Like we said earlier, the supercharged engine is a mélange of tradeoffs.

However, this is a minor point offered primarily as food for thought if you like that sort of thing. The engine builders who know supercharged engines still agree that blower cams, in general, should have relatively short duration, wide-lobe centers, and slightly advanced overall timing.

CHAPTER 8

Chevrolet has come a long way since ball-and-stud, stamped-steel rocker arms, hasn't it? Given major improvements in factory roller-cam valvetrains, the one area of concern when adding a supercharger might be valvespring pressure. However, these small, light beehive springs and retainers are excellent to the factory rev limit of 6,400 rpm. If you plan on some 8,000-rpm weekend racing, we'd recommend a stouter valvetrain, all around.

As far as the rest of the valvetrain is concerned, other than the importance of increasing valvespring pressures (as mentioned in the cylinder head section), you can use the same parts in a supercharged engine that you would use in any other performance engine. Hydraulic lifters should be fine for most street blown motors, but be sure to use a good-quality anti-pump-up type (most are these days). A hydraulic lifter that "pumps up" would hang a valve open, with the same consequences mentioned earlier. Today's modern engines with hydraulic roller camshafts generally have superb, lightweight valvetrain components, as seen in our accompanying engine build-up photos.

Fuel System

In previous editions of this book, we spent several pages on a section titled "Carburetion," including step-by-step photos of how to rework Holley and AFB-type 4-barrels to work on top of GMC blowers. While plenty people are still planning to bolt a big GMC on top of a big V-8 with a pair of big 4-barrel carbs—and there's absolutely nothing wrong with that—we'd have to say that the majority of people bolting blowers on vehicles these days are integrating them with some sort of electronic fuel injection. Plus, we'd also have to say that even the carburetion market has shifted toward suppliers who offer specific or "pre-modified" carbs already tailored to certain applications, rather than the old school where end-users are buying used carbs at swap meets and rebuilding them at home. So we're not going to show you how to rework carburetors here.

In fact, we'll start with a statement made in previous editions, which still holds true: trying to pre-scribe any sort of carburetor (or other induction system) tuning in a book like this is exactly like asking a doctor to cure your ills over the phone. If your symptoms are common enough, the doctor might be able to phone-order you the proper prescription to make you better. But without physically examining you in person, the doctor can never be sure of exactly what's wrong with your particular body. The same goes for carburetors (or EFI), in fact, for the entire "tunable" package of an engine, which includes the fuel and ignition systems, as well as cam timing and profile, valve adjustment, blower drive ratio, and several other factors. And of course the tuning of any particular engine, blown or otherwise, depends on factors such as vehicle weight, transmission type, rear-axle ratio, rear tire diameter, and the type of driving you normally do, not to mention local elevation, typical weather conditions, and several other such factors. Are you getting the picture?

The point is that we cannot give you specific recommendations on how to tune your specific supercharged engine combination, nor how to retune carburetors or electronic fuel injection to do so.

However, we can make a couple of broad generalizations that hold pretty true. The first, and most basic, is that carburetors and today's most common type of electronic fuel injection (which uses a MAF sensor) work on the same principle. They "read" the amount of air flowing through them, and add the correct, proportional amount of fuel to it.

Granted, they do it in very different ways, and carburetors (which do it mechanically, by the venturi effect) may not respond quite as quickly and as accurately as EFI, but they both do a pretty good job of automatically adjusting, by themselves, when you add a supercharger to the system. That is, the supercharger (when it's in boost) blows more air into the engine. Either a carburetor or the MAF sensor of the fuel injection reads, or senses, this air increase immediately, and automatically injects more fuel into the airstream to keep the air/fuel ratio correct. It's really pretty simple. In fact, to be honest, in most cases where somebody starts fiddling with either carburetor jets or circuits, or reprogramming an EFI on their own lap-top computer, they can cause more problems, in a hurry, than solve fine-tuning bugs.

It might sound like a broad over-generalization, but in a very large number of cases, street-level superchargers will work just fine with unmodified carburetors or with factory electronic fuel injection, as is. Many of the street supercharger systems covered in this book are specifically designed to work with factory EFI systems, without modification, at least partly to maintain full smog-control compliance. Others come with a hand-held, plug-in computer module that reprograms the factory computer fuel and spark parameters in a one-time "flash" operation. The companies that do offer larger throttle bodies, higher-flow injectors, and so on, generally offer a similar unit to re-flash the stock computer, or a secondary computer module to plug into the system to operate it correctly.

In the case of EFI or carburetion, the bottom line is that either must be able to flow enough air to keep up with what's being pumped by the blower; then it must be able to add enough fuel to mix properly with that amount of air. The vast majority of street superchargers making less than 10 pounds of boost will not exceed the flow limits of stock EFI systems, and carburetors come in plenty of sizes. In either case, one limiting factor you might overlook is the fuel pump, which must exceed the needs of the system, as must any other component of the fuel-delivery system, from tank pick-up, to line size, to filter flow capacity.

But in these days of the "systems approach" to street supercharging, the company supplying the system or kit should either include whatever fuel system upgrades you need (such as higher-flow EFI injectors and/or pump), or be able to give you specific recommendations on what works with their components (such as correct carburetors to mount on their GMC-style blower). Beyond that, for finer tuning, we recommend one of the many dyno-tuning facilities around the country, which can run the vehicle under loaded and unloaded conditions, and read fuel mixtures at the tailpipe, among many other criteria.

As far as carburetion is concerned, draw-through systems on top of Roots or similar blowers are straightforward. However, in a blow-through system with a centrifugal blower, you have two options. If the carb is contained in a pressure box, as in Paxton and Vortech systems, about the only consideration is a non-collapsible float. In the rare cases where the blower pressure is pumped directly into the carb top through a "hat" or "bonnet," some sort of seals (O-rings) must be installed on the throttle blade shafts. ProCharger uses such a configuration primarily for high-boost/racing applications, and various specialty carburetor shops can provide properly modified carbs for such specific use. In fact, "blower" carbs tailored for racing or street are available from many such shops/manufacturers, including Holley, which makes sense since they now sell blowers, too.

Air Cleaners and Intercoolers

The same thing applies to the air-inlet side of the blower systems as to the rest of the fuel/air system: it has to be able to freely flow as much air as the blower will pump. If the air filter restricts airflow in any way, you're defeating (or at least hurting) the purpose of the blower. Further, the whole purpose of supercharging is to provide a *denser* charge of air to the engine, and that cool air is denser than hot air. So placing the air filter and/or air inlet where it can breathe the coolest air possible (i.e., fresh air as opposed to underhood air) is only logical.

Continuing this line of logic, the only possible arguments against incorporating some type of intercooler in a modern street supercharging system would be cost, lack of space, or logistics. Obviously, the heat exchanger located between the blower and the intake ports must not restrict airflow. And whether the system is air-to-air or water-to-air is largely a matter of packaging, complexity, and opinion (for drag racers, overall weight is a concern, but we're discussing street systems here). We show the various types of intercoolers (or charge-coolers, or after-coolers) offered by the different manufacturers. They work. Whether you use one is mostly a matter of whether it fits on your car or in your budget.

Ignition

We've already discussed ignition timing in relation to pinging or detonation being one limitation to boost. In any performance (or economy) engine, you want as much ignition advance as possible, short of pinging. Increased air charge density or heat (both products of supercharging) might limit ignition advance. With a mechanical distributor you can physically change initial advance and the mechanical and/or vacuum advance curves and totals. If you have electronic ignition (with or without a distributor), you—or more likely someone else—will have to reset these parameters electronically.

Beyond that, the ignition system's one job is to fire the spark plugs. Increased air charge density in the cylinder makes it somewhat harder for the spark to bridge the plug gap. High-boost racing engines need super-high-voltage ignitions. But street engines making 5 to 10 pounds of boost shouldn't tax the capabilities of modern electronic ignitions at all. Obviously, like the fuel and air-intake systems, you don't want limiting (or defective) elements anywhere in the ignition system, from cap/rotor, to wires, to plugs, and to coil(s). But the bottom line is, the ignition either fires the plugs under all running conditions—including full boost—or it doesn't. If it doesn't, you'll know, and you should upgrade the system.

Exhaust

This is the appropriate place to end this book, and the message is much the same as it has been throughout this section. If the blower is pumping more air into the cylinder, the exhaust has to be able to flow more spent gases out. If there is any restriction in the exhaust system, it will simply fight what the blower is trying to do. If you look at any supercharged race cars, you'll see that big, open, individual headers are the only way to go. That's not possible on the street.

But the race car example should tell you two things. First, "tuned" headers, in terms of primary tube diameter and length and collector size, mean little on a blown engine. In general, bigger is better. Headers are better than stock manifolds. And if you plan any weekend racing, easily opened collectors are a good thing. Otherwise, second, make the rest of the exhaust system, for street use, as unrestricted as possible. End of story.

This is what the engine looked like when Duttweiler delivered it back to the Magnusons. Not much different than when it left, but with some stouter innards for insurance and the knowledge that everything is balanced, clearanced, torqued, and sealed the way it should be. That's what blueprinting is.

 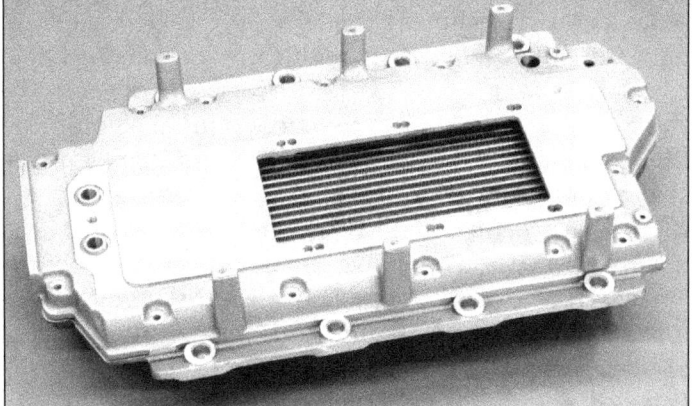

The first step to installing the supercharger on the otherwise completed engine was to mount the 2-piece intake manifold, which contains the heat exchanger for the water-to-air intercooler.

BUILDING THE STREET-SUPERCHARGED ENGINE

Our engine builder is Ken Duttweiler (Saticoy, California), who knows plenty about highly pressurized high-performance engines. The rebuild subject is a Gen-3 6.0L LS aluminum V-8 from Maureen Magnuson's 2005 Corvette. It was rated at 400 hp stock, but had been driven 20,000 miles with the addition of an MP 112 Magna Charger. In fact, this is a perfect example of what we suggest: bolt the street-boost supercharger on a good, fresh, stock engine and drive it. Maureen and Jerry thought they heard a small knock, plus they wanted to install the new TVS 4-lobe MP 2300 Magna Charger on it, so they decided to tear it down, blueprint it, and install a set of new, stronger rods and pistons just for insurance. As the engine was torn down, no obvious reason for a knock was found.

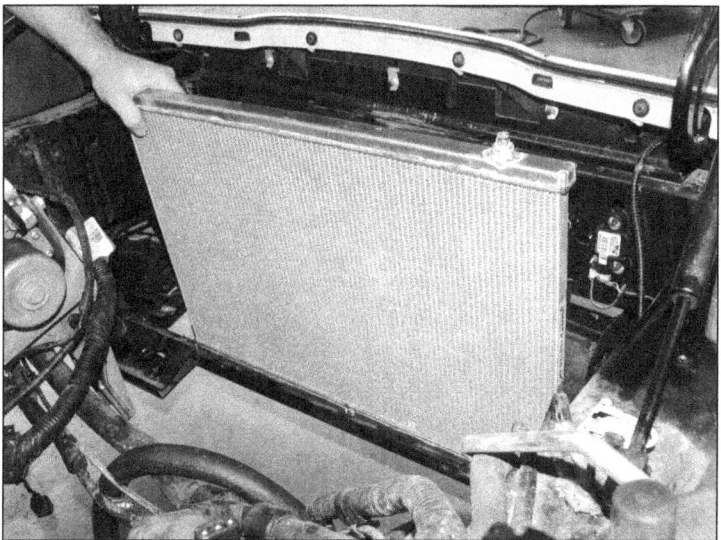

This isn't exactly how it mounts, but this photo gives you a look at the size and general placement of the "radiator" portion of the intercooling system. It mounts in front of the engine radiator.

And here is what the completed package looks like, all buttoned up. Wouldn't you know the boss would go for the all-business, as-cast blower setup instead of any polish or paint? Maybe sleeper is more what he has in mind. We now know it's strong and it's plenty stout. Take it easy, Maureen.

Source Guide

Accessible Technologies
ATI ProCharger
14801 W. 114th Ter.
Lenexa, KS 66215
(913) 338-2886
www.procharger.com

Blower Drive Service
12140 E. Washington Bl.
Whittier, CA 90606
(562) 693-4302
www.blowerdriveservice.com

Dyer's Blowers, Inc.
7665 W. 63rd St.
Summit, IL 60501
(708) 496-8100
www.dyersblowers.com

Eaton Performance Products
(269) 781-0469
supercharger@eaton.com

Edelbrock Corporation
2700 California St.
Torrance, CA 90503
(310) 781-2222
www.edelbrock.com

H&H Flatheads
4451 Ramsdell Ave.
La Crescenta, CA 91214
(818) 248-2347
www.flatheads-forever.com

Hampton Blowers
11255 Woodruff Ave., Unit C
Downey, CA 90241
www.hamptonblowers.com

Kenne Bell
10743 Bell Ct.
Rancho Cucamonga, CA 91730
(909) 941-6646
www.kennebell.net

Littlefield Blowers
1114 Kimberly
Anaheim, CA 92801
(714) 992-9292
www.littlefieldblowers.com

Magnuson Products
Magna Charger
1990 Knoll Dr.
Ventura, CA 93003
(866) 751-4477
www.magnacharger.com

Mooneyham Blowers
1935 11th St., Unit N
Upland, CA 91786
(909) 985-4425
www.mooneyham-blowers.com

Paradise Wheels, Inc.
(vintage Paxton blowers)
920 Rancheros Dr., Ste. E
San Marcos, CA 92069
(760) 740-0954

Paxton Automotive
1300 Beacon Pl.
Oxnard, CA 93033
(888) 9-PAXTON
www.paxtonauto.com

The Blower Shop
26846 Oak Ave., Unit C
Santa Clarita, CA 91351
(661) 299-5483
www.theblowershop.com

Vortech Engineering
1650 Pacific Ave.
Oxnard, CA 93033
(805) 247-0226
www.vortechsuperchargers.com

Weiand-Holley
1801 Russellville Rd.
P.O. Box 10360
Bowling Green, KY 42102-7360
www.weiand.com

Whipple Superchargers
3292 N. Weber
Fresno, CA 93722
(559) 442-1261
www.whipplesuperchargers.com

www.ingramcontent.com/pod-product-compliance
Lightning Source LLC
Chambersburg PA
CBHW051416070526
44584CB00023B/3458